JOHN—H̶ ̶...̶y job, and an off-again, ̶...̶ ̶to turn over a new leaf ̶...̶ ̶75. He didn't know som̶...̶ ̶ve him killed.

ARLENE—She had fled her ̶...̶ ̶r her husband broke her jaw. Some said she took a lover before she went back to John. Did she secretly want him dead . . . or was she an innocent victim too?

PEZZANO—He went to the police a few days before the murder with a warning. He said someone had tried to hire him to kill a trucker named John Mudd. So why didn't the police warn the victim he might be gunned down?

STEVE—He lived across the street from the Mudds . . . and was much more than a neighbor to Arlene. Mean and lean and tough, he told a friend that he wanted to give a holiday gift to his girlfriend. Her husband's murder.

JOHN JR.—He was supposed to have been asleep on the couch, but did the frightened five-year-old really see the man who killed his father? Fifteen years later he said he had a flashback—he recalled everything that happened that night. Including the killer's face.

AT LAST, HERE IS ALL THE EVIDENCE: WHAT THE SNOWY FOOTPRINTS SHOWED . . . WHERE THE PRIME SUSPECT REALLY WAS . . . AND WHAT SHOCKING FACTS THE POLICE OVERLOOKED.

FIND OUT THE VERDICT IN . . .

TOTAL RECALL MURDER

TOTAL RECALL MURDER

by Earl Bohn

A Dell Book

Published by
Dell Publishing
a division of
Bantam Doubleday Dell Publishing Group, Inc.
1540 Broadway
New York, New York 10036

ISBN: 0-440-21587-0

Printed in the United States of America

Published simultaneously in Canada

September 1995

10 9 8 7 6 5 4 3 2 1

RA

To Emilia, Philip, and Evelyn, whose childhood happiness becomes more precious whenever I think about the lousy, rotten things that happen to so many kids, John L. Mudd Jr. among them

ACKNOWLEDGMENTS

I wish to thank Bob Dvorchak of the Associated Press for introducing me to the editors at Dell, the editors themselves for their patience and support, the detectives, court personnel, and attorneys who endured hours of interviewing and otherwise aided in the research for this book, and my wife, who graciously kept smiling while I was closeted away in my office at times when normal people would have been helping around the house or, better yet, having fun with their families.

AUTHOR'S NOTE

In telling the story of John Mudd's murder, his son's startling account of recalled memory and the first degree murder conviction of Steven Slutzker, I have relied almost exclusively on official sources. Primarily, they include evidence entered into the record of criminal court proceedings, tape-recorded interviews conducted by police investigators, interview accounts typewritten after the fact by the investigators who conducted them, and transcripts of depositions taken in connection with civil litigation. I also gathered material from my own interviews with some of the persons named in the book. Dialogue that occurred in court, in taped police interviews, and in the civil proceedings is quoted verbatim. In other places I have reconstructed dialogue based on the investigators' typewritten accounts of their interviews and the recollections, as told to me, of the persons who were involved in the conversations.

Load the clip, Pull the slide, Aim, and squeeze

Patches of grass the size of king-size bed spreads pass for lawns in Wilkinsburg, one of the squat, red-brick boroughs that stand shoulder-to-shoulder on Pittsburgh's southeastern flank.

The distance between homes is often only enough for one person to carry a garbage can from the back of the house to the curb.

There is just enough chlorophyll in Wilkinsburg to distinguish it from the city of Pittsburgh proper, but there is no mistaking Ardmore Boulevard for a rural delivery route.

From the time Wilkinsburg wakes up in the morning until it goes to sleep at night, cars, trucks, and buses lurch from one traffic light to the next along Penn and Braddock avenues and the matrix of streets that feed the main thoroughfares. The growl of straining engines, the grinding whine of gear boxes, the clatter of bouncing undercarriages, and the pleading of rubber tires against brick and asphalt pavement merge into a continuous rumble. The round black mouths of a hundred thousand tail pipes pump a brownish-gray perfume of petroleum exhaust out over the borough.

The solid houses of Wilkinsburg were built for the wage earners and middle managers of the mills, foundries, factories, and warehouses of the 1920s, '30s and '40s. Since then, many of the homes in the area have been redone as apartments for the retirees, graduate students, and data processors of the service economy of post-steel Pittsburgh.

In 1975, the evolution of the housing stock was being helped along by Stephen Gerald Slutzker, an independent electrical contractor, and Joseph Keith Lindsey, a carpenter. The two twenty-six-year-olds worked for Lindsey's father-in-law, Ray Lynn, creating three apartments in each of four buildings on Buena Vista Street.

Lindsey and Slutzker worked together on the project in September and October that year. Lindsey stayed on after Slutzker finished the wiring.

One day in December, Lindsey was working alone in the basement of one of the four buildings. A thick blanket of clouds, typical of Pittsburgh's weather in summer and winter, blocked most of what little light was still available in late afternoon from the weak December sun.

Lindsey heard footsteps and looked to see the skinny electrician with the big nose.

"Hey, how's it goin'?"

"Okay, Steve. How you doin'?"

"Not bad. Not bad. How's the job? Things movin' right along, I see."

"Yeah, it's comin'. So, what brings you back here?"

"Need a favor. I just bought this, and I need you to show me how to use it."

Slutzker took the brown paper bag he was carrying and laid it on a makeshift table of two-by-four boards laid across sawhorses. He reached into the bag and pulled out a gun.

Slutzker knew that Lindsey had been a marine.

Before the Corps discharged him into civilian life in 1969, it had trained Lindsey to use firearms. Since he'd been assigned to work in communications, Lindsey's primary weapon had been the .45-caliber automatic Colt pistol.

The gun that Slutzker laid on the two-by-fours looked a lot like a .45 ACP, though smaller. The caliber was not immediately apparent to Lindsey. It had wood grips, and it wasn't blued as many pistols are.

"Do you know how to load it?" Slutzker said.

"Yeah, I'm pretty sure I can. Got any shells?"

The bag contained a box of cartridges, marked .32 caliber. Lindsey picked up the gun. He pressed the magazine-release button and let the clip fall out of the bottom of the stock into his hand. He put down the gun and picked cartridges out of the box, pushing the cartridges, base first, against the spring-loaded follower in the clip. Then he showed Slutzker how to replace the clip in the stock and lock it in position.

"After you do that, it's just a matter of you holding it by the stock with one hand and pulling back on the slide with the other. Leave go of the slide, you've got a round in the chamber. Aim, squeeze, bingo!"

The lesson took all of three minutes.

Slutzker chatted for a few more minutes about nothing in particular, thanked Lindsey, and left. The carpenter went back to work.

Connellsville is like Wilkinsburg in one way. It was built for hardworking people: coal miners, loggers, farmers, and merchants. But fifty miles southeast of Pittsburgh, higher in the Appalachian foothills, Connellsville gave its people elbow room and greenery. Its homes are made of wood that was cut in the days when pine trees were tall, and you could get thirty-foot-long studs that were really two inches wide and four inches deep. Its builders left big trees and big yards between the houses. They decorated the doors, windows, and roof overhangs with fussy wood moldings.

Connellsville was a place to retreat after work. Wilkinsburg—bisected by a thundering railroad line and throbbing roads—was a place to sleep and eat right in the heart of the pounding congestion.

No one appreciated the contrast between the two communities more than Mike and Donna Pezzano, who had put Wilkinsburg behind them, or so they thought until the phone rang in their home at 3:59 P.M. on December 19, 1975.

"Hello?"

"Donna, this is Steve Slutzker calling."

"Hi."

"Is Mike there?"

The question was innocent enough, but the voice and the name made the hair stand up on the back of Donna Pezzano's neck.

"He's not here, and I don't know when to expect him, Steve."

Donna considered Slutzker to be one of the stray dogs that her husband occasionally dragged home, and the Pezzanos had believed for a while that this was one stray they'd left behind in Wilkinsburg.

Steve was a user, not of drugs or alcohol, but of people and situations, which he manipulated with considerable skill into opportunities for himself.

A lot of people are like that. But Slutzker also had something that a lot of people don't, a personality that could turn forceful and menacing without warning. Those traits, combined with Slutzker's generally high opinion of himself, created a person who is hard to forget. Donna Pezzano was finding out just how hard that could be.

"I need to speak to him."

"Is there something wrong?"

"No, it's just urgent that I reach Mike."

"What's so urgent? Is there something I can do to help?"

Donna didn't really want to help. She wanted to find out what Slutzker was up to.

"No. I have to talk to Mike about something important."

"Is it anything concerning your family?"

Slutzker laughed.

"No," he said.

"So, what's so important that we haven't heard from you for a year and all of the sudden you call us?"

"Well, I want to know if Mike knows any important people."

"What do you mean by important?"

"Just big people."

"You mean here or in Pittsburgh?"

"Well, either down there or up here."

"I guess Mike knows important people, depending on what you mean."

"Listen, if Mike wants to tell you about it, it's up to him. How 'bout taking my number. Ready?"

"Yeah."

"6-7-3-0-0-0-1. I'll be here."

"Fine. I'll tell Mike when he comes in."

"Okay, Donna. I really appreciate this."

The call jolted Donna Pezzano, dredging up uncomfortable images and emotions.

She and Mike hadn't moved solely to get away from Slutzker. Mike's parents had relocated to Ruffsdale, a nearby patch, and his parents had lobbied for their kids to join them. After much cajoling and a gift of $3,000 as a down payment on a big, old $9,000 fixer-upper, Mike and Donna left Norvell Drive in Wilkinsburg for Race Street in Connellsville. The move delighted Mike's family and gave him, an inner-city kid, a chance to experience life in a different setting.

It had the added benefit of distancing Mike and his former best friend, Steve, lessening the likelihood of impromptu visits. Spur-of-the-moment invitations to dinner or coffee had brought Slutzker and his family into the Pezzanos' home often over the previous five years.

Connellsville and Wilkinsburg are only a forty-five minute drive apart, but for a while it seemed as good as 1,000 miles to the Pezzanos.

The distance now seemed a lot shorter to Donna as she

hung up the phone. Her blood pressure slowly returned to normal and her stomach settled down, but the piercing voice lingered in her mind and produced a vague discomfort, a shadow of uncertainty. Though Mike had valued Slutzker's friendship for a long time, Donna had always disliked him. She feared him too much, though, ever to come out and tell him what she really thought.

Even though she was tempted to forget about the call, Donna would give Slutzker's message to Mike because she not only loved him but respected him, despite what she thought was his occasional poor choice in friends.

Mike Pezzano was a streetwise guy from East Liberty, a section of Pittsburgh that is a tough ethnic stew. In any neighborhood, Pezzano could have qualified as a punk. In East Liberty in the 1950s and '60s, he fit right in.

He shared Slutzker's proclivity for big talk. Both liked guns. Neither drank alcohol except occasionally and even then only in small quantities. Both had wild streaks.

It was the CB radio craze of the early 1970s that brought them together. They met on the radio and frequently gathered at the homes of fellow CBers and at Jack Whiteside's, a CB shop, for bull sessions that they called coffee breaks.

Pezzano worked on his own as a painter, roofer, and handyman. He piddled around at a variety of things to fill the gaps in his business. One of his odd jobs was helping Slutzker. Slutzker taught Pezzano the few fine points there are to wiring household fixtures. He also taught him the advantages of getting paid in cash.

Pezzano had a fast lip and a big mouth and with his stocky, five-foot-six frame, he came across like gangbusters. His was not the kind of personality that floated on the periphery of other people's sensibilities. Most people decided right off the bat that they either loved him or hated him.

His favorite threat was "I'm gonna kill you." In truth, though, his machismo was mostly window dressing and his threats mostly bluster. Pezzano had a heart of gold and a burning desire to fit in and be liked. He once ran over a dog that darted in front of his car. The accident shook him so badly that he lost sleep for days.

The wild streak in both of them was part of the cement that held Pezzano and Slutzker together. The fact that Pezzano's wildness usually abated before Slutzker's may have kept them out of real trouble on more than one occasion.

Where they differed was in the source of their bluster. Pezzano's was a shield for his insecurity and was readily abandoned once he became friends with someone. Slutzker's, on the other hand, seemed to spring more from innate arrogance and a hot temper. He didn't hesitate to tell people he was right. He used guns to command respect, and he wasn't above pulling one just to make a point.

Slutzker was behind the wheel one day when he and Pezzano stopped at a gas station at Swissvale and Penn avenues in Wilkinsburg.

The station was busy, and the young fellow pumping gas was having trouble keeping up with his customers. When the kid finally came to their car, Slutzker pulled a snub-nosed .38 revolver and pointed it at the attendant. Pezzano ordered him to put the gun away. Slutzker obeyed.

Another time a dog ran in front of Slutzker's car as he and Pezzano were riding on Universal Road in Penn Hills just outside Wilkinsburg. Unlike Pezzano, Slutzker was not the type to lose sleep over a dog that got caught under the wheels of his car. Quite the opposite. The dog's audacity at crossing Slutzker's path set him off. He whipped out his .38 and fired several shots at the animal as it scampered away.

One of Pezzano's other pursuits was as a part-time, private security guard. It was quasi-police work, and it appealed to his machismo and his appetite for authority. He got interested in the work in the days when Pittsburgh had something called "special police." These were generally law enforcement wannabes who were allowed to wear a facsimile of the city police uniform, use the police firing ranges, rub elbows with real cops, and hire themselves out as guards, usually for businesses and institutions. Pezzano later worked for a private security firm in the same capacity.

He convinced Slutzker to join, and the two spent many hours whomping away with .38s at silhouette targets at the Pittsburgh police firing range in East Liberty. When they worked at it, the two could cut cigarettes at fifty feet, although not necessarily on the first shot.

As outrageous as Pezzano liked to think he was—talking "nigger this" and "nigger that" in the presence of black CB friends—he usually was the more responsible of the two when they were getting their ya-yas out.

Pezzano also had the great benefit of having a good woman with a strong character at his side. Slutzker had married a good woman, but Debbie was fat, and Slutzker brutalized her emotionally and physically because of her weight, snuffing out the good influence she could have been.

But because he was Mike's friend, Donna could accept the braggart in Steve Slutzker. And, besides, she too had CB fever.

It was a nearly perfect pastime for a person who loves to hear his own voice.

Certainly a lot of truckers avoid a lot of speeding tickets thanks to warnings about police speed traps. Neighborhood news can spread faster on the CB than on the TV or commercial radio. And many stranded motorists have gotten help over their CB radios.

But a sizable portion of the jabber on the airwaves, especially during the CB craze of the 1970s, served little purpose other than to exercise the vocal chords and egos of otherwise anonymous people. The CB allowed them to adopt new identities and broadcast their voices and their thoughts through an invisible medium to unseen, uncounted listeners miles away.

So, empty talk in its own right was not something that would readily offend a willing listener and fellow talker like Donna Pezzano, the "Cream Puff" of the Pittsburgh-area CB airwaves.

Slutzker was also full of talk, but his dark side never seemed far from the surface, and Donna thought she could see it better than most people. She has a keen awareness of other people's character, and she doesn't need a lot of time to tune in. As a grocery clerk, she became known for spotting shoplifters in the act. She was especially good at catching old ladies.

The Pezzanos had lived on Norvell Drive, not far from Slutzker's house on Marlboro Street. Steve and Debbie Slutzker were often guests in the Pezzano home. That was Mike's doing, not Donna's. In fact, Donna refused to accept the Slutzkers' offer to return the hospitality. She would not step foot in Steve's home.

She winced whenever Mike announced that he wanted to invite the Slutzkers for dinner. She didn't have anything against Debbie or their daughter, Amy. To the contrary, she felt sorry for Debbie and tried to take her under her wing. Donna readily recognized Amy for the beautiful child she was. Donna's problem was Steven Slutzker.

Of all the things she didn't like about him, the most troubling was the way he treated his wife and daughter. Although Debbie outweighed her six-foot, 140-pound husband considerably, she was no match for his emotional or physical strength. He often lashed Debbie with insults about her weight and appearance. Being blonde and having a very pleasant face were as close as Debbie Slutzker came to glamour. She was kind-hearted and trusting to the extent that she allowed herself to be weak and subservient around Steve.

The Pezzanos and the Slutzkers' neighbors had little doubt that Steve beat her. They believed that he would sometimes send Amy to stay with an older couple on Marlboro Street, who fed the girl snacks while Steve fought with Debbie. On at least one occasion he held a gun to his wife's head during an argument in front of Amy. Neighbors overheard Amy plead with her father, "Don't hit Mommy any more."

People around the Slutzkers could legitimately wonder whether he had more love and respect for his security-trained German shepherds, Harley and Israel, than he did for his wife. At least no one ever saw him hold a gun to the head of either of the dogs.

If the Slutzkers were out visiting and Steve decided he was ready to go home, he expected Debbie to be on her feet immediately. In his own home, Slutzker had no compunction about ordering her to cook food exactly as he liked it, regardless of her own tastes.

Debbie was virtually without self-esteem. Her lack of confidence was debilitating. Slutzker could read personalities as deftly as Donna Pezzano could, and he seemed to use his ability for the pleasure he derived from holding the upper hand. In his wife, Slutzker had a prime target, a woman who was easily led. Slutzker was faster, smarter, tougher and much meaner than Debbie, and he never let her forget it.

With Amy, it was different. His love for his daughter was obvious. His devotion took on the appearance of worship at times, even though he could become unreasonable in demanding that she obey him or pay strict attention when he was talking.

Slutzker's relationships with his wife and daughter gave the impression that he chose to keep Debbie around for little reason other than Amy's need for a mother. Regardless of whether any other reason existed, there was little question that Debbie was there because Steve chose to let her be there. On the day in 1975 that he finally changed his mind, he was brutish, as Amy remembered the incident years later. Steve kicked Debbie out of the house. He forced her to get in her car and drive away, allowing her to take only his check for $100 and the clothes she could fit into a suitcase. Amy watched from the front yard, wailing, her heart broken and tears streaming down her face. As soon as Debbie was gone, Steve stopped payment on the check.

Time and again, Donna Pezzano found that Slutzker loved himself and loved to hear himself talk. He enjoyed spirited conversation. With anyone other than another egotist, he tended to be boorish because of the underlying premise of his conversation, which was his own blue-eyed, brown-haired superiority. He seemed to believe he was the best person, the best husband, the best father, the best electrician, and the epitome of the CBer.

To some of those who knew him, Slutzker's greatest achievement was as a blowhard.

He had one of the most powerful base units in the Monongahela River Valley and took pride in blowing other callers off the channel. His handle was "High Voltage."

Even though the thought of having Steve Slutzker in her home made Donna Pezzano wince, she took comfort in the thought that Debbie and Amy were safe as long as they were under her roof. Except on those occasions, Donna worried about what might happen to them. Her suspicions that Slutzker mistreated his wife were heightened by his tendency to loom over any conversation between the two women, as if he didn't want Debbie to be alone with Donna. Whether he knew it or not, Slutzker had good reason to keep Donna away from his wife. Donna was, in fact, trying to gain Debbie's confidence. Given half a chance, Donna would have tried to instill enough gumption in Debbie for her to leave Steve on her own terms.

Having Slutzker in her home also meant that Donna could argue with him, an exercise she enjoyed not because she hoped to ever change his mind but for the pure devilment of it.

Her CB handle, "Cream Puff," told only half the story of what Donna Pezzano was like. She was plump, five-foot-nine and pretty much a softie—except where Slutzker was concerned. She would go out of her way to lure him into debate, and though she secretly feared his potential for emotional, if not physical, violence, she could be relentless. She rarely hesitated to tell him in so many words that he was full of horse manure.

During one of their get-togethers at the Pezzanos'

home, the conversation turned to a murder case that had been in the news.

"I could murder someone and get away with it," Slutzker boasted.

"Get out of here," Donna said. "Nobody can commit a murder and get away with it."

"I can."

"How do you figure?"

"I'm a Section Eight. I got out of the service on a Section Eight, and I've been in St. Francis."

The Pezzanos could only take Slutzker's word about his military discharge, but Debbie had confirmed to them separately that her husband had been treated at St. Francis Hospital in Pittsburgh for what she described as a nervous breakdown. Steve alternately claimed that he had served in the navy for eighteen days in Orlando, Florida, and that a chaplain got him out because he didn't like the navy.

All in all, Donna Pezzano believed Steve was a wacko who carried himself sanely.

Mike Pezzano's view of him wasn't as complicated. He saw only a guy who'd been a fellow CBer, a close friend and coworker and someone who seemed to deserve his sympathy. But Mike Pezzano became disenchanted with their friendship after Slutzker began stealing things from one of the places they were supposed to be guarding.

The two of them were hired to provide security for Biggs Discount Store in East Liberty. Then they took jobs with Pennsylvania Investigations Security, a private firm. In the spring of 1974, they pulled midnight detail at the Allegheny County Community College Boyce Campus in Monroeville.

Mike remembers that Steve began breaking into file

cabinets and stealing things from the music and communications departments. Faculty and staff filed reports with police about missing tape recorders, stereo equipment, speakers and microphones. Pezzano says Slutzker was also ripping off candy and crackers from the vending machines in the lounge.

Now, in late December of 1975, Slutzker was about to try to enlist his old friend in business darker than Pezzano had ever seen. When it happened, the stocky Italian with the big mouth and the big heart showed his true colors. He put himself at personal risk in an attempt to save Slutzker from himself and to save a total stranger from being murdered. That Mike Pezzano failed in the greatest gesture of kindness he had ever made in his life was no fault of his own.

Mike returned home about an hour after Donna hung up with Steve. She gave him the message, and he returned the call at 4:37 P.M.

They chatted briefly about the breakup of Steve's marriage. Then Steve got to the point.

"Listen, Mike, I wondered if, you know, ah, maybe whether there's someone that, you know, who could do a job for me."

"What kind of job?"

"I need someone to make a hit for me."

"A hit?"

"Yeah."

"You mean get rid of somebody?"

"Yeah. There's this girl. I really like her. We're in love, and her husband's a junkie. An asshole, really bad news. It'd be doing everybody concerned a big favor. He's a known drug addict and a drug dealer. I know for a fact that he beats his wife. He won't give her any household money. He's a child-abuser. His brother's an ex-con who killed a guy. The whole family's no good. His name is Jack Mudd."

"What?"

"Jack Mudd."

"Come on."

"Do you know the Mudds from Claybourne Street in Garfield?"

"No."

Slutzker was losing his audience. Pezzano thought the name sounded fishy. He figured Slutzker was pulling his leg, the call coming out of nowhere, a name like Jack Mudd, a hit. For Christ sake, he thought.

"Hey, I don't know, Steve."

"It has to be done around the twenty-fourth, Christmas Eve. I want her and the boy to have a nice Christmas. I want to make it a nice Christmas for Arlene. I want to be with her. Her old man's a bastard. He's a real loser. He's got a record and all. He's always gone off somewhere. He comes in late. He's always on something. He smacks her around. I've seen the marks on her. And there's other stuff, you know, sexual stuff. She wants out."

"Are you serious? I can't believe this. You're serious, aren't you?"

"So, what do you think? You know somebody? Could you do this? There's money."

Pezzano's disbelief was starting to wither. Slutzker's voice, which was usually intense regardless of the circumstances, told him that he was either serious or was putting on the best act he'd ever seen. But Pezzano knew that Slutzker wasn't an actor. He didn't have to act. He was a character just being Steve Slutzker. Besides, practical jokes weren't a big part of their relationship, and it didn't ring true that Slutzker would call like this just to make a joke.

"What do you want to blow the guy away for? Sounds like you're getting the milk for free. Why do you want to buy the cow?"

"I love her. We want to be together."

Pezzano's mind shifted gears. He was more than halfway home toward believing Slutzker was serious about this crazy plan and was heading straight for big trouble.

"Well, what all's involved, moneywise, I mean?"

"It's five hundred dollars. I've got the money. I've got it on me."

"Is that the best you can do?"

"That's all I've got."

"Well, if I could do this, how would it be done?"

"You've got options. I've got a thirty-two with a clip-on silencer. I've got a rifle with a scope, and I've got a car. The thirty-two you'd have to give back to me when it's over. It's not mine, and I have to give it back."

"Who all would know about this? What about the guy's wife?"

"She's in on it. She knows."

"Where would it happen?"

"The best place would be between Mudd's house and the boulevard, Ardmore. He takes a bus every morning to go to school, electronics or something. See, you don't have to worry about gunfire attracting a lot of attention. I've taken care of that. I fire guns in the morning up in the air and firecrackers. The police got tired of the neighbors complaining, so they don't care anymore. They wouldn't even bother coming up here if someone called. If you want to use the rifle, you could use my bedroom window as the site. He lives right across the street."

"That might work, Steve. It just might work. Listen, let me think about this."

"Can you do it?"

"Let me think it over, but maybe. . . ."

" 'Cause if you can't, I'll find somebody else."

"I'm not saying that. I think I can. Let's plan on me doing it, okay?"

"Okay. Right. That's good."

"But lemme think about this, okay?"

"Okay. I'll call you."

"Yeah."

Later Donna asked Mike about the conversation. Mike froze her out, and she had a hunch at the time that she was being stiffed.

"What did he want?"

"He wanted me to do a job."

"What kind of a job?"

"Oh, a bathroom job."

"Remodeling?"

"Yeah."

"Why would he call you clear out here?"

"I don't know."

"And what else did he say?"

"Nothing."

"Nothing?"

"He said it was worth five hundred dollars."

"Five hundred dollars for a bathroom job?"

"And what did he want to know if you knew any important people for?"

Mike didn't respond.

"That must be some bathroom job," Donna said.

Slutzker called Pezzano the following Monday, December 22, at three minutes to eleven at night. He wanted to talk about the plan and a schedule. Pezzano tried to put him off, but agreed to come to Wilkinsburg the next day, around noon, to go over the plans in detail.

Instead of making the trip to Wilkinsburg, Pezzano stewed all day. He didn't know what to do. Sensing that time was running out, that Slutzker might already be laying assassination plans with someone else, Pezzano went to the police, first to the Connellsville police department, where an officer suggested that he take his story to the state police in Uniontown.

It was right at 9 P.M. when Pezzano arrived at the state police barracks, a clean, crisp-looking building on Route 119, otherwise known as Connellsville Street, just outside Uniontown in North Union Township.

Trooper Donald Mates was on the desk.

Pezzano laid out the entire story.

To the twenty-eight-year-old trooper, Pezzano did not seem upset or especially dramatic, but he was adamant in predicting that Slutzker would find someone to kill Mudd or possibly do the job himself.

Pezzano might have been motivated by more than pure Boy Scout altruism to spill the beans. Believing that Slutzker was capable of pulling the trigger on someone, Pezzano might have wanted to put his warning on the record so that he could not be implicated if Mudd turned up dead and Slutzker tried to point the finger of guilt toward the short ballsy guy in Connellsville. It's possible. But Pezzano was also smart enough to know that by being two counties removed from the scene, having a watertight alibi and a conscience absolutely free of guilt was a defense as good as anyone needed.

"It ain't like I'm turning him in just to be a rat. It's just that I want to stop him before he gets involved in a murder rather than just a conspiracy," Pezzano said.

Mates took Pezzano into a back office and had him tell the story to the supervising officer.

"If you want, I could call Steve from here. You guys could pick up an extension, listen in on the conversation."

They gave Pezzano the distinct impression that they weren't buying the story.

"Well," Pezzano said, "can you at least get in touch with Lieutenant Krueger in Wilkinsburg?"

"How do you know Lieutenant Krueger?" one of them asked.

"I told you, I used to live down there. I've known Krueger from being on the CB radio."

The two officers told Pezzano to have a seat in the waiting area. They disappeared back into the office and emerged a half hour later accompanied by a third officer.

The new one asked Pezzano a lot of the same questions that the first two officers had.

"Well, I don't know what to tell you fellas. I told you why I'm doing this. If you want, I'll go down there if there's any way I could go down and have the Wilkinsburg police there. I could go through with it to a point where I could get my hands on the weapon, to where someone could step in."

"Listen, Mr. Pezzano," Mike recalled one of the officers saying. "Why don't you go home and forget about all this business? I think we can handle this from here. What do you say?"

"You going to do anything?"

"We'll make some phone calls. I think that's the best thing right now. If you hear anything further from your friend, you let us know. Okay?"

Before he left, Mike called Donna. He had to tell her something to explain why he was out so late, so he told her he was at the state police barracks because he'd witnessed a traffic accident. She bought it.

Pezzano left the barracks, and the officers decided that Mates should fill out an incident memo and pass the information along.

Mates called the state police barracks at Carnegie, which handles the Pittsburgh area, and learned that Wilkinsburg did indeed have its own police department. He called there and left word with Officer Hugh Biddle that he needed to speak to Lieutenant Irwin Krueger. Biddle's call got Krueger out of bed.

The next day, Christmas Eve, 1975, Krueger typed a memo to his boss, Lieutenant Bernard McKenna.

Last night I received a call from Hugh Biddle. He said that a state policeman from Uniontown wanted me to get in touch with him. A one Steve Slutzker, who resides at 1516 Marlboro St., wants to hire a hit man for $500.00. He contacted a one Michael Pisano [sic], who resides in or around the Uniontown area. Michael Pisano went to the state police in Uniontown and talked to trooper Mates. Trooper Mates called me. He got my name through Pisano, who is a citizens band operator who knows my son Bill. Pisano told the state police that Slutzker wants a Jack Mudd killed before Christmas and will pay $500.00 and supply the weapon, which has a clip-on silencer on it. He also has the car, which may be stored in his garage. Michael Pisano used to live at 1124 Norvell Dr. His C.B. name is Blue Coat. Pisano is supposed to have a business in or around the Uniontown area. Mudd lives on Marlboro across from Slutzker. Pisano told the state police that he thinks Mudd's wife may be involved. Slutzker goes by High Voltage, or HV. The victim is supposed to be hit between his home and Ardmore Blvd, where he gets a bus.

All pretty straightforward. Except for two details.

First, Krueger's memo to McKenna made no mention of Pezzano telling the state police that Slutzker was a wacko who just might go through with the killing.

Second, the incident memo that Mates filed with his superiors concluded with this line: "Krueger [sic] advised that he knew Slutzker and that he was radical, unstable, and could possibly be capable of committing an act such as this."

Mid-December 1975

Around the same time that Slutzker was trying to find someone to do his dirty work, Arlene Mudd was thinking about Christmas presents, among other things.

She and John drove to see brother Terry and his wife, Donna, on Lindberg Avenue in Lincoln Place. While they were visiting, Arlene suggested to Donna that the two of them go Christmas shopping. Arlene said she had a store in mind.

They traveled the aisles together until Arlene said she wanted to go her own way for a while and would meet Donna back at the spot where they were parting.

Donna found what she wanted and returned to wait for Arlene, but she didn't appear. After waiting for what Donna thought was an appropriate period, she started off to find her sister-in-law. As she came around the end of one of the aisles, she spotted Arlene.

What she saw next was going to become valuable information in a very short time, but Donna Mudd kept it to herself for a very long time.

John and Arlene

John Lawrence Mudd, born March 26, 1947, was a U.S. Navy veteran, truck driver, husband, father, and student of electronics technology.

In 1975 he worked for Pennsylvania Truck Line, Inc., and for Crane Supply Co. A corporate personnel director might describe Mudd in those days as a casual employee.

A person who works forty hours a week and takes a two-week vacation puts in about 2,000 hours in one year. John Mudd Sr. worked about 500 hours in 1975, or one day out of four. His wage was $5.80 per hour, and he earned a little more than $3,000, including overtime, for the entire year.

Measured just in dollars, Mudd's career was going downhill. He couldn't seem to find and keep steady, full-time work even though truck drivers were in demand. It was a time when the American steel industry was still booming, and Pittsburgh was the industry's Mecca. The industry's big collapse would not come for almost a decade, and Pittsburgh and the mill towns of the surrounding Monongahela, Allegheny, and Ohio river valleys were whistling through the graveyard, innocently ignorant to the upheaval that would begin in the early 1980s, eliminating about 100,000 steel and related jobs in the Pitts-burgh area.

But in the early 1970s, there was work for those who wanted it.

Mudd managed to work an average of just one day out of every ten in 1972. He got ambitious the next year and worked nearly four out of ten days. He worked almost five out of every ten days in 1974, for gross earnings of around $5,700.

A dollar went a lot farther in those days. Even so, if the U.S. Department of Labor is to be believed, it took around $2,500 to $2,800 in the mid-1970s to support just one person.

Whether he brought home any extra money from activities other than his occasional work as a trucker is not clear. Mudd was a user and a convicted dealer in narcotics and other dangerous drugs. He served in Vietnam, where he may have been introduced to drugs.

Some drug dealers make tons of money, but those who use and deal at the same time are lucky to break even. If Mudd was doing much better than breaking even on his drug involvement, it didn't show.

He was charged with assault and battery in February 1968 and assault with intent to kill in August 1969. On October 12, 1969, he was charged with assault and battery, resisting arrest, disorderly conduct, and assault and battery with an auto. The next day, October 13, he was charged with assault and battery and resisting arrest.

In January 1970, Mudd was charged with simple assault and robbery and the following March with being drunk and disorderly. The next month, he was charged with receiving stolen goods, larceny, and conspiracy, then in June 1970, he was charged with violating the Dangerous Drug and Cosmetics Act.

John L. Mudd also had a temper that could be nasty. His arrest record suggested as much. So did the black-and-blue marks that Arlene wore at various times during their marriage. When Arlene told his mother that John had given her venereal disease, John gave her a broken jaw as well. He did that at her parents' home in Forest Hills while Arlene was visiting them.

She told people later that she still loved him even though he beat her. She figured that he hit her because he loved her so much.

It would have been difficult to predict that Arlene Dudas would fall for a guy like John Mudd. But once she did, those who knew the inside story about life in the Dudas family were not surprised.

Arlene seemed normal in many ways. Yet she came across as dumpy, lacking in self-esteem, burdened with unresolved emotions, overweight and out of shape. All in all, she was breathtakingly unglamorous.

A charitable person would call her attractive: five-foot-two, 175 pounds, an oval face, big round brown eyes, a thin mouth, and straight brown hair.

Beneath the rounded edges of her personality was a heart that wanted to love and be loved. Too often, though, her heart guided her behavior and left her helplessly hoping for a bright, shining life. It wasn't meant to be.

She is the younger of two daughters of Cecilia and William Dudas of Forest Hills. Dudas was a strict father, and between him and Cecilia, the Dudas girls got a proper upbringing and were well schooled in social mores.

Cecilia, for example, would abide no work being done in her home on Sunday and drummed that belief into her children. Years later, Arlene was still reluctant to wash clothes or do much of anything in the way of housework on Sunday.

Somehow along the way Arlene developed a marked resistance to authority.

Whether Arlene was aware of it or not, dating John Mudd may have been one of the forms her rebellion took against her father. In that regard, William Dudas had plenty of company. The open sexuality and drug use of the 1970s strained relations in many families. Bill Dudas was not unique in being disgusted over his daughter's choice in boyfriends, a skinny navy vet, a young, arrogant, oversexed drug user with a coterie of equally distasteful friends.

But if ever a girl jumped from the frying pan into the fire, Arlene did when she hooked up with John Mudd.

She was studying to become a hairdresser when she discovered she was going to have a baby, which broke her father's heart.

John Mudd Jr. arrived a few months after Arlene and John Sr. were married in 1970.

Arlene found that married life with her new husband was no dream come true. He was as overbearing as her father had been, perhaps more so. John refused to allow Arlene out of the house without him. He wouldn't let her return to beauty school as she wanted. His jealousy was so great that he even forbade her to go to bingo games with her mother and sister.

John may have been just as demanding when it came to sex.

During one of their particularly boisterous fights, Arlene screamed loud enough for neighbors to hear, "I'm not going to be your fuck machine." The argument occurred during a period when the neighbors were noticing a lot of men coming and going at 1515 Marlboro Street.

Despite the turbulence in the household, Arlene showered John Jr. with love. She told people that she couldn't have any more children and that Johnny meant the world to her. It seemed, however, that Arlene's love sprang more from childlike emotion, from her view of men and boys to be cuddled and hugged, than it did from any overwhelming sense of personal responsibility or parental duty.

She read to him often and for long periods. Her joy was visible when she played with him. That, combined with the boy's innate intelligence—his IQ was 125—explained his ability to read by age four. The boy also walked by age eleven months and talked at a fairly early age.

But in many other ways, Arlene lacked maturity, especially when it came to being responsible for her son's welfare.

When Johnny was only a few weeks old, he developed an eye infection that required a hospital visit. Arlene was so repulsed by the infection that she was not able to listen to the doctor's explanation of how to care for her son's eye. The incident was one of the first of many times that Johnny was very lucky to have his aunt Maureen close by.

Maureen listened to what the doctor was saying and then did what Arlene could not or would not: She applied medicine to the boy's eye four or five times a day. To do that, Maureen had to travel from her house to the Mudds'.

Arlene's parents lived on Trenton Avenue in Forest Hills, a twenty-five-minute walk or a five-minute drive from the Mudds on Marlboro Street in Wilkinsburg. Yet it was Maureen Perri who drove the better part of a half hour, longer if there was heavy traffic, to get from Lawrenceville to Wilkinsburg to treat her nephew.

Arlene did not nurse Johnny when he was an infant. She fed him formula and often set him down and propped the bottle, which is considered by some people to be a classic trait of lazy parents. It was not her only irresponsible trait.

Johnny was about three years old when someone left a pot of scalding-hot water near the edge of the table. He bumped the table and was burned badly. The boy was in the hospital for ten days, part of that time in an oxygen tent.

When Johnny was about four and a half years old, Arlene left him alone in the bathtub. She was gone long enough for him to fall asleep in the water and nearly drown.

Arlene may have taught her son to read at an early age, but she apparently forgot to teach him how or when to use a toothbrush. His teeth were badly neglected, requiring an unusual amount of dental work for a child.

Maureen Perri called regularly to see how her brother and his family were doing. She often called in the morning, and many times Johnny would answer the phone. Arlene would still be in bed while Johnny made breakfast for himself.

Once he told his aunt he was cutting oranges.

"What are you making for your breakfast?" she asked another time.

"Peanut butter toast, Aunt Maureen."

"How do you make peanut butter toast?"

"Put the peanut butter on the bread and put the bread in the toaster."

Such were the early years of John Mudd Jr.

The Summer of '75; Love Is in the Air

When the wind stops in Pittsburgh in the summertime, the heat and humidity can become so intense that the sweat dripping down the small of your back makes you shiver.

In neighborhoods like Marlboro Street in Wilkinsburg, the houses stand hip to hip, and the brick, asphalt, and concrete soak up heat all day only to release it all night.

Marlboro Street is an especially efficient heat sink because it is flanked by hillsides that block all but the strongest breezes.

In people who are prone to daydreams and grandiose self-images, weather like that only encourages the yearning for something better, which is what Arlene Mudd and Steve Slutzker thought they had found in each other in the summer of 1975.

The Mudds and the Slutzkers had met a year earlier, in the summer of 1974, when John and Arlene and little Johnny moved into 1515 Marlboro. The Slutzkers lived almost directly across the street at 1516.

The two couples became friends and exchanged visits to each others' homes. Johnny Mudd and Amy Jo Slutzker became playmates.

Debbie worked at Gilbert's Restaurant in the city's Garfield section and helped Arlene get a job there. The two women became especially good friends, and whether Arlene knew it or not, Debbie, for a time, considered Arlene to be her best friend.

Steve sometimes ate breakfast at Gilbert's. Occasionally he noticed that Arlene was wearing lots of makeup. She told him it was to disguise bruises and marks from beatings by her husband.

Steve did favors for the Mudds. He installed a dimmer switch and a ceiling fixture in their dining room.

The couples celebrated New Year's Eve, 1974, together at the Slutzkers' house. It could have been at that party where Steve and Arlene realized they were attracted to each other. By late January, things were so bad between Steve and Debbie that Debbie had to get away. She went to Altoona for a while to stay with her parents.

Slutzker slunk over to 1515 Marlboro Street to tell his new lady friend how tough things were for him. It's likely that Steve played the part of the injured party in his crumbling marriage with Debbie. Had she wanted to know, the neighbors could have told Arlene what really went on in the Slutzker home.

The DeManns, who lived across the street from Slutzker and a few doors down the hill, heard quite a few details about life in the Slutzker household from Debbie and Amy. They knew about the guns Steve kept at home and of Debbie's fear that he might shoot her during an argument. Amy once told Mrs. DeMann that her father had a gun and said "he was going to kill Mommy." Debbie had told them, too, that Steve had suffered a nervous breakdown and had received a medical discharge from the service.

Mrs. DeMann overheard one of the Slutzkers' fights, in which Debbie yelled, "Don't hit me any more" and heard Amy cry out, "Don't hit Mommy any more."

Amy wasn't immune from her father's punishment. Neighbors saw him beat Amy more than once, for things such as falling off of her bike.

As she grew closer to Steve, Arlene poured her heart out to him. She told Steve that she and John hadn't been getting along well for years, that he had used heroin, didn't want to work and sometimes wouldn't buy food or pay the rent. She said John blew his money on pot and pills. He'd take off for long periods without telling her where he would be and often returned at 3 or 4 o'clock in the morning.

Over time, Arlene revealed more about her life with John. She told Steve that her husband slapped her around and forced her to perform sex in ways she didn't like. Steve reciprocated by bad-mouthing John Mudd. He told Arlene that her husband would ogle other women in public when Arlene wasn't around and was cheating on her.

Arlene and Steve started saying they loved each other around April. Steve was also telling other people that his marriage was in trouble. He and Debbie visited his friend Eleanor Padolf, who was "Ma Bell" on the CB and was a traffic reporter for KQV radio. Ellie and her husband conducted what amounted to a counseling session during the visit. The Padolfs listened and came to the conclusion that divorce was probably best.

It was no great coincidence that on April 10 Steve forced Debbie out of the house again. He told his friends that Debbie had left him. Technically, that was true, though in reality, he had kicked her out.

With Debbie out from underfoot, Slutzker didn't have to sneak around. Arlene started seeing Slutzker openly, apparently having little fear that her husband was alert enough to figure out what was going on.

As soon as Mudd left for his electronics classes, Arlene would call Slutzker, most days waking him. He would take Amy to school while Arlene took John Jr. to kindergarten. Then they'd spend several hours together until Arlene had to pick up Johnny. They'd go grocery shopping, run errands, or just drive around. Sometimes they would park and sit and talk or climb into the back. Other times they would neck on Slutzker's front porch.

They always parted before 3 P.M., when John usually got home from electronics school. Steve would run around doing a few minutes of work, then pick Amy up from school.

On Saturdays and Sundays, he rushed around like a madman trying to fit in all the work he'd missed during the week. With John not in class during the weekends, Steve couldn't see Arlene, so he figured he might as well work.

Throughout the summer, Slutzker made a habit of leaving the front door of his house unlocked so that Arlene would have a place to run to if John took a notion to slap her around.

Steve was convinced that Mudd had once stabbed Arlene because of the scar on her abdomen.

Arlene often watched Amy as a favor for her new boyfriend.

Steve and Arlene drove to Ohio one weekend and stayed at his brother Dave's home on North Star Road in Columbus. Arlene had told John that she was visiting a girlfriend.

Steve got a chuckle out of the fact that people thought he and Arlene had been in Niagara Falls when they'd actually been in Columbus. About a month after the Ohio trip, they did go to Niagara Falls. Steve brought back a doll with long braided hair for Amy.

Debbie Slutzker stayed in touch, most often by phone, and mostly to check on Amy, but she drove back to Wilkinsburg from Altoona at least once. She knew what Steve and Arlene were up to, and while she was back in Wilkinsburg in early July, Debbie told John Mudd what was going on between their spouses. John immediately confronted Arlene. She admitted to having an ongoing affair with Steve Slutzker.

Arlene fled to her parents' home. John crossed the street and confronted his rival in his home in front of Debbie. John said he knew everything and that Arlene had confessed.

Steve, confident that his was the superior intellect, wouldn't admit to anything. He called Arlene at her parents' house.

"Yeah, he knows," she said.

"So what am I supposed to say?"

"Talk to him. He knows everything."

"He wants you here too," Steve said.

"No way. I'm not coming over there."

"Well, he wants you to come over."

"I'm afraid of him."

"The four of us will sit down and talk this out."

"Steve," she pleaded. "I'm afraid he'll beat me again."

Mudd must have been having one of his better days, because the meeting apparently ended on a gentlemanly note, with Mudd saying "May the best man win."

It looked for a while as if Slutzker might be that man. Arlene and Johnny moved in with Slutzker. Their first evening together was uninterrupted by any trouble from Mudd. Slutzker took his new family out for ice cream, and everyone had a good time.

The next day, however, Mudd was watching. He saw his son unattended on the porch, bolted across the street, up the steep front lawn, and took the boy.

Mudd's old pal from East Liberty, Elmer Francis, known as "Duke," or "Dukers," moved in and brought with him another member of their old neighborhood gang, Jackie Smith.

Smith was dating Francis at the time, but she had dated several guys from the neighborhood, including

Mudd. When Francis moved out a short time later, Smith stayed.

The presence of the young woman with long black hair must have eased any pain John Mudd felt over the loss of his wife. Over the ensuing days, he did little more than talk to Arlene on the phone except to peep through the windows of Slutzker's house. On one of his trips, Mudd rapped on the glass.

Arlene told Steve not to let him in. "I'm afraid of him. I'm afraid he's going to beat me again."

John whined for a while for Arlene to come back with him, then he went home.

Meanwhile, Steve and Arlene talked about divorce and obtaining custody of Johnny. Both contacted attorneys. Slutzker's attorney began drawing up papers. Arlene seemed more interested in getting Johnny back than divorcing her husband. She was advised that her chances of winning custody would be much better if she were not living with another man while still married to John Mudd.

She moved from Slutzker's house to her parents' place, but she continued to come and go from 1516 Marlboro, usually slipping in the back door and sometimes staying overnight.

On July 24, when Steve had expected Arlene to stay all day, he came home to find a note: "I can't live without my son, so I'm going back to John."

The thought of being rejected was humiliating and infuriating.

Up to that moment, the pact to let the best man win had been working in Slutzker's favor. Now it was no longer convenient to let Arlene decide for herself which of them she wanted.

Slutzker looked out his front window. He could see that no one was home down at the Mudd house. He couldn't restrain himself. He got his Smith & Wesson .38, five-shot revolver, strapped on his ankle holster, and jumped in the van. Instinctively he headed to East Liberty.

He arrived at 5337 Broad Street, home of Mudd family matriarch Mary Mudd, while John and Arlene were still in their car. Steve stopped and called for Arlene to come back to him.

"Tell him," Mudd commanded her. "Tell him. Tell him what you gotta tell him."

It was decision time, and Arlene was petrified. She sat, immobilized in the car. Her eyes darted back and forth from Slutzker to Mudd.

Steve kept calling.

"Don't you move," John yelled. "You're with me."

"Can I talk to you?" Steve said. "I just want to talk to you."

Finally Arlene spoke. "I'm going back to John. I love John."

Slutzker was not convinced. He saw a message in her eyes that was very different from her words.

"Who do you love?" Slutzker demanded. "Who do you love? If you love me, get in the truck. We'll go, and that'll be it."

Mudd was seething. East Liberty was his home turf, Arlene was his wife.

"Get in the house," John told her.

She obeyed and walked toward her mother-in-law's, where Johnny O'Connor, Mudd's uncle, was on the porch, lying on a glider.

Mudd jumped out of the car and approached Slutzker's van.

"Be careful," Arlene yelled. "Just be careful."

Slutzker assumed the warning was meant for him. He

reached down with his left hand and raised his right pant leg. Up came the .38. Slutzker raised the gun as Mudd approached. He knew he wasn't going to shoot, but he had too much arrogance and not enough intelligence to understand that pulling a gun in a street fight leaves only two options: using it and risking any number of criminal charges or not using it and losing face.

"Just stay away from the truck. Get the fuck away from my truck!"

Someone was approaching from back in the line of traffic behind Slutzker's vehicle.

"Jimmy," Mudd yelled. His brother, James, was in the line of cars and was walking toward Slutzker from four cars back.

Events were shifting even further in Mudd's favor.

"Go ahead. Do it!" Mudd said, staring at Slutzker's tormented face. "You won't do it," Mudd snarled, " 'cause you ain't got the balls."

Mudd's mouth proved to be braver than his feet, which had taken him as close as they were going to the pistol that Slutzker was pointing at him.

"Hey! Put that goddamned gun down," a voice yelled. "Mary, get back in the house." It was O'Connor yelling at Slutzker and then in turn to his fourteen-year-old daughter who had come outside.

Slutzker suddenly realized how far out on a limb he was: brandishing a gun in the middle of Broad Street, attempting to win back his lover while his rival, his rival's brother, uncle, and niece watched. Worse, the love of his life was inside. He needed to find a way out.

Slutzker swung the barrel of the gun toward himself and pointed it at his own head. Mudd didn't say a word. He just backed away, perhaps half wishing to hear the crack of the pistol and see Slutzker's head snap sideways.

"I'm calling the police," O'Connor declared, and turned to go inside.

Having lost his dignity and perhaps Arlene as well, Steve now had no reason to stick around, especially when O'Connor was heading for the phone to call the cops, who were never far away in East Liberty. He made one desperate attempt to persuade Arlene to leave with him.

"Arlene!" he pleaded. "Come on. It's going to be too late. Come on. We haven't got much time. If you're not coming, I'm leaving."

He put the gun down and sped away in his van. Jimmy ran back to his car and tried to follow the van but lost it as Slutzker wheeled onto Negley Avenue and headed east toward Wilkinsburg.

The Mudds buzzed about the incident for several hours. John finally loaded Arlene and his uncle into the car and drove to the Public Safety Building in downtown Pittsburgh that evening to file a complaint with police. Somewhere on the drive home, he apparently changed his mind about pressing charges because he never followed up.

"Just forget the whole thing," he told O'Connor. "This is a family matter."

That evening at home, Slutzker received a phone call. It was Arlene's sister, calling to say Arlene wanted to talk to him and would be calling later.

Arlene placed the call from her in-laws' home while everyone else was outside. She spoke softly and kept the conversation short.

"I told John it's all over between you and me, but it's not all over. We just have to cool it for a while. John knows everything, and I'm afraid he's going to hurt me. No more looking out the window waving to each other.

No more calling over to the house. Just let things cool down for a while."

Steve acquiesced.

"I still love you," Arlene said. "Some day we'll be together."

She also had some disturbing news.

John had taken her to a doctor for a shot of antibiotics because he'd found out he had venereal disease, and he didn't want Arlene to get it.

Soon after talking to Arlene, Slutzker got another call. It was Mary Mudd. She was so incensed about his tacky affair with Arlene that she had to confront him. She lit in, saying she was going to file charges against him and calling him a senseless fool for chasing Arlene and trying to break up her son's family.

Mrs. Mudd also unloaded her feelings about her daughter-in-law.

"She's no good," she said. "She's nothing but a whore." To hear her tell it, Arlene brought nothing but misery to her son, who, by the way, was a good person and deserved much better.

"If he's such an angel, then why don't you ask him how come he has VD?" Slutzker blurted out.

"Ah," Mrs. Mudd gasped, "that's not true. Johnny's a good boy. I don't believe that for a minute."

"Ask him, why don't you? Just ask him."

"Well, if he does have it, he got it off that slut Arlene."

"Okay, fine," Slutzker said. "But that's not the way I understand it. But you know what, Mrs. Mudd, I have nothing to say to you. And if you feel you want to file charges against me, do whatever you feel is necessary. It'll all come out in court."

It didn't take long for word to get back to John that the

subject of his venereal disease had been broached with his mother. Worse yet, he found out who had broached it.

Whether he'd given his wife venereal disease was not the point. Mary Mudd was the undisputed leader of the family. She was as strong-willed in her rule over her clan as she was in the belief that her children were good, upstanding citizens. The thought of his mother learning otherwise was enough to send John into a rage.

On top of that, Slutzker could have learned of the VD problem from only one source, Arlene, who only hours earlier had told her husband the affair was over and she was once again his woman.

Arlene was at her parents' home when John caught up with her on July 26. He burst through the door in a rage. As he screamed at her and swung, his hand connected with Arlene's face, breaking her jaw.

John lunged for her and instinctively his hands were around Arlene's neck, squeezing as he continued cursing her. Just as Arlene felt she was going to pass out, Mrs. Dudas threw her substantial frame onto Mudd's back. The maneuver worked. He broke off his stranglehold in order to wrestle free of his mother-in-law. Then he yanked open a drawer, grabbed a knife, and chased Arlene around the house. She escaped to a neighbor's house, and Mudd, having made his point and suspecting that someone had called the police by now, left.

Arlene was taken to Braddock Hospital for treatment, where she was laid up for a week. Steve visited her faithfully. He was at her side for most of the waking hours of every day.

Whether their fears were imagined or not, Arlene and Steve believed that John might make an attempt to attack her again while she was in the hospital. Slutzker, believing himself an expert in such matters, concluded that Braddock Hospital's security wasn't very good.

He gave the nursing supervisor orders not to reveal Arlene's room number or telephone number to anyone. Then he called on the telephone, pretending to be a relative who needed to know where she was. The switchboard operator passed the test, and Arlene continued healing in peace.

She was released during the first week in August. Steve had shopped for a new dress so Arlene would have something nice to wear home. He picked her up at the hospital and drove her to his place.

But having been assaulted at her parents' home in Forest Hills, Arlene soon grew edgy about continuing to live with Slutzker only a few angry strides away from the man who'd made a pretty good show of wanting to kill her.

Arlene moved back in with her parents. It was much less stressful there. Besides, she could continue seeing Slutzker, which she did for the two months that her jaw was wired.

The recuperation gave Arlene time to think about what to do with her life and her family. She spent long periods thinking about her son and all the things she used to enjoy doing with him, especially reading and playing. She truly missed Johnny. Arlene also harbored the thought, more a dream, that John Mudd truly loved her and could be a good husband and father. That must have taken a powerful amount of rationalizing.

At the same time, she was confronted with Slutzker's plans for their happiness whenever she talked to him. On one of their outings, for example, Steve took her to the Padolfs' home in Highland Park. Arlene's jaw was still wired to keep it immobile while the bones healed, so Steve got to do most of the talking for them. He told the

Padolfs they were in love and wanted to get married. They took him aside and told him to cool it.

Steve also talked openly about his plans to Steve Apter, originally a CB buddy known as "Madman" who moved in with Slutzker that summer, including periods when Arlene was staying there.

Slutzker told Apter he wanted to marry Arlene, how he encouraged her to file for a divorce and gain custody of John Jr., and how Arlene wouldn't do that because she knew her husband would oppose it.

Apter's advice was the same as the Padolfs', but he was more blunt.

"She's no good for you," he told Steve. "Forget about her."

"I can't. I love her."

Arlene's emotions rested on less stable ground. She was sinking deeper into a quandary about whether to file for divorce or to legally separate from John while seeking custody of Johnny. So, she did neither.

Slutzker plunged ahead. His divorce papers were filed on August 20, and Debbie was in no position to contest a divorce.

Steven Gerald Slutzker and Debra R. Wenrick had married about seven years earlier, not long before Amy Jo was born in August 1969. Acquaintances remember hearing that Steve and Debbie had met at a dance.

If he ever had much respect for Debbie, it had evaporated long before the summer of 1975. In the divorce complaint, he accused Debbie of being the rotten party, and to add insult to the injuries, physical and emotional, that Slutzker had heaped upon the poor woman, the court found that Debbie "offered such indignities to the person of the plaintiff, the injured and innocent spouse, as to render his condition intolerable and life burdensome."

The findings in the decree were nothing more than archaic, boilerplate language that had survived over the years in the nomenclature of the divorce courts. Nonetheless, it remains on the books in Allegheny County Court to this day, a cruel blot on the record of a woman who suffered uncounted indignities while married to Slutzker. To top it all off, the judge ordered Debbie to pay court costs of $100.

The divorce became final on October 31.

Finally, Steve was free of the ball and chain that impeded his plan for happiness, but just as he rid himself of his spouse, he was confronted with a new problem. Arlene moved back in with John. They were trying to reconcile.

Arlene made the move when it was time for the rubber bands and braces to come off her teeth. That was the only dentist appointment to which Slutzker did not take her. John played the dutiful mate on the trip.

"I'm going back with him because I can't give up my son for you," Arlene told Steve. "That should pacify John."

"But why, Arlene? You can still have Johnny. You don't have to go back to him."

"I'm scared, Steve. I'm afraid he'll hurt me if I don't."

"But you can file charges. I been telling you that all along. You could."

"No. I'm scared. I'm afraid next time he's really going to kill me. If he gets papers in the mail or some kind of a summons he's going to blow up. He's going to get hysterical. There's no telling what he'll do."

"But they'll pick him up and put him in jail before anything could happen to you. You said he's still on parole. He's got a couple years to finish out. If you file charges against him, most likely if things go all right, he'll have to pick up the rest of his parole plus whatever else they give him. While he's in prison, you'd have no trouble getting a divorce."

"Oh, Steve, no. I can't. I'm afraid. If he gets picked up by the cops his family will get him out on bond, and he'll come back and kill me. You saw what happened. I just got my braces off from that. I can't."

The reconciliation went well enough, so far as John Mudd knew. Arlene was back in his bed and keeping his house. What he didn't know is that while he was in classes, Arlene was still sneaking around with Slutzker.

The affair continued as Halloween came and went, although Steve and Arlene were much more careful than before. They avoided using their home phones to talk to each other. They knew that when John had gotten wise, he'd begun calling home. If the line was busy he'd immediately dial Slutzker's number. A busy signal there told him that his wife and neighbor were talking to each other.

As Thanksgiving approached, Steve and Arlene commiserated over the prospect of John being home for five consecutive days from school.

After the holiday, they continued sneaking around together, crying on each other's shoulder—she inclined to dream about a better life, he inclined to act.

As the days passed, the weather became cold and damp, the daylight hours became fewer, and Christmas drew closer.

December 28, 1975

At four in the morning on December 28, 1975, the telephone rang in Mary Mudd's home. It rang twice before the sixty-six-year-old woman picked up.

"Hello?" she said.

No one spoke on the other end, yet Mrs. Mudd could tell someone was there. A few more seconds passed, then a man spoke. He wasn't speaking into the phone but was prompting someone who was supposed to do the talking.

"Go ahead and tell her her son is dead."

There was a pause.

"Go ahead and tell her her son is dead."

Mrs. Mudd hung up.

About four hours later, John and Arlene Mudd got out of bed and ambled downstairs to start the day.

It had been a very cold night, and when dawn came, a high, thick blanket of clouds promised that the sun would remain out of sight for most of the day. There would be little direct light to help the road salt do its job. The pavement throughout southwestern Pennsylvania would remain frozen.

Their Sunday ritual called for them to spend the day at Mary Mudd's home on Broad Street. But since it was Christmas time, John had told his brother Woody that he'd bring the family over to visit before they headed to East Liberty.

Arlene made breakfast. John looked out the living room window, studied the weather, and stared at their car, parked in front of the house.

He called Woody. "My tires are just about shot. If we head up to your place, I'm afraid we'll get hung up somewhere, so I think we're going to go straight to Mom's."

After breakfast, Arlene dressed herself and Johnny while John got himself ready. Then it was off to spend the day at Mrs. Mudd's home.

Around 5 P.M., John and Arlene and Terry Mudd and his wife decided to eat out. Snow was falling again, and they had all planned to visit Maureen and Phil Perri at their home in Bloomfield, which is hardly more than a stone's throw from East Liberty. Mary Mudd wasn't planning to serve a meal, and none of the kids wanted to trek home for dinner only to retrace their steps back to Bloomfield.

They ate at Minutello's, a roomy, casual place on the border between down-at-the-heels East Liberty and trendy Shadyside, where the parking regulations are enforced, even on the side streets and alleys. The restaurant's decor was 1950s diner. The food was Italian and pretty good.

After dinner, they all spent the evening with the Perris. Young John had fun playing with his cousin, Phil, who was only slightly older.

At 10 o'clock, John and Arlene called it a day and said good-bye. Arlene got behind the wheel.

New snow made the whole world seem holy, and at John's request, Arlene drove on Fifth Avenue so they could see the Christmas lights on the houses and apartment buildings and a manger scene that he was particularly fond of. The manger was a disappointment because it was not well lit. Still, the three of them were in a jolly mood by the time they got back to 1515 Marlboro.

John turned on the living room light. It was 10:35 P.M.

"Come on, Daddy. You be coat man."

They all laughed. John did as requested and hung everyone's coat, then pulled the button that turned on the TV. He joined his wife and son on the couch, where Johnny had his Superman sleeping bag and his ViewMaster. The television made a perfect backlight for the scenes as Johnny clicked through the picture disks.

"Mommy, look at this," he said, and swung his head and the ViewMaster in one quick motion toward his mother, accidentally clunking her on the head.

She winced.

"All right, settle down now," John barked.

The boy snuggled into his sleeping bag.

Just as the 11 o'clock news was getting under way, the TV went black, and the living room light went out.

"Go try the switch," John said. Sometimes they had to work the switch in and out a few times to get the TV to come on.

Arlene obeyed. No luck.

"Wasn't the light on in here too?" John said, knowing the answer before he'd finished the question. A fuse must have blown.

He heaved himself off the couch, got out his lighter, and flicked it. In the dim yellow glow from the gold stick in his hand, Mudd walked into the dining room, turned into the kitchen, and walked diagonally across the length of the room to reach the top of the basement steps.

He crooked his index finger and with it flipped up the light switch. No light in the basement. With his index finger and his thumb, he worked the wall switch up and down three or four times. Still nothing. Next his fist hit the wall beside the switch. Maybe the loose wire that had given them trouble before was acting up. A few more thumps made it clear that brute force wasn't going to improve the situation. It may never have dawned on Mudd that the basement light was on the same electrical circuit as the living room light and the outlet that powered the TV.

The light in the fish tank beside him in the kitchen was still on, although its glow was weak, and Mudd's body blocked most of it. He couldn't see much farther than a few feet in front of him.

So, still holding the gold lighter, he started down the stairs.

By the time he reached the last few steps, Mudd's eyes had been in near darkness long enough that the brief white flash probably would have been visible to him if he'd been looking in that direction. But he never saw it. It came from behind him on his right side and slightly below him.

Accompanying the flash was the sound of the first detonation, which reached his ears in about five thousandths of a second, led by an expanding shock wave of air compressed by the hot blast and followed about one thousandth of a second later by a bullet, a small missile, just a third of an inch in diameter with a lead core sheathed in copper. It was spinning clockwise along its horizontal axis and traveling at around 960 feet per second. At that speed, the bullet, weighing less than a fifth of an ounce, hit him with the force of a baseball bat swung by a grown man taking a full cut.

"Oh, hon!"

Mudd's words came out in a tight, loud moan, as much a cry of surprise as pain.

He may have grabbed the wooden two-by-four hand-rail on his right to steady himself, thereby giving his killer an easier target. Not that he was a difficult one by any means, his back illuminated by the soft light of the fish tank and his torso, shoulders, and head silhouetted by the glow from the cigarette lighter he held in front of him. They were weak lights to the eyes of a person who only moments earlier had been watching television in a well-lighted room, but to someone whose pupils were wide open from waiting in a dark basement, they were perfect.

Before losing consciousness, Mudd probably didn't have time to understand that he was being shot, let alone figure out that the shooting had been planned or to guess who was pulling the trigger.

Wham. Wham. Wham. Wham. Wham. Wham. Wham. Seven more shots came in rapid succession.

The oppressive barking of the .32 autoloader drowned out the clacking of the extractor arm as it pulled the empty casing from the firing chamber and ejected them in short arcs forward and to the right. The sound of the shots also drowned out the faint click of each new cartridge snapping into place under the pressure of the spring in the magazine, the dull smack of the firing pin hitting the primer at the base of each shell, and the light jingling of the empty brass bouncing on the concrete floor. The blasts obliterated the sizzling-zipping sound of the bullets piercing Mudd's body at nearly Mach I, puncturing his brain, heart, lungs, and liver, shattering bones and sever-ing blood vessels. Also lost in the cacophony was the *whap* of the copper-jacketed bullets hitting the walls and the floor after exiting the front of John Mudd or missing him altogether.

Next to the guns blasts, then, the loudest sound was

the thump of the body hitting the wooden steps as it collapsed.

Of the eight shots fired, six hit him.

One entered low on his back, just to the right of his spine and an inch or so above the waistline. Unimpeded by any vital organs or big bones, it vectored through him, exiting just below his sternum, the nearly flat, dish-shaped bone midway between his naval and chin.

Three other bullets hit him on the right side. One of those entered about midway between his shoulder and waistline. It pierced the liver, diaphragm, and lung and stopped just under the skin on the right side of his sternum.

The other two hit under his right armpit: One entered the abdomen, piercing the liver and diaphragm and exiting through the left pectoral muscle; the other pierced his abdomen and lung and lodged in his left side.

The only bullet that hit left of his spine entered near a vertebra, pierced his lung and heart, and burst through the sternum, sucking a mist of tiny bone shards and blood droplets through the hole in its wake.

Had only a single bullet struck the target, the killer would have wanted it to be the shot that entered low on the back, right side of the head. It bored through the center of the brain and exited a half inch above the left eyebrow.

For all practical purposes, John Mudd's five-foot-ten-inch, 132-pound body was dead when he hit the floor. The killer probably fired several of the shots after the body landed, considering that spent slugs were recovered from under the body near the exit wounds: one under his chin and another under his torso.

Mudd landed on his left side with his head against the bottom step and his feet almost touching the wall that faced the staircase. Because his left arm was under his neck and head, as if he were using it for a pillow, the snake-and-butterfly tattoo on his arm was hidden beneath him. His left hand was exposed, however, showing the thin, gold wedding band on his ring finger. His gold cigarette lighter lay on the floor, two inches from his nose. His legs were flexed at the hip and knees, like an unborn baby's. His feet rested on a child's toy, a white plastic Winnebago wagon.

The tattoo on his right arm, a woman's head and the letters S-T-E-R," were visible below the short sleeve of his white T-shirt. His blue jeans hid the bunny head tattoo on his right calf. Otherwise, he wore white cotton jockey shorts and blue-green-pink-and-white socks. Only those few clothes and a small, multicolored hooked rug insulated him from the cold, damp concrete floor as the heat radiated from his body and the blood settled in his major organs and body cavities and pooled on the floor beneath his head.

The body was hemmed in by the two concrete block walls in the northeast corner of the basement. A box, which once contained a child's bike, and four plastic garbage bags, bulging with crumpled wrapping paper and the scraps of Christmas, were clustered near him against one wall. Six deformed bullets and seven shell casings were sprinkled around him. The eighth casing was never found.

Upstairs, Arlene Mudd went into a panic. She picked up the telephone in the living room and, instead of dialing the number for Wilkinsburg police, she dialed "0." The operator connected her with Pittsburgh police.

"Pittsburgh police," the dispatcher said.

Between sobbing, screaming, and wailing, Arlene could get out only one word, "Police?"

"Keep on yelling, and I won't know anything," the dispatcher said.

"Police," she screamed again.

"Keep on yelling—"

"Are you the police?"

"Yes, this is the police."

"Oh, please come to 1515 Marlboro. My husband's been shot."

"What's the matter?"

"Oh, my husband's been shot."

"Would you please quiet down till I get the address."

"1515 Marlboro Street. Please hurry."

"1515 . . ."

"Marlboro Street."

"Marlboro?"

"Yes."

"What's the matter?"

"My husband's been shot. Please hurry."

"Don't hang up now. Stay on the line, will you please?"

"Oh, please hurry," Arlene said, calmer but panting.

A third voice came on the line.

"Hello? What's the address?" the radio operator asked.

"1515 Marlboro. A man's been shot," the dispatcher said.

"1515 what?"

"Marlboro," Arlene and the dispatcher said together.

"Hello, ma'am? What is your name?" the dispatcher said.

"Arlene Mudd. Please hurry. I've got to get a neighbor, please hurry."

"Would you please calm down and give me your name. The police are on their way up there," the dispatcher said.

"My name's Arlene Mudd. Oh, God!"

"What is your name?" the dispatcher said, as if to either give Arlene a hard time for being hysterical or to demonstrate that when police departments hire emergency desk operators they run the risk of getting assholes with attitude.

"Arlene Mudd."

"How do you spell your last name?"

"M-u-d-d."

"Let me have your phone number, please."

"242-1204."

"242—"

"1- . . ."

"1-2-0-4"

"0-4."

"Is that a private home?"

"Yes. Oh, please hurry."

"Beg pardon?"

"Hurry."

"Hello."

"Please hurry."

"1550 Marlboro."

"Please hurry."

"And is that a private home?"

"Duplex."

"Duplex?"

"Yes."

"In other words, it's a private home?"

"Yes."

"All right," the dispatcher said. Finally.

"Madonna and Child"

One of the reasons for having a police force is to prevent crime. The mere presence of the police usually is enough to maintain the semblance of law and order in most communities. Very few people will break a major law. They fear they would be hunted down by beefy men with sidearms, handcuffs, and badges hanging from their blue uniforms.

Fighting crime that way, through the deterrent value of police, is infinitely easier than trying to get convictions after the fact.

To a police department, then, it would have to seem like manna from heaven for an informant to step forward and report that a capital crime was going to be committed.

If the informant described the means, the motive, and the time of the killing and named the victim, and if the informant was sober, if he had no apparent motive to lie, if his information was specific and plausible, especially if the informant was a part-time police officer and most especially if the police department receiving the informant's tip thought the would-be killer was capable of killing another person, then bagging a bad guy would be almost as easy as dunking a doughnut and slurping coffee, extra cream, extra sugar, from a Big Gulp cup.

Or, so you would think.

But in Wilkinsburg in December 1975 you would be wrong.

By not warning Mudd that a plot was under way to kill him, by not questioning Steven Slutzker and putting him on notice that his scheme had been betrayed, Wilkinsburg police may have left Mudd's killer with a clear line of fire and the confidence to proceed with the plot.

By not taking decisive action, Wilkinsburg police also invited the wagging of fingers, the clucking of tongues, and the filing of a civil law suit that exposed Wilkinsburg taxpayers to the possibility of a whopping damage award.

The blood was still wet on his basement floor where Mudd lay curled on his side like a baby when something else happened that, rightly or wrongly, reflected on the performance of the borough police department. It had to do with the fact that a police car from neighboring Edgewood arrived at 1515 Marlboro Street before a Wilkinsburg car.

That in itself meant little. In the expanses of Texas, it might be embarrassing to have police from the next town arrive at a crime scene before the locals, but mother nature and local politics long ago decided otherwise for the communities that stand shoulder to shoulder in the hills east of Pittsburgh.

For one thing, the slopes and ravines made it difficult to travel very far in any direction in a straight line. Then there's the matter of the Conrail tracks that bisect Wilkinsburg through the center of the borough.

The embankment on which the track lies is punctured with underpasses, but not at every street. So, depending on the route they are taking, drivers can be forced to go blocks out of their way to cross the tracks.

On top of that, the borders of Wilkinsburg and its neighboring communities are as crooked as a dog's hind leg. So, if you are lucky enough to find a street that leads very far in a reasonably straight line, you could be in Wilkinsburg one minute, Edgewood the next, and Swissvale the next.

Those are some of the reasons that Wilkinsburg, Edgewood, and other municipalities share emergency radio dispatchers. The joint dispatching center also saves money.

In handling Arlene's call, the dispatcher announced "1550" as the address of the shooting. That's where the first Wilkinsburg car was when Edgewood officer Tim Brendlinger drove past the Mudd home and saw something that no Wilkinsburg officer was in position to see.

Brendlinger, a three-year veteran of the Edgewood department, was on patrol with Sergeant Dominic LaBella that night.

The temperature was around 10 degrees, and an inch or so of new snow crunched under the rubber treads of the tires as Brendlinger eased the cruiser down Brinton Road, across broad, four-lane Ardmore Boulevard, and up Marlboro, a one-way street with parking allowed on both sides.

Under the streetlights, everything had a white freshness.

From the passenger's seat, LaBella was peering at house numbers, not knowing that 1515 was the number they wanted even as they passed it on the way to 1550.

Just then Brendlinger glanced to his right and noticed a woman standing on the sidewalk. She held a child wrapped in a heavy blanket. A man was with her. The crisp, cold air was instantly turning their breath into white puffs that were illuminated by the streetlight above them. The scene was all the brighter for the white coating of snow on everything. They stood together, not face to face, but partially turned toward a two-story, red brick house across the street, on Brendlinger's left. The cruiser was moving at about ten miles per hour. Funny, Brendlinger thought, for a woman to have a child outside on a night like this. He did not stop the car.

The Wilkinsburg police had already driven past 1515. The dispatcher didn't correct his mistake until after the Wilkinsburg officers had reached the house at 1550 and tossed an old man, pushing him spread-eagled against the side of their car and patting him down as a potential suspect.

The dispatcher corrected his mistake and announced the right address as Brendlinger approached the Wilkinsburg cruiser. He lifted the gearshift into reverse and backed down the hill. He and LaBella trotted up the steps to the front door, where they met Arlene, whom Brendlinger recognized as the woman he'd seen moments earlier. She was still holding the child, who by now was screaming and crying hysterically. The man who had been with her was gone.

"He's in the basement. At the bottom of the steps," Arlene said, shouting to be heard above the cries of the child and pointing toward the dining room and the kitchen beyond.

With those words began a criminal investigation that should have been over before it began, but which, in truth, wouldn't come to a conclusion for more than fifteen years.

■ ■ ■

Brendlinger and LaBella went inside and followed Arlene through the living room, past the television and the Christmas tree, through the dining room, and to the top of the basement stairs. Arlene, still holding her son, stood between the two officers. With only the glow from the aquarium for light, they could make out a body at the bottom.

"Did anybody come up out of there?" LaBella asked.

No, said Arlene. And the only other way out of the house was the basement door.

Brendlinger left immediately. He went out through the front door, turned right, and descended the slope beside the house, headed for the backyard. He noticed the perfectly fresh snow at his feet.

LaBella waited inside.

Arlene lay her son on the couch in the living room and, still in her stocking feet, went outside and rushed up the street, where Wilkinsburg police officer Dominic Mangano and his partner were getting back into their car after realizing that 1550 was not where they wanted to be.

"My husband's been shot," she blurted out again. "He's lying at the bottom of the steps."

"Why the hell didn't you give us the right address?" Mangano said.

"I did when I called the police," Arlene said, standing there in white socks with no shoes, blue pants, a yellow pullover jersey, and a matching long-sleeve sweater.

By the time Mangano and his partner, Officer Dan Rearick, got to 1515 Marlboro, it was 11:28 P.M. When they entered, LaBella left to join Brendlinger out back.

"There's no foot tracks in the snow," Brendlinger said.

"Then he's still in there," LaBella said and went back inside to inform the others. The undisturbed snow that Brendlinger had found in the yard made it clear that no one had left the house through the basement door in the six hours since it had stopped snowing.

Officers inside were peering into the basement from the kitchen doorway. Flashlights cured the problem of low visibility. Mangano could see four bullet holes in Mudd's T-shirt.

LaBella drew his gun and went down.

Mangano followed, but to make himself a smaller target, he lowered himself onto his belly and slid down the steps headfirst. Only after it was too late did he realize that his tactic could have cost him his life rather than protected it. The staircase had no risers. Had anyone with a gun been hiding underneath, Mangano would have been easy pickings through the spaces between the treads. It seemed a moot point, however. The basement appeared to be secure.

Just then the door to the backyard burst open. The first thing through was the muzzle of a gun. Officers Brendlinger, and Phil Miller followed.

Within minutes, the basement was crowded with officers, beaming their flashlights at anything of interest.

The body was the big attraction. Then came the fuse box. It contained two main fuses and four circuit fuses, the latter in a horizontal row. They found that the one on the far left had been backed out of its socket, accounting for the lack of light in the basement. One officer reached up to the box and turned the loose fuse with his bare fingers until it seated against the metal contact at the base of the socket. Light.

With the Wilkinsburg contingent in charge now and LaBella's shift over as of midnight, the two Edgewood officers pulled out. As they left the house, LaBella noticed that Mangano was taking the boy from Mrs. Mudd. At Mangano's request, a neighbor escorted Arlene away from the commotion of her own home to a neighbor's house, where at least her immediate surroundings, if not her thoughts, would be peaceful. Mangano took the boy to the home of a Wilkinsburg police officer who lived on Marlboro.

"That was her. That was her we saw on the sidewalk talking to that guy before," Brendlinger said to his partner as he eased the cruiser over the snowy streets back to the Edgewood station.

"What do you mean? That was who?"

"The woman, Mrs. Mudd. I saw her. As we drove in. Right before they put out the correct address. I saw her on the sidewalk, holding the baby, talking to a guy. Did you see her? She was on your side."

"No. I didn't see her. I was spotting house numbers on your side of the street. I didn't see her."

Brendlinger dropped LaBella at the station, then turned around and headed back to 1515 Marlboro.

There he passed the information along to the Wilkinsburg officers at the scene. "That's okay. Everything's taken care of. We know who did it," Brendlinger remembers one of them telling him.

■ ■ ■

"Homicide. Warzeniak."

"This is Robinson of Wilkinsburg PD. We've got a homicide at 1515 Marlboro in the borough. Multiple gunshot wounds in the back. I think your guys better come out here."

Ron Warzeniak didn't need to hear many details. He roused the district attorney's people from their homes on a frigid Monday morning on the weekend after Christmas. Detective Joe Dugan was the first to arrive. He was followed closely by Assistant Chief William Jennings, Detective Marian Corcoran, Lieutenant Richard Byers, and Sergeant James Finello. Allegheny County deputy coroners Jim Gregris and Nick Vlasic and photographer Tony Greco weren't far behind.

For the next hour or so, the county investigators measured, photographed, and diagrammed just about everything in sight in the basement. They plotted the distance from John Mudd's body, using the buttocks as the point of reference, to each of the casings and slugs. They noted the holes in him, the blood on and under him, the color of his clothes, his tattoos, and most of the items in the basement.

They collected his wallet from the living room and cataloged its contents: driver's license good until March 31, 1977; Veterans Administration patient date card with a notation for an appointment on November 18, 1975; a Teamsters Local 249 membership card; a card for Penn Technical Institute on Ninth Street in Pittsburgh; two twenty-dollar bills, and one ten. They also found a small amount of white powder that later tested out to be methamphetamine hydrochloride, or speed, which was not unusual to find on truck drivers, and a small amount of marijuana.

They interviewed Arlene Mudd and others in the neighborhood who might know something about what had happened that night.

The deputy coroners bagged the slugs, the casings, and the body in plastic and hauled them to their old stone headquarters at the foot of Fourth and Ross streets in downtown Pittsburgh. In the meantime, the county investigators went with the borough officers to the Wilkinsburg station.

There, over hot coffee and cigarettes, the Wilkinsburg people told the fascinating story of Steve Slutzker, his affair with Arlene, and his effort to enlist Mike Pezzano in using a .32-caliber autoloader to murder John Mudd, the man who only a short time earlier lay in his own blood at the bottom of his basement stairs with holes in his back, holes that just happened to be made by bullets from a .32-caliber autoloader.

They also revealed that Slutzker and Bill Krueger, son of Wilkinsburg police Lieutenant Irwin Krueger, were friends and fellow CBers who often hung out at a home in McKeesport.

All things considered, the officers felt they had more than enough information to consider Slutzker a prime suspect. Shortly after 4 A.M., Lieutenant Byers drove back to Marlboro Street to look for Slutzker at his home.

No one answered his knock at the door. Behind the house Byers found two sets of footprints in the snow leading from the back door.

One set appeared to be an adult's, the other a child's. They disappeared at a spot framed by the imprints of four tires, from which tracks led down the alley and away from the house. There were no footprints in the front of the house.

With that discovery, Byers decided to check the place in McKeesport, but that could wait until after dawn, which wasn't far away.

■ ■ ■

About the time that John Mudd's body reached the coroner's office, two men were walking up to the front door at 1123 Race Street in Connellsville.

Bing-bong. Woof. *Bing-bong.* Woof woof woof. *Bing-bong.* Woof woof woof woof woof.

The bell and the barking woke Donna Pezzano from a sound sleep.

She forced herself out of bed and wove her way out of the bedroom toward the front door. Mike kept right on sleeping.

Bing-bong. Bing-bong. Woof woof woof woof.

Good dog! she thought. You're a pain sometimes, but not now. Give 'em what for.

Donna held the dog by the collar with one hand and with the other swung open the door to see two large men in gray uniforms.

"Mrs. Pezzano?"

"Yes."

They introduced themselves as officers of the Pennsylvania State Police and apologized for disturbing her at such a late hour.

"Is Mr. Pezzano here?"

"Yes. Why?"

"We'd like to talk to him."

This was mighty strange. Two state troopers at the door in the wee small hours of the morning. Donna Pezzano was still too sleepy to ask any more questions. She climbed the staircase and shook Mike.

"Wake up, Mike. There's two state troopers here who want to see you."

"Huh?"

"There's two state troopers here. They want to talk to you."

Mike focused his eyes on Donna for a moment, then got out of bed.

"What's going on?" she said.

"I don't know."

"Are you in trouble?"

"No."

Mike padded downstairs with his wife close behind.

"Mr. Pezzano, we're sorry to disturb you at such a late hour, but we need to ask you a few questions."

Both officers looked at Donna in silence.

She got the hint and left the room. From a distance she could hear parts of the conversation. She could tell by the tone of Mike's voice that he was agreeing with whatever the police were saying. Then she overheard one of the officers say ". . . right to remain silent . . . right to have an attorney present . . ."

If there was any grogginess left in her, the realization that her husband was being given his Miranda rights snapped her out of it. She strode back into the room, spitting recriminations at the two officers.

"Hey, wait a minute!" she said, her throat tight with fear and aggravation. "Are you arresting him? How dare you barge into our home—"

The dog instantly took up the cause, loudly squaring off with the intruders as he backed his big hind end as close as possible to Donna and Mike.

Donna was still yelling as the officers explained that they were required to recite Miranda rights even though they wanted only to ask questions.

Donna began to understand. Her husband wasn't going to jail.

"Could you give me a few minutes to talk my wife?" he said.

The officers nodded.

Mike took Donna into another room and related a story that he'd been keeping from her for more than a week.

Donna was slack-jawed as she listened. Steve Slutzker had called on the nineteenth looking for a hit man to kill someone.

Mike had tried to learn as much as he could about Slutzker's plan and made his own plan to prevent the killing. He told Donna about his conversations with the state police and with Slutzker. He told her about Slutzker's romance with the dead man's wife.

He also relayed the information that the two officers

had come to report. The person who was the target of Slutzker's plan had died earlier that night. He'd been shot repeatedly in the back. Mike's voice and face betrayed his shock.

He was gripped not so much by the news that a stranger had been murdered but by the notion that his intuition told him Slutzker had been serious, and his intuition turned out to be exactly on target.

"The district attorney's office will need to speak with you in Pittsburgh in a few hours," one of the troopers said when Mike returned.

"I'll be there."

■ ■ ■

At 8:30 A.M., Wilkinsburg's chief, Harry Hodgins, and his two lieutenants, Krueger and Bernard McKenna, along with Finello and Byers from the county piled into their cars, cranked up the heaters and the cigarettes, and set out for McKeesport. They knew exactly where they were going and whom they were going to see. They had the Krueger connection to thank for that. They had good reason to believe Slutzker would be there, because Billy Krueger had been in the home of Pat and Janet O'Dea a few hours before the shooting and was told that Steve was sleeping in one of the bedrooms.

"Forty minutes through traffic. Not bad," Byers said as Finello stopped the car at a one-and-a-half-story bunga-low at 1504 Grandview Avenue. The winter wind barreled in unimpeded from the valley on whose southern rim Grandview Avenue was perched. The cold air was almost as good as a cup of coffee for suppressing their fatigue, although the aching in their knees, lower backs, and eyes told the five officers that the feeling of being refreshed was largely imaginary.

They clomped onto the wooden front porch and knocked. Janet Marie O'Dea answered the door.

"Yes, Steve's here," she said, letting the officers in.

Slutzker appeared moments later, a look of studied innocence on his face, which was turned upward to meet the gaze of Finello, who at six-foot-five, and 245 pounds dwarfed Slutzker, who was no midget himself.

Children, including Steve's daughter, were playing with Christmas toys in the living room.

"There's been a shooting in your neighborhood on Marlboro Street," the big one said.

Before Finello could get another sentence out of his mouth, Slutzker turned and started walking away.

"I'll get my coat," he said matter-of-factly as if the detectives had come to enlist the aid of a special agent in the investigation.

Finello and Byers exchanged looks and arched eyebrows.

"I'll be back in a little bit," Slutzker said to Janet O'Dea as he and the others stepped toward the front door.

Finello informed Slutzker of his right to remain silent and have an attorney present against the prospect that anything and everything he said could be used against him in a court of law.

"No problem," Steve said. "I understand about all that, the Miranda rights, due to me being a special policeman for the city of Pittsburgh. I'm out of Station No. 5."

"That's good, Steve, because you'll appreciate the fact that we'd like to ask you a few questions."

"I understand."

Byers held the back door of the car open for Slutzker

and got in beside him. Finello got behind the wheel and headed downtown.

"Steve, do you own any guns?" Byers asked as Finello made a right turn off Grandview and nosed the car down steep, corkscrewing O'Neill Boulevard heading toward Route 30 and the Penn Lincoln Parkway to Pittsburgh.

"Well, I have this one." He casually reached past his knee and pulled up his pants leg, revealing a .38 Smith and Wesson, five-shot revolver in an ankle holster.

Byers was a stereotypical gumshoe: double-knit slacks, a cheap blazer, shirt and tie—often with the knot loose and the top button open. He was rarely seen without a cigarette wagging from the side of his mouth, and the smell of smoke and coffee hung about him, all of which usually gave him a scruffy, don't mess-with-me-because-I-don't-give-a-damn-about-anything image.

When Slutzker produced the gun, however, Byers' tough-guy expression gave way to a rosy flush in his face.

"It's legal. I've got a permit to carry it," Slutzker said, handing over the weapon and the piece of paper as Byers swallowed hard.

Finello loosened the steel grip he had instantly assumed on the steering wheel, but he continued to watch the rearview mirror for as long as he dared while driving on the descending curves of Eden Park Boulevard. He wondered how quickly the Wilkinsburg officers following them would react if something happened.

"Uh-huh," Byers said, the sheepishness receding from his face. "Your permit's good until August of 1976."

Small consolation, Finello thought. How could he and his partner be so stupid? he asked himself in silent exasperation. Here's our prime suspect in a vicious, cold-blooded shooting death, and we don't pat the guy down?

Byers emptied the revolver: four wad cutters and one wax load.

The moment was not lost on Slutzker.

"It's old ammunition," he explained in a slightly patronizing tone.

"Steve, do you own any other guns?" Byers asked, almost afraid to know.

"Uh-huh. I have a four-inch Combat Masterpiece that I carry in uniform."

Byers looked Slutzker in the eye and didn't have to utter the question on his mind.

"It's back at my place," Slutzker said.

A .38 and a .357 Magnum. No match there, Byers thought. That doesn't prove anything.

"How well did you know John Mudd?"

"Not too well," Slutzker said, and went on to confirm things that Byers and Finello already knew for the most part.

Finello pulled through the Forbes Avenue archway of the county courthouse onto a courtyard paved with Belgian block. The courtyard was once used for public hangings.

The officers ushered Slutzker to a windowless room on the fourth floor and seated him in a chair with his back to the door.

As the interview continued, Slutzker dropped one bit of information that the detectives hadn't heard before. He said he had done electrical work in the Mudd home.

Other than that, he dodged the zingers that the detectives threw at him in an attempt to trip him up. This was obviously a suspect who wasn't going to break down and confess as some do.

Slutzker said he left his home Sunday around 4:30 P.M., drove to the O'Deas' place, and stayed until the police showed up the next morning. He said he never left the house at any time and played cards and drank shots and beers until he got drunk.

He said he passed out on the O'Deas' bed and slept there until his hosts told him to move to the couch in the living room so that they could go to bed.

Satisfied that they'd gotten all there was to get from Steve Slutzker for the moment, Finello looked him straight in the eye and asked, "Did you ever tell anyone that you were in love with Arlene Mudd?"

"No comment."

"What do you mean, no comment?"

"Exactly what I said."

Finello and Byers left the room for a minute or two then returned.

"Steve, would you be willing to take a polygraph test about the things you've told us?" Byers said, wanting to gauge Slutzker's reaction to the question as much as he'd want to see the results of the test.

"I don't believe in the polygraph. I just don't have any faith in them. Besides, I don't think I need to take a polygraph. My word should be good enough," he replied, fidgeting slightly in his chair and avoiding their stares.

At that moment, Finello and Byers, without uttering a word to each other, came to the same conclusion that the Wilkinsburg officer had voiced to Tim Brendlinger at the Mudd house in the small, dark hours of the morning.

■ ■ ■

At 8:36 A.M., six minutes after Finello and Byers walked out of the Wilkinsburg police station on their way to pick up Slutzker in McKeesport, Detective Marian Corcoran began typing on a sheet of translucent onionskin paper in a conference room on the fourth floor of the Allegheny County Courthouse. She was transcribing, word for word, the story Michael Pezzano was telling to Assistant Chief Jennings.

Pezzano, like just about everyone else involved in the case, was operating on only a few hours' sleep.

He was nervous too, but he was a diamond in the rough, and Jennings treated him accordingly. Not that criminal investigators prefer to question cooperative, voluntary witnesses. Some detectives truly enjoy hammering away on suspects.

Pezzano had come out of the woodwork with a tip—more than a tip, a mother load of detail, which had it been heeded would have reduced the Mudd affair to a simple solicitation-to-commit case if that much.

Jennings started with the easy preliminary questions. Pezzano was thirty-two, born on April 5, 1943, married with three children, a self-employed painter on public assistance for the moment.

Mike laid it out just as it had occurred. He even took an excursion through his law enforcement experience with Slutzker.

"I was a special policeman when I met him four years ago, and he became a special policeman. We had a contract with Biggs Discount Store in East Liberty. Then we got a job with Pennsylvania Investigations Security. We pulled midnight detail at Boyce Campus in Monroeville as security guards.

"I quit because Steve was robbing electronic typewriters, file cabinets, ham operating equipment, out of their electronic lab, and robbing the candy and pinball machines down in the lounge."

"Do you know where this stolen equipment is?"

"Last I knew, it's in the first bedroom on the left on the

second floor. He converted it into an office. He sold a lot of the equipment."

At 10:40, as Pezzano, Jennings, and Corcoran were putting their signatures on the typed transcript of their interview, Finello and Byers were finishing with Slutzker. Pezzano was released to return to Connellsville, and the team of detectives met in the office of Jack Stack, chief of detectives.

"I think we've got our man," Finello said.

Stack's tight lips worked a big, cheap cigar back and forth across his teeth as he listened from behind a dark oak desk. "Well, how do you think we should proceed?"

One of the detectives suggested attacking Slutzker's alibi and searching for the weapon.

Stack's bald head, wreathed with a crescent of reddish hair, nodded. "Okay, but among other things, Pezzano's story will have to be corroborated."

Stack ordered a check on all handguns registered to Slutzker and all toll calls by Slutzker, Pezzano, and the O'Deas beginning with the week of December 15.

"Also," the chief said, "get the woman in here. If Pezzano's right when he told us she was involved, then we'll need her formal statement."

The detectives trooped out of Stack's office. Finello immediately called Arlene.

"I'll get my dad to drive me in," she said.

The big man and his chain-smoking partner sat down together and, aided by more caffeine and nicotine, planned the interview with the widow.

■ ■ ■

Captain Bob Meinert volunteered to drive Slutzker back to McKeesport. He had just come from the coroner's office, where he'd viewed the first stage of the autopsy on John Mudd.

Mudd's body was laid out on one of four stainless-steel tables, each ringed with drainage troughs, in the main autopsy room on the ground floor of the old stone building.

Following normal procedure, forensic pathologist Dr. Earle Davis and associate pathologist Dr. F. A. Malak first opened the white plastic bag, removed the body, and checked every nook and cranny of the bag for anything left inside.

Then they removed the man's clothes and spread the pieces out to dry, especially the soaked T-shirt, so that the blood would not putrefy.

Then they looked the body over from head to toe.

They noted the tattoos and cataloged the entry and exit wounds created by the bullets. They used X rays to spot the two slugs still in him and felt them just under the skin with their fingers.

One of them tried to get fingernail scrapings, but Mudd's nails were too short. They clipped pubic hair, swabbed the orifices, and drew blood. They took photographs of each step.

Meinert knew what was coming next. He didn't stick around.

The pathologists examined the inside of every orifice for injury and evidence. Killers leave a surprising variety of items in the openings of their victims' bodies: coins, medals, small statues, buttons, food. As it turned out, Mudd suffered no such minor indignities.

Once they were satisfied that they had missed nothing, Davis and Malak carefully washed the body. They numbered each bullet wound, recorded a description of it, and measured its location. They noticed no stippling of gun-

powder on Mudd's clothes or skin and concluded, therefore, that the muzzle of the gun was at least thirty-six
inches away for each shot.

The internal exam began with the standard Y-shape
incision on the chest. Using a scalpel, they cut through
the skin beginning near each shoulder to a point just
above the breastplate. From there they made one cut
toward the pubis. It was a straight cut except where it
detoured around the naval.

The deep, bloodless incisions created two big flaps of
skin, which they pulled aside to reveal the rib cage and
organs of the lower body cavity. They removed the two
bullets that ran out of energy just before bursting through
the skin on his front side.

From one of the glass-front cabinets that line the walls
of the autopsy room, one man reached for a two-handled
device resembling a bolt cutter. One by one, each rib
yielded to this instrument with a smart, loud *crack* until
the pathologists could remove the breastplate and expose
the heart and lungs.

Then they cut out each major organ, examined it for
disease and trauma, weighed it, and set it aside to be
dissected and analyzed more closely later.

Then they examined the head, beginning again with
the scalpel. They started the incision just below the hairline forward of the ear, drew it back and down, following
the hairline around the back of the head and over to the
other ear.

They pulled the skin up over the top of the skull and
down as far as the brow.

They saw where the bullet entered and the starburst
pattern it created on the rim of the hole.

Amid the whine of a high-speed motor, one of the
pathologists pressed an electric saw against the forehead

and began a series of cuts. The notch he left in the skull cap would enable them to align the piece and secure it later when the skin was replaced and sutured. After the cutting, a wide blade popped the skull cap off.

The collection of blood around the wound to the brain told them that Mudd was alive when the head shot was fired.

It took nearly three hours for all of that work to be done, and Meinert had lacked the time, the need, and the fortitude on the Monday after Christmas to watch. He knew he could read the report, so he'd opened the big heavy wooden door, walked through the white-tiled hallway, and went back to the detective bureau to collect Slutzker.

■ ■ ■

Bill Dudas merged with westbound parkway traffic near the WTAE television studio on Ardmore Boulevard, taking Arlene to be interviewed by Finello and Byers. Within minutes, Detective Bliss Zenner turned his car off Ardmore onto Marlboro Street. His job was to canvass the neighborhood for witnesses.

He started with Ken Raynor and his wife at 1501. The only information they could contribute was that they heard yelling and hollering at about 11:30 P.M. the night before.

Alice Horgan of 1511 had considerably more to say, but little of consequence.

At around 11:30 Sunday night she heard what sounded like three gunshots and looked out the bedroom window but could not see anything. She heard Arlene screaming, saw the police arrive, and saw Arlene being led to a neighbor's house.

The house at 1515 Marlboro was the source of nearly continuous trouble and arguing since the Mudds had moved in, Mrs. Horgan said. She'd heard that it was Debbie Slutzker who told John Mudd of the affair between Steve and Arlene. Mrs. Horgan also knew of Arlene's broken jaw and the period when she lived with Slutzker.

Slutzker made terrible threats against his wife and daughter, she said. "He appears to be very weird. I wouldn't put anything past him."

The neighborhood had been a good bit quieter in the last few months, but maybe that's because the weather was colder and doors and windows were shut, she said.

The Sullivans at 1517 were the ones whose house Arlene entered looking for immediate help after calling the police and her brother-in-law Jimmy.

Yes, they said, they had left their living room light on and the front door unlocked while they were out for dinner with Dan's mother in Wilkinsburg and later a visit with June's sister in Allison Park.

The guy who lived across the street was nuts, they told Zenner.

The Sullivans suspected that Slutzker had been throwing firecrackers out the window around 7 A.M. many mornings.

H. J. Mann at 1509 had been hearing the same noises in the morning for the previous two weeks. He thought they were gunshots, not firecrackers. He never called the police about them.

Mann said he was a member of Teamsters Local 249 and had tried to get John Mudd work. Mr. Dawson at 1526 told of having overheard Arlene tell Mudd that he was not going to use her as a sex machine or as a "fuck machine." Mann told Zenner he'd seen a lot of men going in and out of the Mudd house.

The interviews were getting juicy, but they weren't enough to go to court with, Zenner thought.

Cynthia DeMann at 1503 heard what she thought was a car backfiring at approximately 11 P.M. She thought she heard it six times. She saw nothing the first time she looked outside, but on her second peek she saw Arlene Mudd and a man with her. Then the police arrived, she said.

Mrs. DeMann had learned about Steve and Arlene's affair from Debbie Slutzker, who also reported that Steve had been in St. Francis Hospital for mental treatment.

DeMann told Zenner she'd heard Debbie and little Amy Slutzker plead with Steve not to hit Debbie any more.

■ ■ ■

Meinert didn't particularly relish the role of being chauffeur to a suspected killer. It wasn't his style. He was the dapper captain of the DA's detectives: three-piece suits, not a hair out of place, and always a gentleman.

Meinert so prided himself on being proper in his appearance, bearing, and language that he once helped turn a criminal case in the department's favor just by being himself. It was a case in which a criminal defendant claimed that he was browbeaten by detectives into confessing. The man testified that Meinert was one of several detectives who verbally abused him to the point that he confessed just to stop the onslaught. Meinert, in particular, had cursed a blue streak, the guy said.

On hearing this, the prosecutor knew he had a winner. He introduced a parade of witnesses who testified that Meinert was the one man in county law enforcement who was never heard to utter a foul word and was never expected to in this lifetime. Hearing that, the judge admitted the suspect's confession into evidence.

By driving Slutzker back to McKeesport, Meinert was preventing the bleary-eyed Finello from getting back behind the wheel of the car. It also allowed for a third set of ears to listen to Slutzker's story in hope of finding important inconsistencies.

Steve stuck tightly to his story.

Figuring that he had stiffed Finello and Byers, Slutzker's mind began to drift to other matters. He grew sullen and less responsive as they got closer to Grandview Avenue.

"I'll go with you," Meinert said as he stopped the car at the O'Deas' house. "I want to talk to your friends."

The couple agreed and invited Meinert inside. They went to the kitchen, where Janet did most of the talking.

The O'Deas had moved not long before to McKeesport from Wilkinsburg. They'd met Slutzker through CB radio and had been friends with him since around October.

Steve had been at the O'Dea home on and off through the Christmas season and was there Christmas Eve and Christmas Day as well as Sunday, the twenty-eighth. He came for dinner, she said, and left by himself around 7 or 8 P.M. and was back in an hour.

Slutzker had gotten drunk, so the O'Deas put him to bed in their room and let him sleep there until 1 or 1:30 Monday morning, when they woke him. The three sat in the kitchen drinking coffee. They all went to bed some time later.

They said it would have been virtually impossible for Steve to leave the house a second time that evening without them knowing. They didn't remember any phone calls coming in either. He could have made calls from the phone in their bedroom.

Janet and Patrick indicated they'd be willing to take a polygraph exam if it was necessary.

Meinert thanked the couple, left the kitchen, and was heading for the front door when it occurred to him to ask Slutzker for permission to search his van, which was parked outside.

Slutzker agreed and readily signed a consent form that the captain pulled from his folder.

It was a worthy thought, but Meinert found nothing in the van that connected Slutzker with the crime. He left McKeesport with not much more information than when he arrived.

■ ■ ■

By ten minutes to 2 o'clock, the twenty-four-year-old widow Mudd and her father were seated in a conference room with Assistant Chief Jennings and Sergeant Finello, who asked the questions. Detective Marian Corcoran sat at a typewriter, a stack of onionskin at hand.

It was somewhat unusual to allow a witness of this kind, someone who might be involved in a murder, to bring her father to an interview. But the detectives decided to grant her request. It just might keep her off guard and encourage her to cooperate.

Finello led her through a long description of the family's activities on Sunday morning, the gathering with her in-laws, the drive home, the Christmas lights on Fifth Avenue, and the fun with "coat man."

"I had walked into the kitchen to get a drink, and I noticed the kitchen window open," she said. "Johnny came walking in, and I said did he open the window for anything, and he said, 'No.'

"So I questioned little Johnny, and he said, 'No.' So I

shut the window, and I told Johnny that it didn't just get opened by itself.

"Then little Johnny laid on the love seat in the living room and covered up. We put the television on and we were laying on the couch together. I was facing him. My son came over. He had his ViewMaster, and he was showing us pictures through it. He went to show me, and it hit me on the head, and Johnny said to him, 'Go sit down now and go to sleep,' because he was getting too jumpy.

"I was facing Johnny because my head was hurting from when I got hit by the ViewMaster, so then we were kissing, and he was making jokes and then all of the sudden I opened my eyes after kissing him and it was dark in the living room."

They tried the on/off switch on the television. Mudd flicked the wall switch a few times at the head of the basement steps. He pounded the wall.

"I turned the dining room light on just a little bit in case Johnny would wake up that he wouldn't be scared. I then walked towards the kitchen, and I was going to get some matches and go down with him, and I heard Johnny walk down a couple of steps. He was halfway down, and I heard a noise. I didn't think it was a shot until I heard it again. I heard Johnny say, 'Oh, hon.' I called to him, and he didn't answer. So, I walked to the cellar door and looked down and seen him laying on the floor."

Arlene said that's when she called the operator and was connected to Pittsburgh police.

"I was looking out the door, afraid that someone would be out there. I still had the phone in my hand, and I called his brother Jimmy. I told his wife that Johnny had been shot. She said to calm down, 'Jimmy's on his way.'"

Arlene described seeing lights outside from her neighbor's house and running to their front door.

"I left my door wide open. I rang their bell one time. I opened the door because I was scared. I wiggled the doorknob and it was open and I went in. I yelled for help and nobody answered."

She said she looked in their kitchen and on the second floor. Finding no one home, she returned to her house.

"I got some knives out from the drawer and I put them on the floor with me and I called Terry because we were with them that night, and I told what happened.

"Then I seen a police car coming past the house and I ran up the street to get him. They came down and they wouldn't let me in the house. I told him my son was sleeping in there, and they went and they got him for me.

"Then we went to a neighbor's house, and then I just sat there and waited. I kept asking about my husband and finally they told me he was dead, and they took my son to somebody's house and then my dad came and then we went to the police station. That was it. We just stayed there."

Finello wanted to know more about the shots she heard.

"They were loud. It sounded like something fell. I heard one noise and I didn't know what it was. I was walking towards the door and heard another one. Then I heard, 'Oh, hon,' and heard another shot. When he said it you could tell something was wrong because it sounded like a groan. I could understand him and I heard him. I called out to him and he didn't answer."

Arlene told the detectives that her husband carried a $10,000 life insurance policy on himself, but it was her understanding that when they split up that summer he'd removed her as beneficiary.

She described the incident on Broad Street the previous July in front of Mary Mudd's house.

"Do you know anything about Johnny's mother, Mrs. Mudd, getting a threatening phone call?" Finello said.

"Yes. All I know is yesterday down at his sister Maureen's house, she mentioned it. She said someone called her mother at four o'clock in the morning and wouldn't say nothing on the phone. And then she heard someone say, 'Tell her her son's dead.' "

"Did Steve Slutzker ever tell you that he loved you or wanted to marry you?"

"He said he loved me, but he never mentioned marriage."

"Was there hard feelings between Johnny and Steve?"

"From what Steve told me, he said that he didn't want any trouble. When I went back with Johnny he said if that's what I wanted he wouldn't stop me, and Johnny never said anything about doing anything to Steve, but he didn't care for him because he broke our marriage up. I don't think he hated him, I just think he didn't want to be bothered with him."

"Did Steve ever talk to you about killing Johnny?"

"No."

"When was the last time you spoke to Steve?"

"It was outside a couple of weeks ago. All he said to me, was I happy? I said, 'Yes.' I told him I didn't want no trouble, and he said he told me he'd never force me into anything I didn't want. He just walked away and I just walked away."

The interview was over before 3 o'clock.

■ ■ ■

On Tuesday, December 30, Finello called Debbie Slutzker at her residence on East Maple Court in Altoona. She told him she'd spoken to Steve the day before by phone and asked him if he had anything to do with Mudd's death. " 'No,' " he said.

The former Mrs. Slutzker said she planned to go back with Steve in January for Amy's sake.

The previous summer, John Mudd confronted Steve about a trip he had made with Arlene to Niagara Falls, Debbie said.

"What do you know about the relationship between your husband and Mrs. Mudd?" Finello asked.

"He and Arlene were in love," she said.

Meanwhile, Zenner continued his interviewing on Marlboro Street. He spoke with Colletta Ward of 1536 early that afternoon.

At around 11:30 Sunday night, a police officer told her husband, Dennis, who was standing outside 1515, to take Arlene away from in front of her house. Dennis took her to his house.

"She was crying hysterically and saying 'My husband was shot' and 'He was calling me.' She kept repeating those two things," Mrs. Ward said.

To anyone who came to the Wards' home, Arlene said, "How's my husband doing?"

■ ■ ■

After the visit from the state police and Mike's interview later that morning, the Pezzanos could think about little besides the Mudd case. It wasn't until late on Tuesday that it finally occurred to Mike to get back in touch with his old friend.

"Steve?"

"Yeah."

"It's Mike. Whaddya doin'?"

"Nothing. Sittin' around here. What's up?"

"So tell me, when am I going to get the invitation to the wedding?" Pezzano snickered.

Slutzker gave a nervous little laugh.

"I heard about this guy Mudd. I heard somebody iced him. Is that right?"

"Ah, yeah. I don't know. Yeah. I guess they did. What can I say?"

It was clear that the subject was an uncomfortable one for Slutzker and that the conversation wasn't going to go anywhere.

"Well, what're you doin' right now?" Pezzano asked.

"Nothing."

"Well, Donna and I had a big fight today. She's not talking to me. Whaddya say, I could take a ride down if you're going to be home. If you want."

"Yeah, you could come down. How about bringing a six-pack and we'll have a few beers," Slutzker said.

"No can do. No cash."

"Well, okay. Come on down anyway."

Pezzano arrived at around 7:30 P.M.

They made their hellos. Slutzker was cordial, but subdued and ill at ease.

Pezzano brought up the killing.

"It was fate. It was just fate," Slutzker said.

"That's funny, don't you think? It's kind of funny that fate means he gets shot with a thirty-two and you told me about the thirty-two."

"It was just an act of God," Slutzker said.

"Right. Right. But what if the police get the wife under questioning? What if she breaks down? What if she squeals?"

"There's no problem there. We've got things pretty well worked out together. She loves me. The police can't break her down. And they're definitely not going to get anything out of me."

"How'd you do it? Did it happen like we planned?"

"I wasn't there. I gave the whole thing up when you never called. It was an act of God. Somebody else must have had it in for him.

"I wasn't even in Wilkinsburg that night. I was in McKeesport. I was drunk on my ass, man."

"Well, do you have any idea who did it?"

"Probably someone who he had screwed out of money he owed. He owed a lot out on dope."

They talked some more. Slutzker explained why he hadn't wanted to say much on the telephone when Pezzano had called.

"It's being tapped," he said. "I'm sure it is."

Slutzker picked up the phone and called Debbie, his ex-wife.

He sweet-talked her, saying he'd realized what a mistake he'd made, that he loved her, that Amy needed her, and that he wanted to put their family back together.

"Why'd you do that? You and Debbie getting back together or something?"

"I'm going to have her come back," he told Pezzano after he hung up. "I want her to come back and start New Year's with us to smooth things over, get everybody off my ass for a while. This'll all blow over."

■ ■ ■

On Wednesday, New Year's Eve, after two good nights' sleep, Finello was ready to dig into Slutzker's alibi. He drove back to McKeesport to question Janet and Patrick O'Dea.

The substance of their story remained the same, although some of the marginal details had changed from Monday morning.

Slutzker's absence after dinner lasted only about forty-five minutes, not an hour. They didn't know whether he drove away in his copper-color van or merely sat in it. He also went outside one other time, but for a much shorter period.

He returned from his longer absence at around 7 P.M. By 8 he was asleep in their bed, they said.

Bill Krueger, also known to the O'Deas by his CB handle "Dr. Crossbones," and Jerry "Kilowatt" Schwartz stopped by around 9:30. Steve slept through their visit.

Janet O'Dea was "Lady Shamrock" on the radio, Patrick was "Mr. Shamrock."

They said that after the murder, Slutzker told them that his affair with Arlene had ended several months earlier and that he'd traded angry words with Mudd but the argument had nothing to do with the killing.

Finello left Grandview Avenue for the second time thinking that the O'Deas were not the most appealing alibi witnesses, but they had a story, and they were sticking to it.

■ ■ ■

Three days later, on Saturday, January 3, the phone rang in the sergeant's home. It was the desk man at the bureau. James Mudd had something to report, and he insisted on talking to Finello.

He returned the call and learned that a person who sounded just like Steve Slutzker had called the Mudd residence in East Liberty and gotten Mary Mudd on the line.

" 'I'm coming down there, and I'm going to kill you and everyone in your house,' " the caller said.

The call came the day after the Mudds buried John.

"Mr. Mudd, here's what I want you to do," Finello said. "I want you to call the Pittsburgh police and report to them what you just told me. Okay?"

"What're they going to do about it?"

"I can't say for sure, but that's what I want you to do. There's some things I need to do."

Mudd did as instructed. Finello talked to Stack. The chief wanted the matter pursued.

Finello met two city officers at the Mudd residence around suppertime. They compared notes and agreed there was probable cause to arrest Slutzker.

The officers left to get an arrest warrant. Finello reported in to Stack, who told him to stay put with Mrs. Mudd until the warrant arrived. Instead of the warrant, Finello got a phone call at the Mudd home at 8:30 P.M. from one of the city officers. He had the warrant but he and his partner were unable to go to Wilkinsburg to serve it.

At Finello's request, Chief Hodgins in Wilkinsburg dispatched two officers to retrieve the warrant in Pittsburgh and serve it on Slutzker. That happened at 11 o'clock in the presence of Slutzker's attorney, H. David Rothman.

Slutzker was arraigned that night and ordered to appear at a preliminary hearing on Tuesday, January 13.

Earlier in the day, Slutzker apparently had made a stop at the Dudas home in Forest Hills, because when Arlene's mother went to the mailbox at noon she found a small blue case and two envelopes addressed to Arlene, none of which bore postage.

The case contained a star sapphire ring, which Arlene recognized as the one Steve had offered to her on her birthday the previous November. One envelope contained a poem and a typewritten note saying "Cheer up. Write.

Will wait forever. All my love." The other envelope contained a poem that Arlene had given to Steve.

Arlene gave all three items to Detective Tim Logue on Tuesday, January 6, the same day Slutzker was released on bond. He walked out of the county jail in downtown Pittsburgh at 3:30 that afternoon. Five minutes later, Finello was on the phone to Jimmy Mudd warning that Slutzker was free.

Finello didn't reach Arlene to warn her until 5:30. It was his second conversation with her that day; a few hours before Slutzker's release, the sergeant had questioned her for an hour and a half with Assistant Chief Jennings listening and Detective Corcoran tapping away at the typewriter.

Unlike her earlier conversation with police, Arlene was represented during this one by her attorney, Joe Esper of Forest Hills.

There were no preliminaries this time, only the recitation of her rights under the U.S. Supreme Court's Miranda decision. Then Finello got right down to it.

"Recalling Sunday, December 28, 1975, shortly after the incident occurred, I understand that you were standing outside the house and talking to a gentleman in a tan coat. Do you recall who this man was?"

Finello was basing his question on Cynthia DeMann's statement to Zenner about what she saw the second time she looked outside the night of the killing.

By whatever means, Arlene was smooth as silk in handling the question. She said it was her neighbor, Dennis Ward, who escorted her to his house well after the police arrived. Arlene did not mention the man Brendlinger had seen her speaking to across the street before the Wilkinsburg police arrived.

"He was a gentleman who had come down with the

police, and he tried to calm me down. They, the police, pulled their guns out, and I knew my son was on that couch sleeping and that was right by the door, and I wanted to go and get him.

"They, the police, told me they would bring him out. So they did, and my son was half sleeping and he started crying. So then I took him in my arms and this guy took me to his house."

Could she describe the man?

"No, but he had two daughters there and an older woman, who I assumed was his mother. They kept saying to calm down, your husband's okay. They asked if I wanted a drink or anything. All I wanted to do was to go down by the police. I kept asking for my brother-in-law, Jimmy Mudd. At that time all these guys looked so familiar. I don't know who came in but they told me my husband passed away. I got upset and the baby got upset. Someone took the baby and said they were taking him to a guy by the name of Nick and that he was a police officer, which I knew he was, but I didn't know where he lived."

Finello again took her over the moments when the shots were fired.

"Johnny flicked the light switch by the cellar on the top and kept it up. He didn't know that the fuse was burned out too. We reported to the real estate that you had to put the light on and then bang on the wall and she, the real estate woman, said that it was a bad connection.

"After he did this I don't know how many steps, I assumed four steps or so, I heard a noise, and I heard the second noise. I realized then what it was. I heard Johnny, and I swear this, called me in pain, and he said, 'Hey, hon,' and that's all he said. It sounded like he was in pain. Then I heard another noise. I realized then it was shots, that that's what they had to be.

"I held my ears and kept screaming for him to answer me, and I was screaming 'Johnny! Johnny! Answer me.' Between that I heard a noise in the cellar. I then left the kitchen into the living room and took the phone to the door. I thought if somebody came up from the cellar at least I could run out the door or if they went around the door, I would see them."

Arlene said Slutzker never had a key to her house as far as she knew, even during the time she lived with him. She'd given her set to her husband, who loaned them to his live-in pal, Dukers.

Steve was, nonetheless, familiar with their house and its wiring because he'd installed the dining room ceiling fixture and the dimmer switch, she said.

He'd also been in the Mudd's basement. It was with John, however, at a time when her husband was trying to sell her old Kirby sweeper. The two men went downstairs to look it over.

After a few routine questions, Finello hit her with a tidbit the detectives had picked up along the way.

"Did you see Steve at Children's Palace on Christmas Eve?"

"Not Christmas Eve, but approximately a week before Christmas," she said, not missing a beat, even though she'd told them in her interview December 29 that the last time she'd seen Slutzker was two weeks before the murder.

"I didn't say a word to him," she continued. "He stared at me. When he seen me I was walking in the aisle. My sister-in-law, Donna Mudd, was with me, and we were looking at toys. Little Johnny was looking at the boys' toys, and when I seen Steve he was with his daughter. So, I went to get little Johnny so that he wouldn't go up and say something. I didn't want Steve to go up and say something to little Johnny, because little Johnny was afraid of Steve. So we all stuck together then and we got in line to get out of there.

"Steve was in a different line, and he kept staring, like real sad like, and I told Donna not to look. He got out of the store, and he sat in his truck. He watched us walk to the car, and as we pulled out, he pulled out and followed us down the highway and then he passed us. He took an exit off, and we kept going straight. That was it."

Finello was by now into the heart of the plan he and Byers had laid. He was throwing out the hardest questions he could, given the information he had and the drift of the detectives' suspicions.

"Did you know that you were the beneficiary on the insurance policy?"

"At one time I was. As far as I know, Kay Mudd is the beneficiary, because Johnny told me she was. Johnny mentioned to me that he was going to have it changed back to my name, and the insurance man said that he would go out and get the papers, and we said that there was no hurry. I still believe Kay Mudd is the beneficiary on that policy."

Finello asked next how much light she had when she looked down the cellar steps immediately after the shooting.

"The kitchen light was on, the one over the fish tank. It was a little light. The big light was definitely off. When I glanced down the cellar I could see Johnny laying in a huddle, just like his head and leg were bent up. I ran out then, out of the kitchen. I kept screaming for him to answer me, hoping that he would answer."

As to the possibility that the killer could have left the house through the living room, Arlene said she believed she was gone for three minutes on her excursion through the Sullivans' home next door. Her front door was open while she was gone.

"When I got back to my house, I shut the door and I had the knife there and just then that's when the police cars came by my house with the lights on, flashing. They passed the house."

Finello wanted to know about any threats Steve made against her husband. She did not go out of her way to deflect suspicion from her former lover.

"He never mentioned he would kill him, but Steve said if something would happen to him that would be nice, like a car accident or for him to drop dead, something to that nature."

Finello wanted to hear more.

"See, Steve was a very emotional person. Sometimes he would say something that he didn't even mean, but he said it. Like, he said when I was living with Steve, Johnny came up on the porch at Steve's house, and he tapped on the window. He knew I was in there, and I told Steve I was scared because at that time I had a broken jaw from Johnny. Steve said if he comes in this house, he's going to be sorry. By that, that was what he said, I knew he had guns in the house, and that I think Steve thought if he came in his house he could do something to Johnny."

"Did Steve ever threaten to kill little Johnny?"

"No. He knew my son meant the world to me. He knows I can't have any more kids."

Arlene said she hadn't seen or spoken to Slutzker since the murder, but he called her parents home on Saturday, January 3.

"My dad answered the telephone and thought it was Beverly's boyfriend. He asked for my little sister, Beverly. Then he said, 'How's Arlene taking it? Is she very upset?

Where is she? How could I talk with her? Is she going to church tonight?"

"When she got off the phone she said it was Steve. That's when my parents got hysterical because they knew he was up at the mail box. So we left the house that night."

Finello asked her if Slutzker was in love with her.

"He told me that he loved me, but he never meant it, because he was calling his wife all the time behind my back. Then he told me when I found out he was calling his wife that he did not know who he loved."

"Were you in love with Steve?"

"I think I felt sorry for him."

Arlene offered to take a polygraph test, then initialed and signed the transcript. Three minutes later she thought of something else to say.

"I wanted to add that when I was living with Steve that he said if Johnny was out of the way that things would be okay. I got upset, and he said he meant if he got hit by a bus or a car or got into drugs or got upset over losing me. He thought he would hurt himself because I had left him. I can remember telling Steve I didn't want no harm to come to Johnny because I loved him still, in a different way, and that I wouldn't even press charges against Johnny when he broke my jaw because I felt that he did it because he loved me. He just broke my jaw in a fit of anger. I knew Johnny was sorry after it happened."

The little amendment was just the kind of kicker you'd expect to get from a cooperative witness. Maybe letting Arlene bring her dad to the first interview was paying off after all. Unfortunately, she'd said nothing that opened the door to substantial evidence implicating herself.

The case was moving forward only by increments now. On Wednesday, the seventh, Finello had the Pezzanos back for further questioning. Mike was going to be the star witness when charges were filed, and the investigators wanted to explore his story thoroughly, as much to familiarize themselves with the details as to continue probing for inconsistencies that would be exploited by the defense.

Donna went first. She described the nature of their relationship with Slutzker and her impressions of him. She recited key portions of her conversation with him on December 19.

Finello asked Donna if she'd be willing to turn over records of her telephone calls and she readily agreed. He did not ask her if she would be willing to take a polygraph.

When it was Mike's turn, Finello walked him through the entire affair once again. He finished with his star witness after forty-five minutes. Finello didn't ask Mike to take a polygraph either.

Two days later, Bell Telephone Company produced phone records documenting the telephone numbers for Patrick T. O'Dea on Grandview Avenue in McKeesport, Michael Pezzano on Race Street in Connellsville, and Slutzker Electric Company on Marlboro Street in Wilkinsburg.

The records showed calls on December 19 from the O'Dea house to Pezzano at 3:59 P.M. and from Pezzano to the O'Dea house at 4:37 P.M.

A call went from Slutzker's phone to Pezzano at 10:27 P.M. on December 22 and one from Pezzano to Slutzker at 6:42 P.M. on December 30.

■ ■ ■

The search for all guns registered to Steve Slutzker turned up a .32 automatic Savage pistol, model 1917, owned by Norman Slutzker in Westmoreland County. One of the residents on Marlboro Street had told Zener that Steve Slutzker had a brother, whose car was seen occasionally in the neighborhood.

The job of finding that gun fell to Detective Joe Dugan. On Saturday, January 10, he filled out an application for a search warrant, citing as his probable cause the statements of "Michael Pezzano, a private citizen and prudent person."

He drove to Youngwood and got Magistrate Ernie Johnson to sign it.

At 6:45 A.M. on January 12, Dugan called the state police barracks in Greensburg to notify them of the search at Norman Slutzker's house on Fosterville Road outside Greensburg.

A half hour later, Dugan and Bliss Zener were on the Slutzkers' porch. The man and his wife invited the detectives to come in. Dugan explained why they were there and handed over a consent form. Slutzker was shocked by the news about his brother and the murder investigation. He readily signed, waiving his Fourth Amendment right to refuse a search of himself or his property.

Then he handed Dugan his .32 automatic, which he'd been wearing since answering the door. Dugan emptied the gun of the four rounds in the clip and held on to the weapon.

Slutzker said he and his wife were in New York on Sunday, December 28, and the gun was hidden in the house. He was sure no one removed it.

Slutzker volunteered that he owned another gun and produced a Sturm & Ruger .357 Magnum. It was a nice-looking weapon, but Dugan and Zener had no interest in it and handed it back. The holes in John Mudd weren't that big.

Their business with Norman Slutzker was finished, but since it never hurts to ask a few questions, the detectives chatted Norman up for a few minutes.

He said he hadn't seen much of his brother Steve or his father in several years and last spoke to Steve by phone around the first of the year. Steve hadn't mentioned the recent trouble.

At 7:45 A.M., Dugan and Zener were getting back in their car to find breakfast. There was no sense in getting caught in rush-hour traffic and turning a forty-five minute drive to Pittsburgh into a ninety-minute headache.

Fifteen minutes after Dugan started his engine, Finello and Detective Bill Vukovich pulled up to 1516 Marlboro Avenue and turned off theirs.

Slutzker was sitting in his van with his daughter and talking to county Lieutenant Richard Byers and Wilkinsburg officer Paul von Geis.

"Steve, turn off the motor and step out of the vehicle, please," Byers said when the other county detectives walked up to the van.

No sooner had Slutzker closed the door behind him when Finello spoke.

"Mr. Slutzker, I'm placing you under arrest for the murder of John Lawrence Mudd. You have the right to . . ." he went on.

Slutzker listened to his Miranda rights, less cavalierly this time than when he'd first heard Finello recite them on December 29. The suspect, now on his way to becoming a defendant, nodded and said he understood his rights.

"We have a warrant to search your house," the big detective said, handing over a copy of the affidavit accompanying the warrant.

If Slutzker paid attention to what he was reading, he

saw that Pezzano had ratted him out. He made no comment out loud on that, but he immediately denied any involvement in Mudd's death. He said he was in McKeesport the night of the killing, and he said he didn't own a .32-caliber handgun or any .32-caliber ammunition.

The officers began the search, joined now by Wilkinsburg Chief Hodgins and Lieutenants McKenna and Krueger.

Slutzker asked the officer guarding him for permission to go upstairs and get his money. He said that he had $500 and wanted to give it to a friend. He was allowed to get the cash and call his friend, Ellie Padolf. She agreed to come to his house and pick up Amy and was there in forty-five minutes from her home in nearby Highland Park. Ellie sent Amy upstairs to pack her clothes. Slutzker gave Ellie his daughter, his dog, his keys, a list of things to do, and the $500, which he asked her to deliver to his father, Louis Slutzker.

Byers, Vukovich, and Krueger headed first to the master bedroom, where Slutzker told them they'd find two .38-caliber revolvers. They found a Smith & Wesson with a six-inch barrel and a S & W snubnose.

In the bedroom and stashed throughout the house, the detectives found handsful of .38- and .22-caliber ammuniton and empty shells, gun cleaning kits, and large firecrackers.

They found two certificates issued by the Connelly Technical School for electrical wiring, dated 1971 and 1972.

Krueger produced the only item of any possible significance to their investigation: a single live .32-caliber shell. It was on the second shelf of the closet in Slutzker's bedroom.

An hour and a half after reciting Miranda rights for the

umpteenth time in their careers, Finello and Vukovich watched Slutzker slip his green corduroy jacket over his white-and-red sweater. They escorted him to their car and drove to the Wilkinsburg police station to make a record of his arrest.

A short time later, they went through the same process, plus a photo session, at the county courthouse. From there they went to the morgue, where Deputy Coroner Roy Bauer arraigned Slutzker on a charge of criminal homicide. Then it was on to McKeesport, where Magistrate Charles Johnson arraigned him on a charge of criminal solicitation to commit murder in connection with the phone call from the O'Deas' house to Pezzano on December 19.

By the end of the lunch hour, Steven Slutzker, twenty-five, was an inmate in the old brown stone jail on Ross Avenue in downtown Pittsburgh.

Closing the Barn Door . . .

Never let it be said that rural communities don't have crack law enforcement organizations just because they're located in the sticks.

On January 13, 1976, Bedford County sheriff Fred W. Hoover took decisive action to make the world a safer place. He directed his chief deputy, Al Shuler, to write a letter to Slutzker in care of the Allegheny County Jail.

The letter informed Slutzker that Bedford County was revoking the permit, issued the previous August 15, that made it legal for Slutzker, a resident of Wilkinsburg, two counties removed from Bedford, to carry a concealed pistol anywhere in Pennsylvania.

"Please be advised to, by return mail, send us your

copy of the permit. On conclusion of present case, permit application will be reviewed by this office."

And just so that the hotshot homicide investigators in Pittsburgh would know that Hoover and his boys were on the case, Shuler copied Sergeant Finello.

In the middle of January 1976, Joe Lindsey was still working on the Buena Vista Street project in Wilkinsburg. He was chatting with one of the other workers, who mentioned in passing that a guy he'd known growing up in the Garfield section of Pittsburgh had been murdered. The police had arrested a suspect.

The news would have gone in one ear and out the other except that the other worker mentioned the names. The guy who got murdered was John Mudd Sr., and the suspect was Steven Slutzker.

Lindsay paused for a moment.

Holy mackerel, he thought.

Then he went back to work.

■ ■ ■

A few miles from Buena Vista Street, Steve Hairston heard the same news. He'd talked to Slutzker on the phone on the sixteenth or seventeenth of December and concluded that the substance of their conversation was something the police should hear.

He called the Allegheny County Detective Bureau around 3 P.M. on January 13. Finello got on the phone. Within the hour, Finello and Vukovich were at the Texaco station on Bennett Street in Homewood, where Hairston held one of his two jobs.

"My handle's 'Black Derby.' Some people know me as 'Chief Red Pepper.' That's how I met Steve, through the CB."

"What did Mr. Slutzker say to you exactly when he called, Mr. Hairston?"

"He needed someone iced."

This could be good information, Finello thought. It was the first interview of the day that seemed to be breaking in the detectives' favor.

In a telephone interview with Jerry Schwartz a few hours earlier, Finello had failed to do any damage to Slutzker's alibi. Schwartz, who was at the O'Deas' the night of December 28 with Bill Krueger, said the same thing as every other member of the McKeesport connection.

"Me and Bill got there around eight o'clock. When we got there, Steve's van was parked outside in front of the house. When we went in, Janet said Steve was asleep up in the bedroom because he had too much to drink."

Schwartz said he saw Amy Slutzker playing with the O'Dea children, but he never saw Steve. He and Krueger left at 11 or 11:30 and again noticed Slutzker's bronze-color van.

Schwartz said he had the impression that Slutzker sometimes would stay overnight on his visits to the O'Dea home.

And late the same morning, Corcoran interviewed Krueger. She got more detail than Finello did, but nothing of great consequence. The only items of interest were that Krueger saw a bottle of Seagram's Seven on the buffet in the dining room but no beer bottles. He said that as far as he knew, Slutzker did not stay overnight when he visited the O'Deas.

Krueger said that in a conversation after the murder Slutzker said he didn't know why the police picked him up. He said they had asked about the Mudd shooting and released him because they didn't have anything on him.

Otherwise, Krueger remembered seeing the O'Dea daughters Clare and Norma, their children, and Amy Slutzker at the O'Deas'. The adults watched television and talked on the CB while he and Schwartz were there.

On their way back to Wilkinsburg they heard on the CB that police were on Marlboro Street, Krueger said. Finding the street blocked with police cars, they parked and walked to the home of a CB buddy named "Kingfish." Krueger called his father to tell him where he was, then left after five minutes or so to drive Schwartz to his home in Squirrel Hill. After a cup of coffee, Krueger went home.

Unlike what they'd learned from Krueger and Schwartz, Hairston's statements would very likely be useful in court even though the interview didn't break any new ground.

Stephen Emerson Hairston was an assistant engineer at WAMO radio station and a part-time attendant at the Texaco station. He lived on Laketon Road in Wilkinsburg and had known Slutzker and Pezzano for a couple years.

He said Slutzker had talked to him by phone around 7 P.M. on the sixteenth or seventeenth of December.

He wanted to know if Hairston knew anybody could do a job for him. Hairston recounted the conversation for the detectives:

"What kind of a job?"

"I need somebody iced. It's something between him and me. And there's a woman and children involved."

"No, not offhand, I don't, Steve."

"Well, how 'bout you think about it? I'm having some trouble with someone out here, and I need this done by Friday. There's a place near the house here that would be good to do it. That'll be the easiest way. The job pays. There's money in it for the guy who does this."

"Man, I can't think of anybody who could do it, Steve. But I'll tell you what, I'll think about it. How 'bout that?"

"Okay. You think about it. I'll get back to you."

"Okay, man."

"All right."

Slutzker called again on Thursday, December 18, to find out if Hairston had been able to do any good.

"No go, man. Sorry. The only guy I know who would know anybody like that got himself killed not long ago."

"Well, I'm going to find somebody else, then," Slutzker said.

Hairston had heard a lot of jive bullshit in his time, and he was inclined to believe that this was more of the same until he picked up the *Pittsburgh Post-Gazette* on the morning of December 29.

"It rang a bell with me," he told Finello and Vukovich, "because Slutzker said to me 'His name's going to be mud.' "

"Thank you, Mr. Hairston. We'll be getting back to you soon on this," Finello said.

■ ■ ■

By Tuesday, January 13, the coroner's inquest was only a week away, and Slutzker's alibi was holding up. The evidence against him was circumstantial. Sure, Slutzker solicited two men to kill John Mudd and was rebuffed by both. Mudd ended up dead anyway. It was no stretch of the imagination to conclude that Slutzker did it. But how could anyone know beyond reasonable doubt that he actually did it? In the absence of compelling evidence to the contrary, the DA could reasonably hope for a conviction, but there was, in fact, compelling evidence to the contrary.

That evidence came from Slutzker, Janet and Patrick O'Dea, Bill Krueger, and Jerry Schwartz, who were singing the same tune. Individually, none was an ideal alibi witness. But together, even a skeptic would be forced to admit that their story created reasonable doubt. Besides, where was the weapon? The fingerprints? The eyewitness to the crime?

Unless the detectives could crack that alibi, the prosecution would need a sympathetic ear on the bench come January 22, and Stack had to know it.

A good criminal case has the heft of solid oak or the smell of new leather. Those elements weren't here.

The chief ordered his detectives to pull out all stops in the search for more evidence.

At 10 A.M. on the fourteenth, Lieutenant Byers interviewed Patrick O'Dea at the detective bureau, while Finello talked to Janet. Bliss Zener and Detective Robert Miller interviewed Ellie Padolf.

The grand dame of Grandview Avenue must have known she had the advantage in her interview with Finello because he got little more than her statement that Sunday, December 28, was the first time in many visits that Slutzker had stayed overnight in her home. She also recalled one other time, one Thanksgiving Day, when

Steve drank heavily in her presence. Janet also allowed as how Steve had a bad temper.

Patrick O'Dea was more verbose but no more helpful: The liquor he and Steve drank was, in fact, Seagram's Seven, and the beer was Stroh's. Slutzker seemed depressed. He left the house twice for twenty minutes each time between 6 P.M. and 7 P.M. and explained that he was writing in his truck.

He became tipsy and was in the O'Deas' bed before 9 P.M. and stayed there until they roused him at 1 A.M., gave him coffee, and sent him to the living room couch for the rest of the night.

The O'Deas said Slutzker told them the detectives took him in for questioning Monday morning because he had been dating the victim's wife.

Eleanor Padolf told Zener and Miller everything she could think of about Steve Slutzker. There was little for a prosecutor to hang his hat on.

Ellie and her husband had met Debbie Slutzker and Arlene Mudd. Steve told the Padolfs he wanted to marry Arlene. They told him to cool it. Ellie called Steve as soon as she read the paper on December 29 and came right out and asked him if he did it. " 'Absolutely not,' " she quoted him as saying.

Debbie Slutzker had been staying with her parents-in-law and went to Ellie's house as soon as Ellie told her she had Amy. Louis Slutzker and his wife arrived at Ellie's around 3:30 P.M.. Ellie gave Mr. Slutzker the $500. Steve's parents visited him at the jail then stopped back at Ellie's around 7:30 before checking into a motel. Debbie returned to the house on Marlboro Street.

Meanwhile, a representative of Bell Telephone security responded to the bureau's subpoena *duces tecum* of two days earlier. Stack typed a report based on the records

Bell produced about phone calls made from the O'Deas'
house during December.

Someone had called a dairy in Export and W&W Electric in Apollo on the third; Cridders Corners on the fifth;
W&W Electric again on the seventh; England, the Federal Communications Commission in Gettysburg and the
FCC in Washington, D.C., on the fifteenth; Vandergrift
and A&B Electric in Cridders Corner on the seventeenth;
Pezzano in Connellsville on the nineteenth; and W&W
Electric and the Vandergrift number again on the twenty-
first.

At noon on January fourteenth, Mrs. Mary Mudd, accompanied by her daughter, Patricia Hill, and son, Terry,
submitted to an interview with Vukovich in the county
courthouse.

Mrs. Mudd described the incident with the gun in
front of her house the previous summer. She also described the phone call before dawn on the day her son
John was murdered. Someone had been coaching the
caller to say "Go ahead and tell her, her son is dead."

She told Vukovich the voice in the background could
have been Slutzker.

Terry Mudd repeated what he'd heard from one of the
Marlboro Street neighbors about Slutzker receiving a
"Section Eight" discharge from the service.

While Vukovich was interviewing the Mudds, Finello
and Byers were picking through the details of Hairston's
story in another room on the fourth floor of the courthouse. They'd already heard the best of it. Marian Corcoran typed every word, nonetheless.

After Vukovich finished with the Mudds, he bolted a
sandwich, gulped a cup of coffee, and interviewed John
Mudd's uncle, John O'Connor.

O'Connor recalled getting up from the glider and see-

ing Slutzker pointing the gun at Mudd from two feet
away. He said he walked to within ten feet of Slutzker,
who then pointed the gun at him.

Immediately after the interview, Detective Joe Dugan
collected the report the Pittsburgh Police Department
filed about John Mudd's visit the evening after the gun-
pointing incident on Broad Street.

There was only one person left on the list of subjects to
be interviewed, and the detectives still had not unearthed
anything that advanced the evidence beyond the circumstantial case they had on the twenty-ninth of December.

Steve Apter was the last up before the inquest on January 22. Finello had him in at 8:30 A.M. on Thursday, the
fifteenth.

Apter's statements were nothing more than window
dressing. He'd met Slutzker at the home of a girl named
Debbie Radakovic, whose handle was "Confused." He'd
heard Slutzker say he couldn't end the affair with Arlene
because he loved her. He'd learned about Mudd's death
the day after it happened. Ellie Padolf had called him. He
was so curious about whether Steve did it that he called
him to ask. "No" was all he said. Finello's interview with
Apter was over in short order.

From then until the following Thursday, the main order of business was to help Assistant District Attorney
John Nickoloff prepare for the inquest.

There was also a routine matter of charging Slutzker
with a second count of solicitation to commit a felony
stemming from Hairston's statements. That was done on
Friday, January sixteenth. Squire Raible in Wilkinsburg
issued the arrest warrant to Finello and Vukovich at 11:30.
They got Slutzker out of jail at 2 P.M., arraigned him before the magistrate, and had him back in jail by three
minutes after 3.

The last thing left for Finello to do was type a list of the witnesses whose testimony would be needed to establish the prosecution's case.

■ ■ ■

Allegheny County is one of only two counties in Pennsylvania that retain the archaic practice of letting the solicitor for the coroner decide whether police and prosecutors have enough evidence against a defendant to go to court on homicide charges.

In all other counties, homicide cases are treated no differently from any other crime. The preliminary hearing is conducted by a magistrate at ground level of the judicial branch of government.

When the coroner's solicitor presides at an inquest, he acts as a judge. With this exception, the coroner's office is a part of the executive branch of government, not the judicial branch. It investigates the cause of death when anything besides natural causes is suspected. Coroners and their deputies pick through evidence at the sites of homicides, working shoulder to shoulder with police and prosecutors for evidence. They confer with law enforcement officials in determining whether evidence warrants filing charges against suspects. They testify for the prosecution at trials. Yet for some reason, the attorney chosen by the winner of the election for coroner in Allegheny County gets to sit behind the judge's bench and rule, or impanel a six-member jury to render a verdict, whether homicide cases may proceed to criminal court. If nothing else, the practice allows one more attorney to have a high-profile government job and gives the coroner one more patronage job to pass out.

The Mudd inquest went to a Pittsburgh attorney

named Stanley Stein. It was his first inquest upon being appointed solicitor for the coroner, and at a few minutes after 10 A.M. on Thursday, January 22, 1976, he called the proceeding to order.

The only charge before Stein was one count of criminal homicide. The two charges of solicitation to commit murder would be handled exclusively within the judicial branch.

John Nickoloff, an assistant district attorney, was the prosecutor. He called Assistant Chief Jennings to the stand first. Jennings described the scene as the county detectives found it when they arrived in the first hours of December 29.

Domenic Mangano, the Wilkinsburg police officer, was sworn in next and testified that young John Mudd was sleeping on the couch when he and other borough officers first entered the house.

The boy wasn't just lying on the couch. He was sleeping, Mangano said.

He also read into the record a report written over Edgewood officer Tim Brendlinger's name.

" 'When I arrived on the scene, I was told to go the rear of the above house, 1515 Marlboro Street. I went down the right side of the house, where I was met by Patrolman Miller at the rear cellar door. I told Patrolman Miller that no one came out this way because there were not any footprints in the snow.

" 'At this time I tried to open the cellar door and it was unlocked but would not open. I think I kicked the door with my foot and it opened. At this time myself, Patrolman Miller, and Sergeant Wetmore entered the cellar and found the victim lying at the bottom of the cellar steps.' Signed Timothy Brendlinger," Mangano said, reading from the piece of paper.

When Nickoloff finished his direct examination of Mangano and it was time for the defense to cross-examine him, Slutzker's attorney, H. David Rothman, voiced a suspicion that had been on the minds of a lot of people. "In view of the fact that you couldn't see that the body was there without the use of a flashlight, did you ask her how she knew that the body was there?"

"No, I didn't," Mangano said. "Because at this time our detectives were there and they were handling the case."

In other words, Mangano was taking the position that because detectives Weber and McKenna were there, it wasn't his job to ask questions like that. It was a theme that would recur.

Arlene was at the neighbors', across the street at 1536, for about twenty minutes before Mangano went back to that house.

"Did you direct any officer to perform any test on Mrs. Mudd to determine whether or not she recently fired a weapon?" Rothman asked.

"Objection," Nickoloff said, before Mangano could answer. "Not relevant."

"He can answer that question," Stein said.

"He could have done a lot of things that are not relevant," Nickoloff said.

"I'm only a patrolman. I have no authorization to order anybody," Mangano said.

Mangano said Wilkinsburg police chief Harry Hodgins is the person who screwed in the loose fuse bringing on the television and the lights in the basement, kitchen, and living room.

Nickoloff put Arlene on next. She was a prosecution witness, even though a cloud hung over her head.

She described her family's return from their holiday

outing on the night of December 28, including the open window in the kitchen.

"I went into the living room, where we turned the TV on and my son played with the ViewMaster. My husband and I were lying on the couch together watching TV. My son fell asleep, and I said, 'Let's go up to bed.' He said he wanted to watch the news because of the Viking game, something had happened to one of the referees. He wanted to hear what happened."

She described the moments leading to her husband's attempt to get the basement light to come on and her last conversation with him.

"He said to me, 'Do we have fuses or do we have a circuit breaker?' I told him, I said, I wasn't sure, but 'If it's fuses, we don't have any.'"

She told Nickoloff that she was standing in the doorway between the kitchen and dining room when she heard the noises. She said she was about five feet from the basement door.

"I was screaming hysterically. I didn't hear as many gunshots as they said were fired. I never heard that many. Like I heard the three I knew of, but I never heard the other ones. I didn't hear them at all."

"And you called the operator, did you?"

"Yes. I just picked up the phone. I have push buttons, and I just pushed the operator. I asked for the Wilkinsburg police. Evidently they must have given me Pittsburgh."

Recalling her trouble with the person who answered, she said, "He couldn't understand me and asked me to repeat it again, and I did."

"Did you say 1515 or 1550?" the prosecutor asked.

"1515 Marlboro Street."

"If there was any misunderstanding, it was on his part, then?"

"Yes."

Arlene said that before she spotted the neighbors' lights and went to their house, she called her brother-in-law, Jim Mudd.

After returning from the Sullivans' empty house and grabbing knives from the kitchen drawer, "I glanced down the cellar steps, and I called my husband. He didn't answer," she said.

"Could you see down the steps?"

"A second, and I seen him. I got hysterical again, and I took the knives and made another phone call to my brother-in-law, Terry Mudd. Then I seen the police cars coming past the street, but they passed the house and I couldn't understand why they hadn't stopped at my house. They went above the street, and I opened the door and called and told them that something had happened. They all came back down and they all went in from there into the house."

Arlene said she never talked with Steve about marrying him.

"Were you afraid of the man, Mr. Slutzker?" Nickoloff said.

Rothman objected but Stein permitted Nickoloff to proceed. He asked her about the argument on Broad Street.

"I was a little scared when he pulled the gun out, but my husband said, you know, that he didn't think he would ever use it. It was just more talk than anything. Because if he were going to use it he would have done so. That's why my husband never followed up with the charges," she said.

"From the time that you left Steven Slutzker at about

the time the gun was pulled and threats were made, up until the time your husband was killed, did you ever have any conversations with defendant Steven Slutzker?"

"No conversation," Arlene said. "I had seen him occasionally outside, and he had asked me if I was happy with my husband, and I said, yes, that we were back and things were fine."

"Did he ever express his love for you?"

"No."

"At any time during the time that you were living with Steven Slutzker, did he ever mention anything about it being nice if something happened to your husband?"

"He said that, you know, that if something would ever happen to him—I don't know what he meant by it, but he just said if something happened to him like if he got hit by a bus or something like that, a car accident or something, because at that time my husband and him didn't care for each other."

"Did you ever speak to this defendant Steven Slutzker after your husband was killed?"

"No."

She said Slutzker never asked her to divorce Mudd, but she said she spoke to attorney Joe Esper about the possibility of her and Slutzker getting custody of Johnny.

Arlene said that she and John were getting along very well when he was killed.

"Things were smoothed over," and Steve was "most definitely" out of her life. "As far as he led me to believe, it was over."

Under questioning by Rothman, Arlene said she visited Neighborhood Legal Services and started a divorce action against John. A hearing was scheduled for November 16.

"I don't think I really asked him. I think I told him I was going to get one," she said. "It was something we just didn't talk about. I mean I had mentioned it and he didn't want it, and I don't think I really wanted it and was something that never happened."

The incident on Broad Street occurred the day she left Steve. John drove her to her mother's house, where she stayed for a while before moving in with her friend, Margaret Rocco, in Carrick. She said she returned to John in mid-October, probably the second week. After that, she had no more sex with Slutzker, and the only times she had sex with him occurred while she was living with him.

Rothman switched his questions back to the killing.

Arlene said she would have been able to hear someone opening and closing the basement door from where she was, but heard no such noise.

John sounded frightened when he called as the shots were being fired.

"I went to the living room and I was screaming and I picked up the phone and I took it to the door and I pushed the operator and I called the police."

Rothman asked the obvious. "You did not go down the steps to see?"

"No."

"Well, you didn't know whether your husband was dead or alive, did you?"

"No."

"You didn't know whether he needed help?"

"No."

"And you did not go down to see if he needed help?"

"No."

"All right. You went to the telephone?"

"Yes . . . the one in the living room."

"Now, how ever long it took you to make the call, what did you do then?"

"I called my brother-in-law after that call."

"All right. Then what did you do?"

"Then I looked out the door, my living room door."

"From wherever you were making the telephone calls, if anybody had come out of the cellar and gone out your front door, you couldn't have missed him, is that right?"

"Right."

"Did anybody do that?"

"No."

The front door locks automatically when it closes and would have been locked from the moment they got home and closed the door, she said.

"When did you go to the doorway to look down the cellar steps to see where your husband was?"

"After I came in from the neighbors' house, I went in to get some knives out of the drawer. I left the neighbors' door open. Nobody was there."

"Do I understand then that after you called your brother-in-law, you went out the front door?"

"Yes."

"And you had not yet looked down to the cellar to see what shape your husband was in?"

"No. I had called for help. I was waiting for them."

"You didn't make any attempt to see whether or not you could aid your husband?"

"I kept calling to him."

"I understand that. And there was no response?"

"No."

After finding no one home at Sullivans', Arlene said she went back into her house and called another brother-in-law, Terry Mudd.

"There's a third call that you made now?"

"Yes."

"You still had not looked down the cellar steps to see how your husband was?"

"I had looked in when I came in before I made the call, I went into the kitchen to get a knife because I came back into the house."

"You went to get a knife?"

"Yes."

"For protection?"

"Yes."

"Because you didn't know if anybody was in the house?"

"No."

"Well, did you get the knife after the first two calls and before the third?"

"After the second two calls, after I left the house and came back again."

"The first two calls?"

"I left and came back in, and I then got the knives. I then glanced down the cellar steps."

"That's when you glanced down and it was dark down those cellar steps?"

"Yes."

"It was pitch black?"

"No, it wasn't pitch black. I could see."

"What could you see?"

"I could see him laying down there."

"You could see a figure lying there?"

"Yes," Arlene said, her voice cracking and tears coming.

"Give her a second," Stein said.

"But I assume you could not see whether he was wounded?" Rothman continued after a moment.

"No."

"Is that right?" Rothman asked.

"No."

"Then you made the third call to Terry. Is that right?"

"Yes."

"How soon after you made the call to Terry did any policemen arrive?"

"Almost immediately."

"Where were you when the police arrived?"

"I was standing in front of my door, as they passed the house. As they passed I opened the door and I called to them, and they came down to the house."

"Were you aware of the fact that one of the officers had taken the baby out of the house?"

"Yes. He gave him to me."

"Where did you go with the baby?"

"Up to the neighbors' house up the street."

"Which neighbor?"

"I don't know. I never seen him before. It was just somebody that happened to be out and they invited me in."

"What did you do at the neighbors' house?"

"I sat there, and I waited while the police came back and forth."

"How long were you there without any police officer being there?"

"I don't know. I don't think at all, somebody was always there."

Rothman followed with more questions about when Arlene first washed her hands after the shooting. It was a dead issue. The police never tested her hands for gunpowder residue, and there was no hope at all now of finding any residue if it had been there in the first place. But Rothman pursued it anyway.

She said she did not wash them until she got to her parents' home. She was understandably vague about when she showered.

Next the defense attorney wanted to hear more details about why she left Mudd that summer.

"Did anything happen in August or late in July between you and your husband that caused you to move in with Steve Slutzker?"

"What do you mean by that? What do you mean 'what happened'?"

"I'll rephrase it. Why did you decide to leave your husband and your baby and move in with Steve Slutzker?"

"I just did."

"Had your husband mistreated you in any way?"

"I know what you are implying. I don't want to answer that."

"I'm not implying anything, ma'am. I'm asking a question. Did your husband visit upon you any mistreatment that caused you to leave him?"

"He didn't cause me to leave him. I was already left from him. It's just that something happened that I didn't go back to him right then."

She explained that when she left Mudd around mid-July, she moved in with her parents.

Nickoloff objected. He was already concerned about the direction of the questions. The prosecutors had not filed any charges against Arlene. Their theory of the case centered on Slutzker as the killer, acting alone.

Rothman was well aware of that also. The more scrutiny he could apply to Arlene's state of mind and actions, the more doubt he could cast on the case against his client.

"Objection, your Honor. That's getting pretty far afield here. We're dealing with this defendant, this witness, and this deceased. Not with this witness's mother."

"All kinds of people have all kinds of motives, your Honor," Rothman replied.

Stein allowed the question. "I think that the total issue of motive here should probably be explored."

Rothman continued. "What caused you to leave your husband and go to live with your mother before you started even living with Steve Slutzker?"

"We had an argument."

"What was the argument about?"

"Objection!" Nickoloff said.

"Was it about the divorce?" Rothman continued, trying to ignore the prosecutor.

"It wasn't about the divorce when I left at that time," Arlene said.

"What was it, a desire for a divorce?"

"I have an objection on the record, your Honor."

"Let's limit the question to specific events," Stein said.

"Was there any physical abuse? Did he physically abuse you?" Rothman asked.

"Broke my jaw."

It was time to go on a little fishing expedition and try to rattle Arlene. "Okay. Did you ever have a discussion with Steve Slutzker about the fact that you wanted a divorce from your husband, but he wouldn't give you one?" Rothman said.

"No."

"Do you have a friend whose nickname is Red who works in a pizza parlor?"

"No."

"No such person?"

"No."

Nickoloff objected. "No showing of relevance."

"I'll sustain the objection unless you tie it in with some of the previous testimony," Stein said.

Rothman went right back to work on Arlene. "Did you have any conversation with Steve Slutzker about a desire on your part to have him help you find somebody who could kill your husband?"

"No."

"No such discussion?"

"No."

"Did you know by name or in person either a Mr. Pezzano or a Mr. Hariston?"

"No."

"Had Steve ever mentioned those two people to you?"

"No."

"Were you ever living with Steve at a time when a Mr. Apter was also living in his household?"

"Yes."

"When was that?"

"When I was staying there in August."

"Were you ever in the house after the two-week period?"

"Yes."

"You were?"

"Yes."

"When was that?"

"I don't recall. I just know that I seen him once or so after that to talk to him."

"Was that at his home?"

"Yes."

"Did you have relations with him at that time?"

"No."

"Did you ever have sexual relations with Steve Slutzker in his van?"

"No."

"Never?"

"Never."

"Have you ever fired a weapon?"

"No."

"I mean at any time?"

"No."

"How far do you live from Columbia Hospital?"

"I don't know."

"That's in Wilkinsburg, isn't it?"

"Yes."

"At any time did you call a hospital or a physician before the police arrived?"

"Objection. There is no connection," Nickoloff said.

"I sense that you might be trolling a little far afield. So I'll sustain that so we can get on with it," Stein said.

"While you were making these phone calls, did you believe that your husband was dead?"

"No."

"Did you know he was dead?"

"No."

"When is the first time you told any police officer about your relationship with Steven Slutzker?"

"That's not relevant. I object," said Nickoloff.

"Sustained."

"Did you tell the police anything about Steve Slutzker that led to his arrest?"

"No."

"The night of the shooting, did you ask the police to make inquiry at the Slutzker home to see if Steve was there?"

"No."

"As you went out of your home on the evening of December twenty-eighth, after you heard the noises that you say you heard, do you remember making any mental note of whether or not there were any lights on in the Slutzker home?"

The question really got to Arlene.

"What would I want to do that for?" she snapped at

Rothman. "I didn't look across the street. I don't know what you are implying."

"Take a second until she controls herself," Stein said. "Do not argue with the attorney, Mrs. Mudd. Please try and answer the questions."

"When did you first tell the police the comment that you recited here today about Steve saying something to the effect that it would be nice if your husband met with an accident? When did you first tell the police that?"

"That was after a while, a couple of days."

"Monday, December 29, when you were interviewed by the detective bureau in downtown Pittsburgh, the afternoon after the shooting, did you recite anything about your relationship with Steve Slutzker or anything that Steve Slutzker might have said to you?"

"I don't think so."

"Did you love Steve Slutzker?"

"No."

"Mrs. Mudd, I notice from this statement by Steve Slutzker, according to you, to the effect that it would be nice if your husband had an accident. When was that made?"

"In the summertime."

"In the summertime. When you were living with him or even before that?"

"I was living with him."

"While you were living with Steve, did your husband ever come over to the house, which was right across the street, and create any scene and ask you to come back?"

"I had talked to him."

"Was Steve Slutzker there at the time?"

"No."

"Did you tell him you weren't coming back?"

"I told him I'd call him."

"Did you know, Mrs. Mudd, that once your husband had evidence that you were living with another man that it might be pretty difficult for you to get a divorce?"

"Yes."

"Who told you that?"

"I just knew it."

"How did you know it?"

"Because you know things like that."

"Did your lawyer tell you that if you were guilty of adultery you couldn't get a divorce easily?"

"No."

"Who told you that?"

"I just know it."

"And, of course, your husband actually was a witness to the fact that you were living in another man's house."

"Yes."

"That's all I have."

Now it was Nickoloff's turn to question Arlene again on redirect. Since Rothman had introduced the recorded and typed statements Arlene gave to the detectives, the prosecutor wanted to extract the comments that would help his case.

"Mrs. Mudd, according to your statement here, the January 5 statement, you state "I wanted to add that when I was living with Steve, he said, 'If Johnny was out of the way that things would be okay.' Do you recall giving that statement? Saying that?"

"Yes."

"Could you tell us what was meant by that?"

Alarms went off inside Rothman's head. "Wait a minute! Wait a minute! She can recite the exact words. What is meant by that is for the court to decide."

Stein was not impressed by the objection. "I think she

can recite the exact words and she might be able to indicate to us what she thought was meant by it."

"What did you take that to mean?" Nickoloff asked.

"My husband and I were having a lot of problems and fighting. It's just that I think it was just that we were fighting so much that he said if he wasn't around we wouldn't be fighting."

That probably wasn't quite what Nickoloff wanted to hear.

Failing to hit a bull's-eye there, Nickoloff tried in a different spot. "You stated that your husband caused your jaw to be broken. Is that correct?"

"Yes."

"Did that upset Steven Slutzker?"

"I don't know."

"Did he even know about it?" Rothman interjected.

"He knew about it," Arlene said.

A mistake. Don't ask any questions to which you don't already know the answer. Trial Tactics, first-year law school.

Rothman had only one item to ask about on recross examination, the kitchen window. It was open about three inches when the Mudds got home that evening, according to Arlene. No, she answered, she had not noticed any footprints on the sink, the counter, or the kitchen floor.

Donna Lee Pezzano was first on the witness stand after lunch. Nickoloff led her through the story that the detectives knew almost by heart.

In response to Stein, she said she never did find out what Slutzker was talking about when he asked whether Mike knew any "important people."

Then Mike Pezzano climbed onto the witness stand and recited his side of the story, the climax of which was his decision not to meet with Slutzker as planned on Tuesday, December 23, but to go instead to the state police and spill his guts.

Nickoloff wanted to know why Pezzano strung Slutzker along the way he did.

"Well, I liked Steve. We got along pretty well, and I mean I considered him a friend. He trusted me at the time, and I kind of trusted him. I figured the guy is going in for a murder rap. I tried to prevent it. I figure if they can get him for actual murder, they could get him for conspiracy where he won't end up in jail for the rest of his life.

"That's the only reason I actually went up to the police in the first place."

After the Pezzanos, Hairston described his conversations with Slutzker.

When it was Finello's turn to testify, neither Rothman nor Nickoloff asked him whether anyone had compared the .32-caliber shell found in Slutzker's bedroom to the .32-caliber casings and bullets used in the murder.

Stein raised the subject after both attorneys were finished questioning the detective.

"Was any effort made to compare those thirty-two-caliber ammunitions?" the judge asked.

"Compare them to what?"

"To each other . . . the one and the thirty-two-caliber shells found at the scene?"

"I don't know," Finello had to admit.

"Where is that single thirty-two-caliber shell now?" the judge asked.

"In the crime lab," Finello said.

With that, Rothman piped up. "Other than the single thirty-two-caliber shell, was there any other evidence of thirty-two-caliber ammunition found in the house?" he asked.

"No, sir."

"Thank you," Rothman said to Finello.

The defense attorney should have thanked Stein as well, because the judge had just answered the biggest question on his mind: Was there any physical evidence linking Steven Slutzker to the murder of John Mudd?

In more ways than one, Nickoloff was just about finished. He presented Bell Telephone Company records, which Rothman agreed were accurate. They were entered on the record.

Rothman rested the defense case without entering any evidence. He had good reason to let the prosecution's case sit there all by itself. "I respectfully submit to your Honor that all that's been proved here today are two cases of criminal solicitation.

"There is absolutely no evidence as to who, in fact, committed the killing, and you cannot circumstantially infer that because of prior solicitations that that's a prima facie case of murder."

If he could have read Stein's mind, Rothman would have stopped talking right there. But he had to go on, so as to heap as much suspicion on Arlene Mudd as possible.

"Then, of course, you take that in connection with Mrs. Mudd's testimony, which is absolutely incredible. We have nobody leaving the cellar door, according to the police and her. She would have had to have seen anybody leave the house while she was making the telephone calls, the front door being locked. She's the only person in the house at the time of the shooting, and she never even makes any attempt to call a physician or to see what shape her husband is in. I submit, your Honor, because she knew he was dead, because she either did it or had somebody else do it that she let out of the house.

"There is a stronger case on this record to hold Mrs.

Mudd than there is to hold my client. There is no prima facie case of murder, and I respectfully submit that the charges be dismissed."

Only one thing puzzled Stein. The crime lab reports, whose accuracy both attorneys had stipulated, mentioned a .32-caliber Savage pistol.

"Is that part of this record?" he asked.

Rothman filled the judge in about Norman Slutzker's gun. It was tested in the crime lab. The lands and grooves in its barrel did not match the marks on the bullets that killed Mudd.

And while the words "thirty-two caliber" were in the air and Rothman was talking, he kept going. "And the single, thirty-two-caliber shell, which your Honor asked about, I didn't know about it. But apparently, there has been no comparison made."

Stein looked at Nickoloff. "What do you have to say?"

"No. I have nothing to add," the prosecutor said. But in fact, Nickoloff must have realized just how much trouble his case was in, and he had a lot to say.

"I would mention here," Nickoloff continued, "that I think the question before us is whether or not there is a body of credible evidence here that the grand jury should pass upon based upon the words of this defendant. I think there certainly is."

Nickoloff recapped the high points of the testimony: Slutzker had described for Pezzano his plan involving a .32-caliber gun; Slutzker had fired his gun and set off firecrackers to make the neighbors and police think the sounds were just a part of life on Marlboro Street; he had a motive in his desire to be with Arlene; he told Pezzano of his plan to have Debbie come back and live with him until the trouble blew over; he'd done electrical work in the Mudd house so could easily have been familiar with the fuses and the circuits they controlled; and immediately after the killing he believed his phone was tapped.

"I suggest that by implication there is guilty knowledge here," Nickoloff concluded.

It was time for Rothman's "Yeah, but . . ."

Slutzker's reluctance to talk about the Mudd murder to Pezzano on December 30 could just as easily be explained as Slutzker's anxiety over having solicited a hit man. It didn't necessarily mean Slutzker pulled the trigger or that he even succeeded in finding someone to kill Mudd.

"All that Mr. Nickoloff has been arguing, your Honor, is simply proof of a solicitation and a motive. Mrs. Mudd had a better one than this defendant.

"But motive doesn't make a prima facie case. It's sheer speculation about who, in fact, did this killing."

By picking the appropriate pieces of information that had been submitted into the record—as all attorneys do—Rothman was able to claim that Slutzker tried first to hire Hairston, then Pezzano, then "after Pezzano failed to show . . . he dropped the idea."

Stein weighed in. "I understand the effect of his subsequent statements would not bear very great weight. Nevertheless, I am concerned that the alleged plan that had been worked out is apparently not the plan that was carried out.

"I'm a little concerned that no effort was made to compare the thirty-two-caliber shell that was found at the residence with any of the shells or bullets or slugs that were found at the scene."

That failure seemed to clinch the issue in the judge's mind. He said the .32-caliber shell taken from Slutzker's bedroom was "the one piece of evidence that might make a link between Steven Slutzker and the scene of this crime.

"I don't see that there are facts making a prima facie case of murder or of homicide here," Stein concluded.

Nickoloff and the detectives were stunned. The prosecutor managed to avoid babbling, but there was not much he could say. His best shot was to argue that there was enough here to let a grand jury decide, but that was a thin argument. "It's obviously a case of circumstantial evidence in this particular case as to this defendant, but we're not making a finding of guilty or innocent at this time. We're talking about whether or not there is evidence here that a grand jury should consider."

Stein wasn't buying it.

"What is there beyond the solicitation itself?" he asked. "What evidence is there linking him to the crime? I mean, seriously, what evidence is there?"

"He's telling a man whom he solicits to kill that 'there is a pistol I have to get back,'" Nickoloff said. "'It's a thirty-two-caliber we're going to use.' He names the man. He says it has to be done. 'If you can't do it, I'll get someone else.' The man ends up dead with thirty-two-caliber slugs in his back."

The judge interrupted to say he didn't think that was enough to show that Slutzker committed murder.

". . . in addition to the statements on the thirtieth to Mr. Pezzano that he wanted to marry the woman," the prosecutor continued. "The husband was causing the problems. He abused her. He wanted him killed before Christmas, which obviously wasn't done. Pezzano strung him along.

"The inference to be drawn from all of this is that he in fact was the one who set in motion the chain of events that led to the death of Mr. Mudd. Whether or not, in fact, he's guilty of this offense is really not for us to say at this particular time," Nickoloff said. "We think a body of other people should look at it. The grand jury. We should allow them to perform their function in this case.

"I urge you to reconsider," he pleaded.

The prosecutor seemed to be suggesting a new theory of the case. The criminal complaint, in which the charges were spelled out in detail, didn't accuse Slutzker of hiring an unknown person to pull the trigger. The complaint said Slutzker did it himself.

It took a few moments for that to sink in with Rothman and the judge.

"The request is to have the grand jury speculate what you are not allowed to speculate," Rothman said to Stein.

"I understand," Stein said. "I seriously do not see any evidence to tie this individual to that scene.

"Again, I agree that there are elements here with regard to criminal solicitation. I think there are possibly some items of evidence that should be again reviewed and perhaps some effort made to link them to the scene. I think to speculate at all that this person was at the scene at that time is just that, speculation."

"One can view it either way, that he is guilty as the actual perpetrator of this offense or that he is not the actual perpetrator. There are several theories on which one can proceed, either one of which is valid," Nickoloff said.

The prosecutor tried to compare the Mudd case to one in Chicago, where the leader of a street gang urged a thirteen-year-old to kill dope pushers.

Stein waved off the Chicago case. He didn't know the facts and didn't want to get bollixed up in arguing about it. He finally formulated his reaction to the prosecution's newly sprung second theory.

"There is no indication in the criminal complaint that's been filed that there is any theory of this case with regard to setting another person into motion to actually commit the crime," he reminded Nickoloff.

"And there is no evidence linking this person to another person who we can say committed the crime or did the shooting."

"Is it your apprehension that one must set forth the theory of accomplices in a complaint?" Nickoloff asked.

"No. But we don't even know if there was an accomplice there and whether or not if there was an accomplice present that he is linked to this particular individual."

"By this defendant's own words, he could get another to do it," Nickoloff said.

"Yes, I agree," the judge said. "You charged him with that crime of criminal solicitation. You have no evidence, in fact, that he did procure anybody to do it, and I don't see anything other than the words that he used . . . linking him to anything other than a criminal solicitation.

"So, under the circumstances, I don't really think I have any choice here. I would suggest if any effort can be made to link this defendant with regard particularly to this thirty-two-caliber shell, that it be done. I don't understand why it wasn't done before."

That had to hurt. Here was Stanley Stein, the solicitor for the coroner, essentially lecturing a prosecutor and a veteran homicide detective about basic investigative procedure. With Nickoloff on the defensive, Rothman wanted to start talking about bail for Slutzker on the solicitation charges.

"All right," Stein said.

Nickoloff, having caught his breath, wanted to continue the argument.

"Mr. Stein," said Nickoloff, who throughout the proceeding was much less inclined to address Stein as "your Honor," "are you saying that if that thirty-two-caliber shell were of the same type and make as those found in the residence, that you would hold this for court?"

"Without indicating what I would do . . . I would personally consider that a very important piece of evidence."

"Obviously, if it's the same type and caliber, it may not be probative of anything other than the fact that it's the same type of caliber," said Rothman.

"I'll say it would be a very important piece of circumstantial evidence," Stein said.

"I understand."

"I think that concludes this matter, is that correct?" said Stein.

And that was it.

Slutzker had just beaten the homicide charge. If he was convicted on the solicitation charges, the most prison time he'd face would be a few years.

To Pittsburgh's top criminal prosecutors, it appeared that Slutzker, as he had bragged to the Pezzanos, had just gotten away with murder.

■ ■ ■

The prosecutor and the detectives slunk away with their tails between their legs and went through the motions with the solicitation charges.

One of the two counts was dropped. Slutzker was convicted on the other and was sentenced to eleven and one-half to twenty-three months in a state prison. He served eleven and a half months at the Region Five prison in Hempfield Township south of Greensburg.

Stack wrapped up the homicide case by writing a memo to the file, recapping the facts in seven short paragraphs that ended with a hint of self-pity: "The coroner's office stated there were no grounds to prosecute Stephen Slutzker."

That's not exactly what the coroner's office said. Stein ruled that the prosecutors had not presented sufficient evidence to send the case on to a grand jury.

The grounds to prosecute certainly were there. The implication of Stein's ruling was that the police, the detectives, and the prosecutors had left a few stones unturned. Just how many and what lay under them would not be known for years.

■ ■ ■

As Steve Slutzker was entering the prison system, Arlene went off in search of peace and happiness. It is doubtful that she ever found either in full measure. She received none from her in-laws.

Arlene felt shunned by the Mudds. She claimed they boxed her out of the planning for John's funeral. They even forbade her from visiting the funeral home while they were there. What attention they paid her bordered on hostile.

Meanwhile, John Mudd Jr., intelligent, lonely, and frightened, was entering counseling where, it was hoped, his troubled psyche would heal.

The Formative Years

Johnny was five years, six months, and ten days old when his father died.

At that tender age, he had more than enough emotional baggage to carry, thanks to the fights between his mother and father and their separation, his father's use of drugs, and his mother's affair with Slutzker.

On top of all of that, the boy had December 28, 1975, to deal with and the events that followed.

His grandmother, Mary Mudd, understood that his childhood was shattered. She also realized the awful possibilities that awaited him as a teenager and an adult unless some degree of normalcy could be restored.

Mary Mudd was a strong-willed woman, but by New Year's 1976 she was in poor health. Even so, she was the unquestioned authority in her family and was determined to get Johnny away from Arlene. She wanted to pull him into the bosom of his father's family.

Mrs. Mudd wasted no time after the killing of her son to make her move.

She immediately petitioned the family division of Allegheny County Common Pleas Court for custody. Arlene claimed Mary Mudd did not consult her in the matter, an insult that only added to the bitterness that the widow Mudd felt toward her in-laws.

Judge Patrick Tamilia ordered a hearing.

It was not a difficult decision for the judge, even though the Mudds were openly hostile toward Arlene, who had been charged with no crime. They found it hard to believe that she could have been totally free of guilt.

Despite their hostility, the Mudds were stable and cohesive. They were a family. Arlene was a woman alone and living under a cloud.

In addition, Johnny was already close to his grandmother and his aunts and uncles.

By comparison, Arlene was questionable as a fit mother.

There was no way to disguise the affair she'd had with Slutzker or the fact that she had left Johnny with his father when she moved across the street with her new lover.

In weighing the long-term interests of John Mudd Jr., Tamilia had to consider the possibility that Arlene could very soon be wrapped up in the criminal case. The best mother in the world would have had great difficulty caring for a five-year-old if she had no husband, only a part-time hospital job, and a former boyfriend who was being prosecuted for criminal conspiracy and was possibly facing criminal charges herself.

Tamilia issued a restraining order and granted Mary Mudd temporary custody of Johnny. He also ordered psychological testing for the boy and his mother.

Mrs. Mudd lived in Pittsburgh's Lawrenceville section on Broad Street, where Johnny was surrounded by his dad's family. His aunt Nora Mudd and his uncle James Mudd and his wife, Kathleen, also lived there. Mrs. Mudd's daughter, Maureen Perri, lived on Cypress Street, just a few miles away in the city's Bloomfield section.

Grandmother Mudd quickly became the dominant force in the boy's life. Maureen was a close second.

No one may ever truly understand all that occurred in Johnny's psyche beginning with the shots fired hardly twenty feet from him that Sunday night. But whatever was going on inside his head, not much of it was good, and Maureen realized it.

Even before Mary Mudd petitioned the court for custody, Maureen placed a call to Margaret Gillick, a social worker for Catholic Charities, whom she knew from Immaculate Conception School. Johnny attended half-day kindergarten sessions there.

It was not clear to the Mudd family how much Johnny had seen or heard the night his father was killed.

Peg Gillick understood that the boy had been sleeping on the living room couch when the shots were fired. Other accounts had Johnny awake.

Either way, the Mudd family knew only as much as they could learn from the investigators and the newspapers. Had they been able to impanel themselves as a grand jury to investigate Arlene, their seats wouldn't have been warm before they returned an indictment.

The Mudds weren't getting any details from Arlene about what Johnny witnessed. Gillick would have to grope in the dark on that one.

Maureen told her that Johnny had been having nightmares. She also told her Johnny knew that an unidentified man had made threats over the telephone against his life.

Gillick considered the circumstances to be extremely traumatic and agreed to see Johnny immediately.

Her visits with him began in January, the month after the murder. The sessions were held twice a week, at first in Mary Mudd's home because of the threats against Johnny.

From the outset, it was clear to Gillick that he knew quite a lot about what happened. Johnny was sealing over his intense fear. He was trying to protect himself and claimed that nothing could hurt him.

That intellectualizing was to be expected, considering

that he was a very bright child. Even so, the ego of a five-year-old boy rarely is strong enough to deal with a loss as intense as the violent death of his father, a figure toward whom boys his age usually feel some competition.

Johnny knew Steve Slutzker, knew he was his mother's boyfriend and that Slutzker was in jail. He told Gillick that Steve killed his father.

The social worker dismissed Johnny as an unreliable witness because of his age, and she concluded that he had heard so many adults talk and speculate about the killing that despite his intelligence, he could not distinguish between what he knew of his own experience and what he had heard from others.

The counseling sessions were devoted mostly to playing and easygoing conversation.

Johnny's behavior was classic for a child in his circumstances.

In the early sessions, he regressed to the oral stage of a much younger child: he bit, ate, and fantasized about being devoured by animals.

At first, Arlene visited Johnny once a week. The visits usually upset him. The presumption was that the boy was angry with her for having left him and might have begun to think she was bad and that, by association, he was bad too.

At times, however, Johnny's intelligence and perception came to the surface. One occasion was when Arlene sent him a pair of ice skates. The boy noticed the size marked on the box, "for children ages two to four years."

Without missing a beat, Johnny said, "I wonder if she'll still be sending me skates for two-year-olds when I'm twenty-one?"

Gillick was flabbergasted, but she swallowed her laughter.

Johnny seemed to be making progress until around Easter.

The family was deeply disappointed by the outcome of the homicide case. The failure of the prosecution was particularly galling considering Mike Pezzano's warning that Slutzker was plotting the murder.

■ ■ ■

On March 31, Judge Tamilia told the Mudds at a hearing that he would be willing to return Johnny to Arlene if she was cleared in the criminal investigation. Arlene said she would enter counseling.

When the hearing ended, Arlene deliberately hung back, waiting for her former in-laws to leave the building. Even so, several of the brothers followed her in their car as she drove away.

The incident unnerved Arlene. She stopped on the side of the road in a panic, nearly causing an accident.

The brothers claimed they were following her because they had trouble starting their car.

Soon afterward, Arlene received permission to have Johnny for a day. Her idea of helping him come to grips with his troubled life was to take him to the cemetery where his father was buried. There she posed him kneeling with his hands folded, as if praying at the grave, and photographed him. She also posed him in the chapel of the hospital emergency room.

The pictures infuriated Mary Mudd. Arlene had sent them to the grandmother for Johnny to display in his room. The morbid outing left the boy visibly anxious. As usually happened after a visit from his mother, Johnny also seemed hurt and angry over the separation that inevitably followed their brief reunions.

Not much later, Arlene claimed that she was followed by other men, blacks whom she did not know.

The Mudd boys said Arlene was imagining things.

She also complained that the Mudds' would rail against her when she called to talk to Johnny.

Whether imagined or not, Arlene was sufficiently intimidated to cut off contact with her only child. She stopped calling, and she stopped visiting him.

Arlene could have arranged to visit Johnny at the county Child Welfare Services offices. She could have brought one of her relatives with her for the visits. Gillick told her so, but Arlene did little more than cry on the phone when the social worker encouraged her to keep up contact with her son.

"I miss him so much. I need him. I can't wait to have him back so I could put him to bed and hold him and comfort him," Arlene would say.

She did none of those things, but she did work up the gumption to send Johnny a package of small toys, games, and coloring books. He opened them at his grandmother's house. He was overjoyed.

"Mommy misses me," he said. "Mommy misses me a lot."

She did miss him, but not enough ever to repeat the gesture or try to visit him for quite a while.

Gillick gave up coaxing Arlene to mother Johnny.

Right after Easter, Gillick began using family dolls to introduce Johnny to the idea that adults take care of children. He seemed to like the dolls, and the idea appeared to be sinking in.

At the same time, another social worker from Catholic Social Services was trying to coax Arlene to begin her court-approved counseling. Arlene scheduled her first appointment but didn't show. She rescheduled, but again did not attend the session.

By May, Johnny was displaying a good deal more anger, which Gillick interpreted as being directed toward his mother.

During one play session, Johnny picked up a lamp and held it in the air. He declared that he was going to break it.

"I think you're feeling angry," she said.

"No, I'm not. I'm not angry."

"People who feel like breaking something feel angry inside. It's all right to feel angry. Adults feel angry sometimes, and children feel angry sometimes. Sometimes children feel angry at people they love."

He giggled and put the lamp down.

"People who want to break things feel angry," he said.

The incident represented progress in Gillick's patient attempts to help Johnny deal with his emotions. She recognized that he was entering what the child psychologists call the latency stage of development. It's a time when children respond to intense pain or loss with denial or even reversal of affect.

Her goal was to prevent him from completely repressing his painful emotions and at the same time protect him from hurting himself or from believing that it was okay to smash things as a way of expressing those emotions.

"Johnny, of course, has been told that his father was killed in December, and sometimes Johnny will speak of him in the past tense, but this does not mean that he has completely emotionally understood or accepted the death of his father," Gillick said at the time.

"As a matter of fact, developmentally, children who are

still developing through latency need to have parents and will often keep them alive even when the parents are deceased. Johnny keeps his father sometimes quite alive in fantasy and in dreams and cannot even admit to himself that his father is dead. At other times, he is able to verbalize the fact that his father is deceased."

Gillick felt absolutely certain that therapy was crucial for Johnny. Without it, the chances would be greatly increased that he would repress the whole traumatic experience, which would later come out magnified and distorted.

"Johnny really will not be able to completely work out the death of his father until he reaches adolescence or perhaps until he completes adolescence," she said.

Gillick may not have known at the time she made that assessment how right she was. It would take fifteen years to find that out.

For the time being, however, her only course was to take things one step at a time.

During one of their sessions in May 1976, Gillick tried to get Johnny to talk about the feelings he had about his grandmother being in the hospital.

"You must feel sad and miss your grandmother."

"I never feel sad. I don't miss her. I'm always happy," he said.

There was no question in anyone's mind about the boy's intelligence, but one Friday, the day his mother usually visited him before she stopped coming, his maturity and insight again surprised Gillick.

"I don't think Mommy wants to see me. That's why she doesn't visit me," he said. Then, with barely a pause, he asked, "What do you think?"

"I really don't know why your mother has not visited

you, but she told me that she loves you very much and misses you."

"Does Mommy still have the flu?"

"I don't know whether she still has the flu or not, but I don't think she's still sick," Gillick said. "I think we both know that your mother has some problems to work out before she'll be able to take care of you."

"Today's not really Friday," Johnny said. "This isn't really Friday."

"You must feel sad and miss her."

"I never feel sad. She shouldn't visit me anyway."

One or two sessions later, Johnny started leaving midway through the playing.

After weeks of this, Gillick told him she thought he might be afraid that she was going to leave him and not come back. He denied being afraid, but he stopped leaving early.

Johnny was usually a good student and liked school, but toward the end of the school year he disliked it and said he didn't want to go.

Mary Mudd spoke to his teacher at Lawrence O'Toole and learned that his feeling about school changed after a little girl showed up wearing a blouse very much like one he remembered his mother wearing.

Also around this time, Gillick stopped using the family dolls. She reasoned that they were too intense for him, particularly since the family with which he identified most no longer existed, and what was left of it wasn't visiting him anymore.

He preferred Play-Doh. He also used paints, with which he created poisonous snakes. He was still waking up crying from nightmares.

Having settled into a routine with Johnny and his family, albeit a routine that was worrisome and frustratingly slow in making progress with the boy's therapy, Gillick by now had time to reflect on Johnny's new home life.

It could have been better, not just in the abstract but within the bounds of what was available to Johnny.

Mary Mudd was becoming more depressed over the death of her son. In turn, she was more deeply angry and bitter toward Arlene. She seemed overprotective of Johnny and rarely punished him or scolded him. His aunts and uncles yelled at him and forbade him to do or to have certain things, but Johnny was smart enough to rush to someone else and appeal. Too often he got what he wanted.

The police investigation was still under way, and the case seemed to be not much closer to a resolution than it had been in January.

Everything was leading Gillick to the conclusion that she should change course and no longer support the proposition that had appealed to Judge Tamilia, that Johnny be permitted to live with his mother if she was not charged.

Gillick had seen enough of Maureen Perri and knew enough about her household to appreciate that living in a stable home, one with the normal configuration of mother, father, and offspring, would be better for Johnny than any of the alternatives.

No other child his age or even close lived at Mary Mudd's. Maureen and her husband had a boy, Philip, who would be starting third grade in the fall when Johnny would be starting first, both at Immaculate Conception.

Tamilia had scheduled a hearing on June 2 to take up the question of Johnny's custody. Gillick laid the groundwork for selling the court on her new thinking by having a long conversation in late May with Arlene.

For a woman who professed to want her son back as

badly as Arlene did, she put up no resistance when Gillick told her of her plan to ask the court to send Johnny to live with his aunt Maureen. Arlene accepted the news without protest. Her only comment was to wonder whether Johnny would find Maureen's husband, Philip, to be too strict.

"Mother seemed to accept this because it seemed to me that she realized that the judge would not return him to her because the judge had expected her to be arrested on charges of suspicion in the case, and the judge wanted that to be cleared up before Johnny returned to her," Gillick wrote in her log.

"Since this had not happened and since Arlene had even gone so far as to quit her job at Mercy Hospital because of her intense fears of being followed and because she had not followed through on the visiting of Johnny or with her own counseling, I felt that I could recommend only that Johnny go and live with Maureen."

Gillick knew that Johnny would be a tougher sell. She started preparing him in late May for the next change in his circumstances. In the early conversations, the boy seemed quite definite about wanting to return to his mother. Gillick wondered whether his feelings were motivated by guilt about his anger toward Arlene.

Gillick explained that it was the job of the judge to decide what was best for him. One of the choices, she said, was for Johnny to live with his aunt Maureen, uncle Phil, and cousin Phil.

Johnny listened but said nothing.

Gillick also laid the groundwork with the Perris. She visited them right before the hearing. They would request custody.

On June 2, all of the parties assembled at the Shuman Juvenile Detention Center for the hearing. It wasn't known until everyone was in the hearing room that Arlene hadn't planned to attend. Only her attorney was there, and the explanation was that Arlene was afraid to come to court because she thought members of the Mudd family would hurt her or harass her.

Emily Stevick, the Catholic Social Services clinical psychologist who tested Arlene and Johnny in March, was not able to attend the hearing either. Instead, she wrote Judge Tamilia a letter supporting Gillick on the question of custody.

Stevick told the judge that Arlene had been distraught on the phone in April, claiming that she was being followed and harassed by the Mudds and was called names and abused when she called Mary Mudd's home to talk to Johnny. Arlene had asked for counseling but canceled and broke appointments with her counselor. By May 27, it had been more than a month since Arlene had seen her son.

"While the psychological assessment made in March revealed that Arlene is neither a bad nor a very sick person, her present behavior accentuates the impulsiveness revealed there and raises serious questions for me about her ability and real desire to mother," Stevick wrote.

"Arlene seeks help when she is very upset and feels quite helpless, but once the crisis is over, she falters. If she were to handle her son's counseling (as well as other responsibilities to him) with equal abandon, he obviously would not continue this vital contact or receive other physical and psychological needs essential to his healthy growth and development."

Stevick said that Arlene was not so disturbed as to be an unfit mother, but "has demonstrated that she has not stabilized herself sufficiently to resume her responsibilities to her son.

"Her behavior, in relation to her son, has been impulsive and irresponsible."

Judge Tamilia read the letter. Gillick made her recommendations and stated her reasoning. The judge agreed immediately.

"It seems that he also had some outside information concerning the entire murder case, which no one else knew anything about," Gillick wrote in her counseling log. "He stated that he felt that there were going to be more investigations into the murder of Mr. Mudd, Johnny's father, and it does seem that Arlene Mudd may play a part in some of this investigation, and he did not feel that it would be good for Johnny to be living with her at that time."

Judge Tamilia entered a final order. Johnny would from then on—barring an appeal by Arlene's attorney, which the judge declared to be of little concern, or intervention by someone else—live with Maureen and Philip Perri and their son, Philip. Their home was on Cypress Street in Bloomfield, a neighborhood whose working-class descendants of European immigrants made it one of the most down-to-earth sections of Pittsburgh, itself a very down-to-earth city.

It's an open question whether Pat Tamilia appreciated what he had just done. Time would show that his decision was one of the best things that would happen for a long time in the life of John Mudd Jr.

Two days after the hearing, Johnny asked his counselor if his mother had been at the hearing. It was an odd question to come from a boy who would not be six years old for twelve more days unless he'd heard someone else talk about the case.

"I explained to him that his mother had not attended the court hearing but had sent her attorney in her place to ask for him to come and live with her," Gillick said. "I had to explain to him just what an attorney was and what that meant, and he listened quite intently and seemed very interested in everything that I said.

"He said he wanted to go live with his mother, and he was not at all sure he wanted to go live with Maureen and Philip. This was very interesting, as Johnny knew Maureen quite well and liked her very much and often went swimming with the family."

Gillick read his inquisitiveness as another indication of insecurity. She devoted their sessions throughout June to preparing him for the move.

On June 18, Johnny's birthday, he made a paper airplane, on which he wrote "thank you" after folding the paper. He wanted to fly the plane out through the window.

"Who are you sending your airplane to?" Gillick asked.

He sidestepped her question for a while, then finally revealed that he wanted to fly the plane down to the porch below, where his grandmother was sitting.

"I think you are going to be very sad when you leave your grandmother, and you will miss her. You're trying to thank her for all that she's done for you, aren't you, Johnny?"

"I'm not sad," he said. He ultimately agreed, though, that the thank-you was intended for Mary Mudd. He was especially grateful for the bicycle she'd given him for his birthday.

Arlene had given him a bike for his birthday the year before, but it stayed at the house on Marlboro Street. For whatever reason, Arlene never took the bike to Mary Mudd's home. He'd been asking for the bike for some time. Arlene probably never knew how much it meant to her son.

Things were getting intense for Johnny in the buildup to moving.

The boy would have been incapable of saying so, but his sessions with Gillick were some of his most secure moments.

It might have been for that reason that in late June he acted out a very long fantasy. He was playing with toy animals. He narrated for Gillick.

A father was killed, and somehow the mother also left their son. The boy was now alone.

As the story progressed, Johnny took the animal that represented the son, put him under the table where the play was staged, and tried to kill the boy.

"Does the baby animal want to die? Does he wish to die so that he can be with his father? He loves his father and misses him very much," Gillick said.

Johnny's movements were sharp. His eyes were quick, and he concentrated on trying to kill the baby animal.

Just then Gillick remembered what one of the family members had told her. He had spoken about wanting to die. Gillick was hoping that she could help Johnny understand that by trying to kill the baby animal he was saying he wanted to die and be with his father.

"I think the father of that animal doesn't want his young baby to die," she said. "His daddy wants him to live a long and happy life."

Johnny persisted.

Gillick pretended that a new family of animals was coming to take in the baby and care for him.

"He doesn't want to go there. No," Johnny said.

"The baby animal is feeling fear and anxiety," Gillick said, unable to move very far beyond the phrases she'd heard in her child psychology classes. "The baby doesn't want to go into a new place and a new situation."

Maybe it wasn't necessary to talk at the level of a five-year-old to be understood by the child. Johnny seemed calmer after she spoke.

The incident was one of the most prominent signs during those weeks in June that Johnny was dealing with the death of his father. Gradually more of his fantasies involved his father's death. He'd even begun talking about it.

At the same time, though, he persisted in not wanting to talk about Arlene. It seemed to Gillick as if Johnny could distinguish between missing his father, who was dead and gone, never to return, and missing his mother, who was alive and able to return . . . if she wanted to. One of his biggest problems seemed to be that Johnny could not explain to himself why his mother was not with him.

"On the other hand, knowing that she is still alive causes him all the more to wonder if his father isn't still alive too and really just not coming to see him anymore," Gillick wrote.

"It's going to be a very long and difficult process in trying to help Johnny overcome feelings of being rejected and unloved."

A doctor named Spears was Peg Gillick's confidant and mentor during her counseling of Johnny. He believed that the most important technique in working with the boy was to keep all of the issues troubling him alive until Johnny was a teenager. That way, he would finally be able to grieve for the death of his father and the loss of his mother. Otherwise, the risks were great that he would repress his dark feelings, only to have them manifest themselves in ways that might destroy Johnny or someone around him.

Dr. Spears also said it would be better for Johnny to be

able to visit his mother so that he could face the reality of her inability to care for him in a very gradual way and not idealize her or identify her in a negative way.

Children have to come to know their parents themselves, and no one else could tell the boy what his mother was like or explain what had happened, he said.

■ ■ ■

Around the same time that Gillick was preparing Johnny for the move to his aunt Maureen's, she prepared him for her vacation. She planned to be away for the first three weeks in August.

"As soon as I told him that, the session began to go very poorly, with Johnny crashing airplanes into things and again leaving the session early."

He seemed angry with Gillick. She interpreted it as more evidence of his fear of being left alone.

She explained numerous times what vacation meant, that she would be away from him but would return.

He seemed to come around to understand what was going to happen and to accept it. Then, on July 27, the next-to-last session before Gillick left, as Johnny was playing on the floor, he sat upright suddenly and blurted out, "Where is my father anyway? Do you think he is in New York?"

"It must be very confusing not to see your father any more," she said.

Then she told him something that Johnny had probably heard many times before but could not fully absorb. "Johnny, listen to me. Your father was murdered last December. Your father is dead. He was buried in a cemetery. I think you visited that cemetery one day."

The boy nodded and his eyes showed that he remembered the day he had spent with his mother.

"Yes," he said. "I know who did it."

Gillick recalled Johnny's next words and recorded them in her log.

"He said that Steve had killed his father and that some day he was going to kill Steve after he was grown up, when he was over twenty-one."

If Peg Gillick understood the significance that her young client's comments would have had to a detective, she apparently set it aside. Instead of probing, however gently, for more details of what he had seen and heard, she stayed strictly with her mission. That was to get Johnny to talk about his feelings, not necessarily about what he knew of his father's murder.

"You must feel very angry at whomever killed your father. But, you know, we're not really sure who killed your father. The police are going to investigate the situation and try to find out who did this."

Her lengthy log notes give no indication that she had much interest in helping the police solve the murder, particularly if doing that required her client's participation.

In fact, she didn't think Johnny would have made a very good witness at the time.

"I do not feel that Johnny is capable of honestly revealing at this point who murdered his father even if he did witness this," Gillick said.

The day Johnny identified Steve as the killer was only a week after the boy sang a chant about a little blind boy who saw everything that happened. During the same play session he was pretending to cut up a toy chicken.

Around that time, the Mudds, in conversation with Gillick, quoted him as saying he knew who killed his father but couldn't tell the police because his conscience wouldn't let him.

"If it is true that his mother had a part in the murder, Johnny would not be able to handle that," Gillick recorded in her log. "He might be blaming it on Steve because he could not handle thinking or revealing that his mother did this."

She reasoned that his mother's involvement in the murder would create emotions that would be harder to deal with than even the murder itself.

"We can only hope that the police will solve the murder as soon as possible so that as much reality as possible can be presented to Johnny so that he will not have to continue to fantasize events that may or may not have happened," she said.

Gillick returned from vacation to learn that Johnny seemed better adjusted in the Perri home. She found that the Perris "seemed to have a very good understanding of children and seemed to be handling what might have been a very difficult situation quite well."

While Gillick was away, Johnny talked a lot about his father and asked lots of questions about him. For example, he did not understand exactly the relationship between his father and Mrs. Perri.

"Mrs. P. is always quite willing to sit down and explain all of these family relationships to Johnny, and since he is quite intelligent, he easily understands."

In Family Court, meanwhile, the custody case was heading to the Pennsylvania Superior Court on appeal. The higher court was scheduled to take it up in November.

Maureen had spoken to Mary Mudd's attorney and learned that no witnesses would be called before the appeals court. Instead, a panel of judges would hear argu-

ments from the attorneys in the case and review Judge
Tamilia's findings.

She learned something else from the attorney that
mattered a great deal to a family of modest means: Arlene
had pleaded poverty when she filed her petition for custody of Johnny. Maureen was told that she and Philip
could be on the hook to pay court costs if Arlene won.
The Perris decided to wing it; they would let the appeal
run its course without an attorney to represent them. That
was a risky tactic, but the risk was a calculated one. Judge
Tamilia had said enough during the original custody hear-
ings to leave the impression that he and the rest of the
judicial establishment would not look kindly on Arlene's
assertion that she was ready to start mothering her son. In
addition, the police were saying, at least privately, that
they were intensively investigating Arlene and that the
Perris should not worry about losing Johnny.

■ ■ ■

John Mudd Jr. did remain with Maureen and Phil
Perri, and he continued in counseling for the next two
years.

He took a strong liking to the murder detective game
Columbo, and for a while the elephant was his favorite
animal because of its size and strength. He did well in first
grade. He talked about his concern that his mother didn't
love him and asked questions about where she might be.

"John still feels anger to Steve, who he blames for his
father's death but on another level he seems to unconsciously suspect his mother. I'm sure he has heard his
relatives suspect her," Gillick wrote.

"Maureen continues to be an excellent substitute
mother."

By early 1978, Johnny was having a great deal of trouble with a teacher's aide who looked very much like Arlene.

He couldn't take his eyes off the aide and grew attached to her.

His themes at play continued to be about death and danger, killing, dying, and coming back to life.

In June, Gillick told Mrs. Perri she would no longer be working at Johnny's school but would be able to see him at her offices in downtown Pittsburgh. They parted company for the summer and agreed to resume in the fall.

In September, Maureen was unable to bring the boy into the city. Gillick kept in touch with her by phone and learned that Johnny's test scores were below his intellectual ability.

Before closing the case in January 1981, Gillick also learned that he'd begun fighting with other children at school.

He would go on to become one of the most aggressive young men in his high school.

Not only was he smart, but John Mudd was quick and strong, assets that would tempt him to use his fists to work out whatever was going on inside his head.

The Shuffle

The Mudd family was outraged that Slutzker escaped a murder conviction.

For the dead man's relatives and friends, it was no stretch of imagination to conclude that someone had screwed up royally.

Why didn't anybody lift a finger to protect Mudd or stop Slutzker once Pezzano had come forward?

Don't the police have procedures to follow when they receive a credible tip about a murder plot? They seem to have plenty of procedures to follow in most other circumstances.

Those questions, and numerous others like them, some not so politely stated, were at the heart of the family's civil complaint—"Mary Mudd, Administratrix of the Estate of John Mudd, Deceased, vs. Borough of Wilkinsburg and Allegheny County"—filed in 1976.

The defendants argued that their actions were justified, even though the murder was carried out much as the informant said it would be. The identity of the victim, the means, manner, location, and time of the killing as well as the motivation for it had striking similarities to the informant's information. The tactics varied only somewhat from the prediction. Where Pezzano said Slutzker had proposed an ambush outside Mudd's house, the killer ambushed Mudd inside his house.

The police explained the outcome as the result of departmental policy, a crushing workload, a shortage of manpower, and the failure of the county police to respond to two phone calls from Wilkinsburg officers. To the great disappointment of Mudd's family, for whom the lawsuit offered the prospect of a financial windfall, the defense prevailed. The borough paid not a penny in damages.

It didn't help the family's cause that in the face of considerable pressure from her mother's attorneys, Maureen Perri refused to allow the attorneys to question John Mudd Jr. If nothing else, he would have been the focal point of sympathy.

A major thrust of the family's case was to establish that police in general and Wilkinsburg police in particular trained extensively in procedures that should have come into play in the hours and days after Mike Pezzano had his chat with Trooper Mates at the barracks near Uniontown.

Lieutenant Bernard McKenna was one of those who should have known because he was the pivot man in the Wilkinsburg department, according to the line of reasoning followed by Richard Spagnolli, one of Mary Mudd's attorneys from the Pittsburgh law firm of McArdle, Caroselli, Spagnolli & Beachler.

"Have you ever taken a course in the proper procedures of how to handle threats on citizens' lives?" Spagnolli asked McKenna in a deposition taken in October 1979.

"That has been touched on at times," the sixty-four-year-old retired lieutenant said. "And as I recall that, you would be taught to be careful how we handled a threat because a lot of the threats you get are not real at all. Maybe someone wants to get even with someone else. And you could set off maybe a string of tragic events by going off half cocked without investigating your report, you know, where it would come from."

McKenna was the head of the department's four-man youth and detective division. As such, he and the other three officers routinely acted on tips from informants and referrals from other police departments about drug dealing. McKenna said he personally staked out the homes of suspected druggies.

On the other hand, McKenna described an entirely different protocol that came into play when the state police relayed the report that a contract murder was being planned in Wilkinsburg by one borough resident against another.

"Well, my job, as I saw it, would be to pass that information on to the head of the department, which would be the chief of police," he said.

There were other things that McKenna believed were not his job to do. Among those things were checking the department's files for information on Slutzker, Pezzano, or Mudd, asking officers in the department if they knew any of the three men, or interviewing Slutzker or, heaven forbid, contacting John Mudd Sr.

"Once I had reported it to the chief, it was his responsibility how he would want to handle it," McKenna said.

Furthermore, the chief's only option, as McKenna described the department's long-established procedures, was to call in the county's homicide detectives.

In other words, McKenna was in the difficult position of trying to reconcile two radically different courses of action as being consistent under department policy.

In one case, the department would act on tips from informants and stake out the homes of suspected drug dealers.

"The narcotics work I referred to, it is easier—as I got the report, the crime had already been committed or was taking place," McKenna said. "It wasn't a potential crime."

Neither is solicitation to commit murder. It doesn't take a law degree to know that, in Pennsylvania, solicitation to commit murder is a felony punishable with the same severity as murder itself.

Mudd lived only a few hundred yards from McKenna's home on a nearby street. Officers Dominic Mangano and Frank Weber lived on Marlboro Street. Weber was one of the officers in McKenna's investigative unit.

McKenna said the role of Wilkinsburg police in this circumstance was to do nothing more than call the Allegheny County homicide detectives.

McKenna said he did not discuss the tip with Lieutenant Krueger, who learned of the tip from the state police, typed a memo, and gave it to McKenna.

McKenna said he didn't ask Mangano or Weber whether they knew Slutzker because it wasn't his job to ask. "I had no reason to at that time unless they had been directed by the chief to investigate Slutzker."

He said he did discharge his duty to talk to the chief. McKenna's description of the conversation suggests a head-bobbing session centering on two overriding points: the department's manpower shortage and the risk of creating trouble where none existed if the tip was found to be not credible.

"I asked him, I said, 'What do you think about it?' I said, 'If it is just an idle threat, we just don't have the manpower to get on these things or protect anyone if there was a need for it.' And he said, 'Many times it is just a threat and that is all it is.' He said, 'I am going to call the county on it. They have more manpower than we have. I am going to give them a call and see if they want to come out.'"

McKenna said he never directed anyone to contact Mudd about the tip because "I wouldn't have done that without some direction from the chief" and "I had too much other work to do."

What other more pressing matters were there on Christmas Eve, 1975? Spagnolli asked.

"I can't tell you what specific investigations we had," McKenna said.

■ ■ ■

Spagnolli got nowhere in his attempt to use Billy Krueger to show that the department should have known more than it claimed to know about Slutzker prior to December 28, 1975.

Krueger was in the interesting position of being the police lieutenant's son as well as a CB acquaintance of Slutzker. Young Krueger had been in Slutzker's home on Marlboro Street at least once, and he had worked during one summer for Pezzano in Pezzano's painting, roofing, and handyman business. He'd also worked for Pat O'Dea.

Moreover, Billy Krueger was an occasional overnight guest in the O'Dea home in McKeesport. He was there the evening of December 28, 1975.

But above all else, Krueger said that in the weeks shortly before Mudd's death, Janet O'Dea asked him if he'd like to make some money by killing a person. Krueger lived at home with his father, but claimed he and the lieutenant rarely, if ever, discussed police business.

"Mrs. O'Dea approached me at her house in McKeesport and asked me if I wanted to earn some extra money for Christmas. She called me on the phone, and I went to her house, because before I had worked for her husband painting.

"I got out there, and I asked her, 'How?' And she told me all I had to do was do away with this guy. I tried to find out who it was or what they were talking about . . . her and her husband . . . and they wouldn't give me any idea who or what or how."

That conversation occurred the month of the killing or possibly the month before, he said. But whenever it was, "I just told them 'Ain't no way.'"

Krueger said he did not immediately tell his father what Janet O'Dea had asked him to do. Billy said he didn't realize until after the fact that Janet O'Dea's proposition might have something to do with Mudd's death.

Spagnolli put young Krueger under oath to try to demonstrate that the names Slutzker and Pezzano were known in the police department in the days between Pezzano's tip and Mudd's death, but Krueger disappointed the Mudds' attorney.

In December 1975, Billy Krueger was living in his father's home at 307 West Street in Wilkinsburg, where the son had his CB base station. Except for two periods, his tenth year in school when he lived in Florida and when he was in the navy in 1971 and 1972, Krueger had always lived at 307 West Street.

He knew just about everybody in the Wilkinsburg police department, including Chief Hodgins and officers Mangano and Weber, and he was a volunteer emergency medical technician for neighboring Swissvale.

When Slutzker was selling a CB radio, Billy Krueger was in Slutzker's house with another CB buddy, "Kilowatt" Schwartz.

Krueger claimed he never discussed the Pezzano tip, Slutzker, or Janet O'Dea's proposition with his father or any of the other officers in the Wilkinsburg police department before the murder.

Krueger said that after the murder, he learned by reading a newspaper that Slutzker was a suspect. Even then, he said he never heard his father talk about the Mudd case.

"My dad doesn't talk about police business at home."

It would seem that the only time the Mudd case came up in conversation between Billy Krueger and his father was when Billy brought it up after a conversation with Janet O'Dea well after John Mudd's death. She was delivering one of her trademark diatribes, this one concerning a young woman named Debbie Radakovic. Janet was under the impression that young Krueger was dating her.

"Mrs. O'Dea had told me before if I go with her—

because she was having problems with her husband or something—she'd give me this and give me that. So, she told me that 'Every dog has her day. She'll have hers, and you'll have yours.'

"I asked her what she meant by that, and she said, 'Well, you remember the Mudd incident? I helped arrange that, and I can arrange yours too.'"

Krueger reported Janet's statement to his father, who sent his son to see McKenna. Based on Billy Krueger's statements, Janet was arrested and charged with criminal solicitation and criminal conspiracy in Mudd's murder. She was acquitted in a non-jury trial, although before being cleared she'd spent more than 90 days in jail, unable to make bond.

■ ■ ■

Harry S. Hodgins told a different story about the goings-on within the police department regarding the Pezzano tip. In addition, he said Slutzker was not entirely unknown to the department.

"Slutzker was known as primarily involved in CB work," Hodgins said. "In fact, the information that Lieutenant Krueger had put on his report to me was Slutzker had a handle, you know, CB handle of 'High Voltage.' A couple of our men—well, several of our police officers, in fact—are involved in CB. They knew the name, and that's about it, you know."

During his deposition on July 25, 1978, Hodgins said he asked Krueger in a conversation that occurred in McKenna's presence, whether he knew Mudd or Slutzker.

"He said, I believe, 'No,' that he didn't know them," the chief said. "This was prior to the murder very definitely."

Hodgins said tax records were also checked to determine whether Slutzker lived in Wilkinsburg.

"After that inquiry, what decision did you make or did your men make?" the Mudds' attorney asked.

"Well, Lieutenant McKenna said that he was going to pursue it a little further to see what he could find out about these two men. While we were still there, I had suggested that it might be possible that if this did check out after, you know, talking to Pezzano, if this story seemed to hold true, that this wasn't just some kind of a prank message, that we might be able to set up a police officer to pose as a hit man."

The discussion occurred on December 24, but it led to no action other than Hodgins saying that he would call his friend, Lieutenant Floyd Nevling of the Allegheny County police detective branch.

"I made a call some time, I believe it was the morning of the twenty-fourth. It might have been close to noontime," but Nevling wasn't in his office, Hodgins said, adding that Sergeant James Miles, whom he also knew, was not available either.

The Wilkinsburg chief said no one from the county police called back, so he called again around 4 P.M. and was told that both Nevling and Miles were gone for the day.

"I guess they may have slipped out early because it was Christmas Eve," Hodgins said.

The chief said he and his officers did not discuss the possibility of contacting Mudd because "we really did not have enough background information on this.

"Certainly the possibility, the information that we had, we felt bore further investigation," Hodgins said.

But that is precisely what Pezzano's tip did not get.

As Hodgins told Spagnolli two and a half years after

Mudd's death, "I can say to you today that from the twenty-fourth until the evening of the twenty-eighth, which was a Sunday night, to my knowledge nothing directly was done other than possibly, again I say possibly, trying to find out some more information about these two men.

"Certainly nothing dramatic was done."

Exactly why the Wilkinsburg and Allegheny County police departments never connected on December 24, 1975, may never be known.

The county police said they had no record of the two calls Hodgins claims he made, including the second time when he left a message for Nevling or Miles to call him if either "came back into the building."

McKenna and the county police weren't the only parties with whom Hodgins didn't seem to be in total agreement on the facts. The chief's own statements conflicted about whether Wilkinsburg had a policy requiring its officers to notify the county police on matters such as Pezzano's tip.

Hodgins said in written answers to questions from the plaintiffs that "police procedure required the borough of Wilkinsburg to notify Allegheny County. Allegheny County was equipped to handle this kind of investigation, whereas the borough of Wilkinsburg was not."

Yet in his face-to-face deposition by Spagnolli, Hodgins said, "It was really no clear-cut procedure as to what, for example, a chief of police of Wilkinsburg would do in a certain case or who he would contact." He said his call to the county police detective bureau resulted from his natural inclination to turn to those who had helped in the past.

Hodgins said he deliberately did not call the county district attorney's detectives, who worked independently of the county police detectives.

Although some of the DA's detectives were solid, effective investigators, the office was marred by its reputation as a dumping ground of political appointees.

"Quite frankly," Hodgins told Spagnolli, "we had had a few experiences with some of their men. I think there was within the Allegheny County detectives at that time . . . there was quite a disparate . . . you had some very excellent investigators, and you had some that were not good at all.

"The problem was that if you were to call them, for example, on a specific case, you had really no control over who came out. You might get an excellent investigator. You might get two or three excellent investigators. You might get two or three guys that might mess up your case."

In the final analysis, it would seem that Krueger made the greatest effort in response to Pezzano's tip, and all Krueger did was to write a memo on a typewriter. Hodgins says he made two phone calls to Pittsburgh, but expressed no urgency in the messages he left. McKenna was consumed with ongoing investigations of such magnitude that he couldn't even remember what they were about. His greatest contribution was, as he stated, to wait for Hodgins to tell him what to do.

Hodgins tossed the hot potato back to McKenna, saying McKenna not only had authority to pursue the matter on his own but also had the assignment to do so.

"On the twenty-fourth, who had responsibility to—if there was going to be any other investigation, who had the responsibility on the twenty-fourth?" Spagnolli asked.

"Well, ultimately I had the responsibility, but at that time Lieutenant McKenna would have, you know, he would have been given and was given the assignment to see what he could find out about the principals named in this situation," Hodgins said.

McKenna couldn't remember receiving any such assignment and didn't believe he had any authority to act or direct his detectives to act without the chief's instruction.

"Since you were not going to work on December twenty-fifth, did you instruct any other officer over which you had control to do any investigative work on this incident?" Spagnoli asked McKenna.

"No, I didn't."

"Did the chief ever instruct you to investigate the substance and basis of the information received from the state police?"

"No, he did not."

Since the members of the Wilkinsburg police department apparently were not overcome by curiosity in late December 1975, it's hard to tell what was motivating them to act, or not act, as they did.

Could there have been hard feelings between McKenna and Hodgins that prevented the two senior officers from working together more effectively?

Wilkinsburg had an opening for police chief in 1973. McKenna was a fifty-seven-year-old lieutenant at the time with twenty years of service on the force, but the borough council conducted a nationwide search for a new chief. Competitive exams administered by the International Association of Chiefs of Police turned up thirty-nine-year-old Harry S. Hodgins from Baltimore.

As it turned out, the Wilkinsburg police were little more than bit players in a drama that starred a cold-blooded killer and made a martyr of an unemployed truck driver with a track record of drug involvement and slapping his wife around.

In the meantime, Slutzker returned to his electrical

contracting business after serving his jail sentence for solicitation. Arlene went through another affair, one that had none of the violent characteristics of the Marlboro Street love triangle of 1975, although it did have a decidedly unsavory quality.

The Gun and the Green Shirt

Some friendships, like flowers, bloom and fade. Dorothea Vantrick's friendship with Clare O'Dea was dormant in the winter of 1975–76. Clare, fifteen, was pregnant at the time and was living with her five brothers and sisters and her mother, Janet.

Spring and the baby boy arrived around the same time, and Vantrick found herself loafing once again with Clare, often at the O'Dea home on Grandview Avenue.

Like her other sojourns into the world of the O'Dea family, this one brought the twenty-three-year-old woman from neighboring White Oak face to face with things she would have been just as well off having never known.

One day not long after Clare had her baby, Dorothea Vantrick walked through the O'Deas' door, ushered by a warm spring breeze.

Pat O'Dea, Clare's stepfather, was sitting on a chair with one foot propped up on another chair. He had splashed hot grease on the foot at the Viking Lounge, a dive at the foot of Grandview Avenue that did its patrons a favor by allowing in virtually no sunlight, the better to hide the grime on the floor and mask the faces of the yunzers who hung out there.

Pat was the second-most important employee after the bartender. He was the Viking's cook, and deep-frying was his most important culinary skill. A cook can deep fry just about any kind of tasteless, oversalted, frozen thing and pass it off as food. As the method of cooking that requires the least talent, deep-frying was the cheapest way for the Viking to sell enough food to meet the Pennsylvania Liquor Control Board's definition of a restaurant and consequently qualify to sell alcohol on Sunday.

Dorothea Vantrick saw Patrick the cook resting his burned foot. She also saw Janet O'Dea, who was holding a handgun.

She also saw a man whom she knew only as "Pepsi."

"Pepsi" also saw the gun.

"You better get rid of that thing or be nailed for it," he told Janet.

Dorothea was also thinking that Janet should get rid of the gun, but for a different reason.

Here was Janet casually waving a gun around as Clare's baby lay in a crib close by.

Also, around this time, Dorothea Vantrick loaned Clare a green shirt.

One day, Dorothea saw Janet wearing the shirt. Dorothea remembered the sight because it was the same day that she heard Mrs. O'Dea explain what had happened to the gun she'd been waving around Clare's baby: Supposedly it had been thrown into the Monongahela River from the Homestead High-Level Bridge.

"The Hog" Delivers a Lead

"Homicide. Payne."

"Detective, this is Dominic Ferraro, chief up here in Sharpsburg. I've got one of the locals here says he's got information about a murder back in the mid-'70s, 1974 or '75."

Bob Payne listened, took a few notes, some in writing, some mental, and thanked Ferraro.

"We'll look into it, Chief," he said, and hung up.

Payne looked around the room and stopped his gaze at the first detective in sight. "Hey, Schwab. Take a ride with me, will ya?"

Payne didn't have the slightest idea what case Ferraro was talking about, and he almost didn't care. The Sharpsburg tipster, Harvey Vogel, was reporting about a collection of old details, including some he heard while drinking with his daughter by his ex-wife.

Well, thought Payne, when informants come by their information under the influence, there's a good chance they only want to kiss up to the police and earn a favor for their next drunk arrest.

Payne and Dave Schwab drove north on Route 28 to the office where Ferraro had a huge fish mounted on the wall behind his desk. They knew the chief was nicknamed "the Hog" for his champion appetite, especially when he or one of his cronies from the Valley were cooking barbecue.

Among the details Vogel served up was his claim that his ex-wife admitted being mixed up in a murder with two men and being paid $1,000 for her part. The murder had occurred in East Liberty or Wilkinsburg. Vogel didn't know where for sure, and he didn't know the victim's name.

Also, he said, his daughter Clare had found a gun under the seat of the car her mother and stepfather drove, and the stepfather had removed the gun before the police arrived.

There were other things. Vogel said that during a brief reconciliation with his ex-wife in 1979, she ambled downstairs one morning with a newspaper in her hand and muttered, "Isn't this a nice birthday present?" The article named her in connection with an unsolved murder.

The ex-wife was Janet O'Dea from Grandview Avenue in McKeesport. Her new husband was Patrick O'Dea.

None of the names rang a bell with either detective.

Chief Ferraro had called the right place, the homicide squad on the Allegheny County police. But he called in 1986, ten years too late for anyone who worked there to readily connect the O'Dea name with the Mudd murder.

Within weeks of Stanley Stein throwing out the homicide charge against Steven Slutzker in 1976, the district attorney's detectives were disbanded. They had known the end was coming even before the lights and television went off in John Mudd's living room that snowy Sunday night.

■ ■ ■

Robert G. Kroner's appointment as superintendent of the county police in 1973 was the beginning of the end for the DA's detectives. Under Kroner, the county police organization grew in size and competence from a park patrol and traffic control group to a legitimate investigative force.

Kroner's achievement probably would not have been enough to seal the fate of the DA's detectives, however. Politics in Democratic Allegheny County were still too mechanized for that in the 1970s, a generation after the reign of Pittsburgh mayor, Pennsylvania governor, and kingmaker David L. Lawrence. Professionalism alone would not have carried the day in any adventure that contemplated eliminating public jobs, especially patronage jobs. No, the times required something irresistible. The times required major scandal, and Allegheny County's pretty boy district attorney, Bob Duggan, provided it in elegant fashion.

Duggan was a public servant who gravitated to the fast, rich life. To obtain it, so the U.S. Attorney's office alleged, Duggan had been reduced to consorting with those who controlled gambling in the Pittsburgh area. A DA like that needs bagmen, and after his chief of detectives was caught and sang about corruption within the department, Duggan was indicted by a federal grand jury. He died the same day he was indicted. It happened along a fence line on his property near Rolling Rock Hunt Club, a playground of the rich, located near colonial Ligonier. The shotgun blast appeared to be self-inflicted.

Jack Hickton was the Pittsburgh attorney appointed to fill Duggan's unexpired term.

Hickton cared greatly about good police work. He also recognized the need to continue cleaning house and reasoned that the DA's office needed more attorneys to prosecute cases. The detectives' salaries, it was clear, could be put to better use. The DA's detectives would be disbanded and their duties bestowed on the county police.

Hickton, however, lost the 1975 Democratic primary election to Bob Colville, an up-and-coming former Pittsburgh beat patrolman who had worked his way up to police chief.

Colville took the oath of office in January, 1976, and soon after announced that he would finish the job Hickton had started, populating the DA's staff with more attorneys and turning the investigative duties over to Kroner's county police. There was irony in Colville's decision, because his campaign included sharp criticism of Hickton for converting the staff as he did. Nonetheless, the DA's detectives who originally investigated John Mudd's murder did so with the shadow of unemployment looming over them.

On a Monday morning in March 1976, the county police officers who were picked to become the new homicide detectives showed up for work on the fourth floor of the courthouse. There, across the crowded room, sat the detectives they were replacing. The new arrivals stood along the wall leading to the door. Those who were now between jobs packed their personal belongings in cardboard boxes and walked the gauntlet to the exit.

Even the political hacks among them—and there were solid, honest men in the DA's squad—had too much class to let their feelings erupt. They held their tongues. The heat in their eyes and the flush in their cheeks said everything.

They took with them their memories and insights about unresolved cases and their recollections about where throughout the many offices, storage rooms, and cubbyholes in the courthouse the case files were stashed.

So, when the Sharpsburg chief called the county on July 9, 1985, Payne and Schwab had not the foggiest idea whether Vogel's information was valuable. They also didn't know where to start looking to find out. No card file or index of cases existed. They did what any street-smart cops would do under the circumstances. They called a newspaper reporter.

■ ■ ■

Schwab called veteran crime reporter Paul Maryniak of the *Pittsburgh Press* the next day.

Vogel remembered that Janet O'Dea's birthday was May 29, but he wasn't sure whether it was 1979 or 1980 when she made the remark about the story in the paper.

Maryniak checked the news morgue, found the article, and gave a copy to the detectives. They, in turn, retrieved the old files from the DA's office and found the case folder. Now they knew what they were dealing with.

Two days later, Schwab and Detective Henry Watson brought Vogel to the homicide offices, which were now located in the West Penn Building, for another interview. This time, instead of handwritten notes, there would be a typewritten transcript.

Vogel, born on the Southside of Pittsburgh and schooled through eighth grade at Lattimer Junior High on the Northside, had six children, Anita Marie, Clare, Norma, Dale, Jennifer, and Victoria. He was living on Social Security disability payments after working at Jones & Laughlin Steel Company.

As Nancy Gilmore typed, Vogel unwound his story.

Some time in 1978, he and his daughter Clare were out drinking.

"She brought up the fact that her mother was involved in a murder. Her and Pat O'Dea got to the car before the police. I don't know which police station. Clare found a gun underneath the front seat, give it to Pat O'Dea, her stepfather, and he was supposed to have the gun. I don't know what they did with it."

Then in 1979, Janet called Harvey. Her car was wrecked and she needed another one. Vogel took her to a used car lot run by his friends. That led to a four-month reunion between Harvey and Janet.

"Come her birthday, she came down and told me, after reading the newspapers, she said, 'Isn't this a hell of a birthday present?' That's when I found out about her being mixed in with the murder, her and two other men.

She told me she used Pat O'Dea's car . . . a 1971 Monte Carlo.

"They were supposed to have gotten a thousand dollars. I don't know if that was to be split or a thousand dollars each.

"That's when I started staying away from her."

"Did she tell you who the other two men were?" Watson said.

"She had some electrical trouble in the house, and her landlord got an electrician to come to the house, and it was one of the men who she was involved with in the homicide," Vogel said.

Before ending the interview, Schwab asked whether this was the first time Vogel had ever told this story to any other law enforcement officer.

"No," Harvey said. "I seen a city of Pittsburgh detective, and I tried to talk to him. I'll not mention his name. He thought it was just domestic problems."

■ ■ ■

Schwab wanted Vogel to undergo a lie-detector test, which Vogel had volunteered to take when he stepped forward with his information. The arrangements were made, and a few weeks later criminalist Tom Myers of the county crime lab conducted the test at the West Penn Building.

During an interview before the test, Vogel walked Myers through the story.

Vogel also said that in 1979, after Janet moved to Rebecca Street in Wilkinsburg, she called Harvey and said that a guy who'd squealed on her during the murder investigation was working in a store on Penn Avenue and that she wanted to get someone to take care of him.

The last significant bit of information that Vogel passed on was that Janet told him that on the day Mudd was killed or the day before, she met two men involved in the murder at a bar. The person who paid the $1,000 was there, although Vogel couldn't tell whether the person who paid the money was a fourth person at the meeting or whether he was one of the two Janet had met.

After interviewing Vogel, Myers attached electrodes to Vogel's skin, fixed a pressure cuff to his arm, and strapped a respiration belt around his chest and back. Then he asked a series of questions that represented five tests that make up a standard polygraph.

"Did you lie to police about your knowledge of this murder?"

"No."

"Did Janet tell you she was involved in a murder?"

"Yes."

"Did Janet tell you a thousand dollars was paid for the killing?"

"Yes."

"Do you remember Clare telling you anything else of importance?"

"No."

"Did Janet tell you that she and two guys were involved in a murder?"

"Yes."

"Did Janet tell you that she used Pat O'Dea's car for the murder?"

"Yes."

"Do you remember Janet telling you anything else about this murder?"

"No."

"Are you deliberately withholding or concealing any information from me about this matter?"

"No."

Vogel's physiological response to the questions, as depicted by the lines of ink on the paper, told Myers one thing. Harvey Norman Vogel was probably telling the truth.

■ ■ ■

Now the detectives knew what case they were working on, but they didn't assign it top priority. It was three months before they could advance the case, and then only by increments.

Watson and Schwab checked for criminal records on Janet and Patrick O'Dea, Steve Slutzker, and Bill Krueger.

Then the detectives set to work reconstructing the case, starting with Arlene. They tracked her down in Punxsutawney, where she was known as Arlene Montgomery, living in an apartment on South Findley Street.

They questioned her about December 28, 1975. The broad strokes were there, but many of the small details had changed.

In the retelling of the story, John Jr. was playing on the floor and Arlene was lying on the love seat when the lights went out. Arlene heard what sounded like someone falling on the stairs to the basement, not anything that sounded like gunshots. She went down the stairs and saw her husband on the floor. The home had three phones, one each in the kitchen, living room, and upstairs bedroom. She forgot there was a phone in the basement. In the confusion after making the phone calls, Arlene forgot John Jr. was in the house. She went next door and was talking to no one on the street that night. It was Slutzker who informed Arlene that he had venereal disease. She lived with her mother during her short separation from John. The gun-pointing incident outside Mary Mudd's home during the summer of 1975 led to Slutzker's arrest. She had never before seen the ring that was placed in the mailbox of her parents' home a few days after the murder.

In addition, Arlene denied knowing a man named Charles Stewart. She said she moved to Baldwin Township after Mudd's death because her former in-laws tormented her on the phone.

"The phone would ring and the party on the other end would moan and groan into the receiver."

Arlene told Schwab and Watson that she suffered a nervous breakdown after the murder and moved from place to place to avoid the Mudd family. Her son was taken from her by the Mudds, and she was forbidden from visiting him.

In early December, a month after their trip to Punxsutawney, the detectives tracked down Bill Krueger in Palatka, Florida, Clare (Vogel) Dugan in Texarcana, Texas, and Janet and Patrick O'Dea at work at the Adam Mark Hotel in Houston.

■ ■ ■

February in Pittsburgh can be a real bitch. In the river basin on the windward side of the Allegheny Mountains, where the moisture from the Great Lakes piles up, sunshine is rare even in summer. In winter, the weather takes on a nasty damp chill that is best defeated by day-long physical exertion, which is not the lot of the homicide detective. February, then, is a great time for a Pittsburgher to visit Houston.

Detective Lee Torbin got the nod to accompany Watson to interview Clare Dugan. No one answered the door at Apartment 315 at 7000 Cook Boulevard at 10:30 A.M. February 18, 1985. Neighbors said Clare and her husband, Jerry, worked at Wayne Barbee's Exxon Station on Southwest Freeway.

Two hours later, Torbin and Watson found Clare working the cash register at Barbee's Exxon. Legally, she said, her name was Clare Eastland. She had divorced Bill Eastland, father of one of her children, who was back in the Pittsburgh area living with their five-year-old son. She said her other child, Patrick, was fathered by John Dunn from Pittsburgh's Crafton area. At the moment, she told Torbin and Watson, she was engaged to Mr. Dugan, a mechanic for Mr. Barbee.

Clare was expecting the visit. Janet had called and said she'd heard Harvey was shooting his mouth off to the Allegheny County homicide detectives, who were on their way to Houston.

"My father is stirring all this up just to cause trouble. I told everything to the police right after the killing," Clare said.

She was fifteen when John Mudd died. She was living with her mother and Patrick O'Dea, five siblings, and her own son, Patrick.

Bill Krueger was one of the CB types who used to drink and party at the house on Grandview Avenue in McKeesport, she said. The name Steve Slutzker was familiar, but Clare wasn't sure whether she'd ever met him.

Clare couldn't remember finding a gun under the seat of the O'Dea car.

"I never said any such thing, and I would remember if I did," she said. "You can't believe a word he says. He's just trying to stir up trouble."

Clare acknowledged that it would not have been unusual for a gun to be under the seat of the car "because Pat had a lot of guns and sometimes there would be a gun in the car." The car would have been his green, 1973 Chevy Monte Carlo.

She remembered Janet being arrested and spending time in jail over something to do with a phone call. Even if her mother had been involved in a murder, Clare said she would have been the last to know.

"My mother and me don't get along. She's a heavy drinker, and she treated me like a slave. That's why I finally left home at the age of fifteen and moved to Texas," Clare said as customers queued up at the checkout counter.

Torbin and Watson backed off, but Clare agreed to take a polygraph exam.

"We'll send a car around to pick you up at 10 o'clock tomorrow morning," said one of the two Houston detectives who accompanied the Pittsburgh team.

■ ■ ■

By midafternoon Watson and Torbin were knocking on the door of apartment 1004, 7000 Cook Boulevard, in Houston.

They knew about Janet O'Dea's arrest, imprisonment, trial, and acquittal.

They were hoping that ten years had softened the iron-sided alibi that Janet and Pat had provided for Slutzker.

The O'Deas were not at home, nor were they on the job as cooks at the Adams Mark Hotel. Janet had been fired and Pat quit, the detectives were told. Whereabouts unknown.

As planned, Clare was in the Houston police offices by 10:30 the next morning. Since the detectives' visit, she'd been thinking about the life she left behind in McKeesport and something had come back to her.

"I recall a conversation that took place right after the killing," she said. "I don't know who all was there or even who said it, but I remember that my mother and Pat were there, and they were involved in the conversation. It had to do with the killing, and someone said that the gun used in the killing was thrown over the Homestead High-Level Bridge.

"That's all I remember."

She said Pat O'Dea had at least four handguns that she knew of when they lived in McKeesport, but when shown a revolver she could not recognize it as different from an automatic.

Clare had known Bill Krueger pretty well. In fact, she'd dated him for a while. He often had a gun with him when he visited the O'Deas because he was in his security guard's uniform.

She didn't recall Jerry Schwartz and she'd never heard Slutzker brag about having been discharged from military service for being crazy. She didn't usually pay much attention to the CB crowd that hung around the O'Deas. That's because Janet kept her too busy waiting on everyone.

Clare said Janet was being her typical self when she came home drunk one day not long after the Mudd murder and went into a rage because she thought the house was messy. She was particularly exercised about a towel in the middle of the living room floor, Clare said. Janet slapped her and pushed her down a flight of stairs.

"That's when I decided to move out," Clare said.

Moving to Texas only interrupted Clare's circumstances because Janet followed her in 1980. Clare said she and her husband, Bill Eastland, lived with the O'Deas until the day her mother came home, picked a fight with Clare, and charged at her with a butcher knife.

The Eastlands moved out that night. The young couple split soon afterward, and Bill moved back to Pittsburgh with their son.

After hearing that story, Houston police detective Carl Phillips emerged from the polygraph exam and said that as far as he could determine, everything Clare said was true.

■ ■ ■

An hour after the polygraph exam ended, Torbin and Watson were in the living room of the O'Deas' apartment, along with a detective sergeant from the Houston police.

Janet interrupted their explanation for the visit. "I knew you guys were coming. Harvey told Norma that you were coming here, and my daughter called me.

"You know that little son of a bitch is just trying to cause trouble for me. He's never gotten over the fact that he didn't get the kids and their mother did," she said as preamble to a tirade against her ex-husband.

Asked to recount the events of December 28, 1975, Janet talked about her relationships with Slutzker, Krueger, and Schwartz. "Out of the three, I was closest to Billy. He was like a son to me because I treated him good."

Eventually Krueger got the wrong idea about Janet and made sexual advances toward her, she said. He had to be rebuffed and told that theirs was not that kind of relationship. After that, things were fine between them until he testified against her at her trial.

"Now I consider him to be nothing but a fucking little liar."

She glossed over the events of the evening of the killing, explaining about the CB party she and Pat held and about how they got drunk and went to bed.

Janet denied that she or Pat owned any guns at the time.

"Pat is a resident alien, and it's illegal for him to own firearms," she said. "The only real gun that was ever in my house when I was with Pat was the gun Billy Krueger carried when he worked as a security guard.

"You guys ought to know better than to believe anything Harvey Vogel tells you. That little prick . . ."

She railed on for a few moments. The detectives brought her back to earth with questions about her reunion with Vogel.

"I didn't move in with him. He moved in with me. He needed someone to take care of him, like a mother," she said. "I was living in Apollo at the time, and we were talking decently back then."

She said Harvey wanted to patch things up, and she figured she'd go along with him for a while. "I never intended to get back with him. I was just using him to get a new car?"

"He bought me a car, which I sold after he paid it off. Then he bought me another car. After he paid for that, I sold it too and then bought myself a good car and left him.

"I took advantage of him and got what I wanted out of him. That's what's really bugging him. That's why he's still trying to make trouble for me."

"Were you living with Harvey at the time of your birthday that year?" Watson said.

"Yes."

"Did you ever tell Harvey that you were involved in

Mudd's killing and that you received money for your part in it?"

"Never. He's a damn liar."

"Have you ever been involved in a conversation during which someone mentioned throwing the gun that was used to kill John Mudd off the Homestead High-Level Bridge?"

"No."

"Have you ever heard any conversation like that?"

"Never."

"Have you ever told anyone that you heard something like that?"

"No."

"Did Pat ever mention finding a gun under the front seat of his car?" Torbin asked.

"No. That never happened or I'd have known about it."

"Could Steven Slutzker or Bill Krueger have used your car the night of John Mudd's murder?"

"Steve never left my house, and Billy never drove my car."

"Why would your daughter Clare say she found a gun under the front seat of Pat's car?"

"I have no idea. Go ask Clare. That girl had a lot of problems in her life back then. I doubt she could get anything straight about what happened that long ago."

Janet refused to take a polygraph exam, explained that Pat had found work with a construction company, and ushered the three officers out of her apartment.

They were back the next morning around dawn to question Patrick.

He denied that there ever was an incident with a gun as Clare described, and he said he never heard anyone talk about throwing a gun off the bridge at Homestead.

The rest of the story came out the same as it had a decade earlier.

Pat said he'd submit to a polygraph but only at some later date.

■ ■ ■

After interviewing Patrick O'Dea, Torbin and Watson made phone calls from the Houston homicide offices, then left for the airport. The words and faces of Janet and Patrick O'Dea were on their minds for much of the plane ride to Florida.

They were in the Putnam County sheriff's office in Palatka, Florida, by 6:15 P.M. with a captain, who drove them to a housing project on Husson Avenue. Apartment K-77 was empty, and none of the neighbors claimed to know where Bill Krueger, his wife, and their two children had moved. All they knew was that Krueger's father was living in the area.

Back at the sheriff's office, the detectives were fingering local telephone directories looking for "Krueger, Wm . . ." when a call came in. "I understand someone wants to talk to me," Krueger told the captain.

■ ■ ■

By 8:10, Krueger and his father were in the station. Bill had moved from Palatka to Satsuma, although he used a mailing address in San Mateo. He'd come to Florida about two years earlier, thinking the Mudd affair was entirely behind him.

Krueger had been a reserve Allegheny County deputy

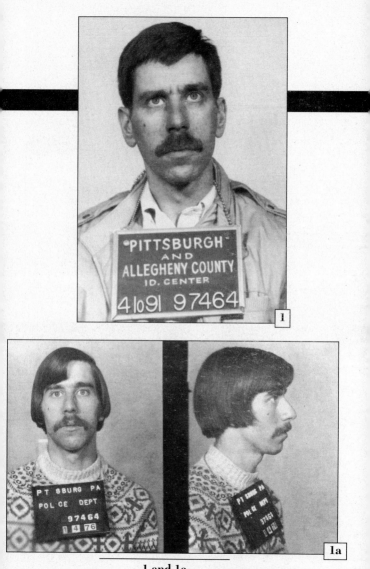

1 and 1a
Stephen Slutzker

2
Arlene Mudd

3
John L. Mudd Sr. age
17, upon enlisting in
the navy

4

The home on Marlboro Street in Wilkinsburg, where Stephen
Slutzker lived in the mid-1970s. It is directly across the street
and slightly uphill from the home where
John and Arlene Mudd lived.

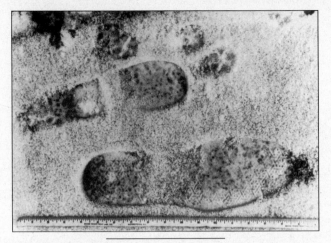

5

Footprints of an adult and a child in the snow leading from the back of Stephen Slutzker's house to the spot in the rear alley where he parked his van. Police thought the footprints were suspicious because it hadn't started snowing that evening until after the time Slutzker said he'd left for McKeesport.

6

1515 Marlboro Street in Wilkinsburg, where John and Arlene Mudd lived

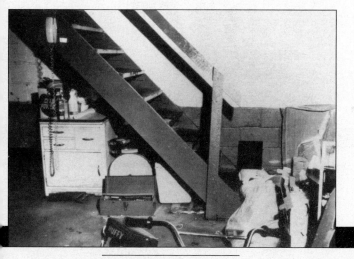

7

The basement staircase where John Lawrence Mudd took his
last steps. The victim's body, with face blacked out, lay at
the bottom of the steps.

8 and 8a

Allegheny County police detectives Regis Kelly and Lee Torbin, whose relentless investigation into the past led to the successful prosecution of Stephen Slutzker.

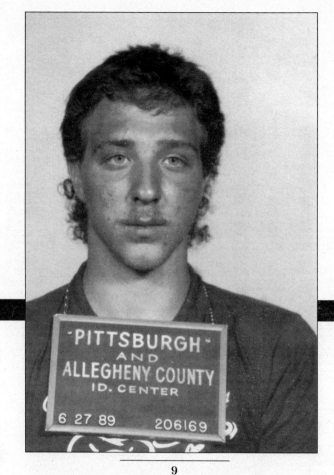

9

John Mudd Jr. was overwhelmed one night by sudden mental images of his boyhood home on the evening 15 years earlier when his father was murdered.

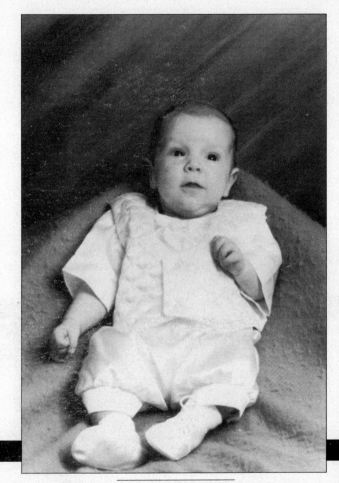

10
John Mudd Jr.'s son, John Lawrence Mudd III

sheriff and had a permit to carry a gun. Yes, he admitted, he did wear his uniform and gun sometimes on his frequent visits to the O'Deas. He went there often to talk and drink.

He'd worked with Pat O'Dea painting a motel in the Monroeville area, and he and Janet talked about opening a CB repair shop together.

"Shortly before Christmas of 1975, Janet called me at my place and asked if I'd like to make some extra money," he told Torbin and Watson. "I said 'Sure. How?' and she told me to come over and 'We'll talk,' which I did."

Krueger got there some time that evening. Janet and Pat were sitting at the kitchen table. Janet showed Krueger a small, short-barreled revolver, possibly a .32, he said. Janet asked if he'd like to make $500. Krueger said he would.

" 'All you have to do is get rid of a guy. That's why I'm showing you the gun.' "

Krueger said he backed away from Janet's proposal and never discussed it with her again.

On the night of the killing, the O'Deas told Krueger that Slutzker was there, and Krueger said he saw Slutzker's van parked at the house but didn't see Slutzker at any time. Also, he was sure that Amy Slutzker was not in the O'Dea house.

Toward the end of an evening of drinking and talking on the radio, a CB personality named "Kingfish," who lived on Marlboro Street, reported that police were in the neighborhood and had "kicked in the wrong door."

Krueger said that's when he and Schwartz left the O'Deas. The pair drove to Kingfish's house and learned of the killing.

Bill said that some time after Janet was released from jail, he ran into Clare Vogel at the Wilkinsburg carnival. He couldn't tell Torbin and Watson exactly when the chance encounter occurred, but he remembered that it was the last carnival the borough held.

"Clare said her mother and Pat would like to see me again and she said why didn't I stop up the house some time. I hadn't seen any of those people since the night of the killing, and I had no intention of going up there again because I didn't need the trouble.

"But while I was talking to her I asked her, I said, was anything going on about the murder, and she said, 'Between you and me, Steve did it.' "

Krueger said he didn't question Clare further.

"Bill, do you know Clare's father, Harvey Vogel?" Watson said.

"No, I don't."

"Did you know John Mudd or his wife?"

"No."

"Did you know that Steve Slutzker and John Mudd's wife were having an affair?"

"No."

"Were you sexually involved with Janet O'Dea?"

Bill Krueger's face twisted into a look that didn't require any further response to the question, but he spoke anyway. "Are you kidding? No way. Did you ever see her?"

The detectives asked a series of questions about Jerry Schwartz, but Krueger considered him as only a sometimes friend, believed Schwartz's father was a photographer but knew little else.

He agreed to take a polygraph test.

■ ■ ■

Back in Pittsburgh, Watson and Schwab reviewed the state of the investigation with other members of the homicide bureau.

The juiciest tidbit was Krueger's version of his conversation with Clare Vogel at the Wilkinsburg carnival. But that was hearsay for the moment, and in two interviews Clare had demonstrated that her grasp on the details of the Mudd affair was rather weak.

She had been good for the detail about the Homestead High-Level Bridge, but that appeared to be a dead end. Clare couldn't remember telling her father about having found a gun under the seat of Pat O'Dea's car.

That being the case, the odds were long that she'd remember the comment Krueger attributed to her, and even if she did, it was doubtful she would be able to explain how she knew that "Steve did it."

At first, the interviews with the O'Deas seemed to be of little value except to provide fodder for after-hours storytelling about the characters who make up the world. But as the detectives thought it over, they realized that Janet had been adamant that Slutzker never left the house. Pat, on the other hand, left the door open to the possibility that Steve could have left without anyone knowing about it.

They figured that the issue should be pursued when they could interview the O'Deas separately.

For the time being, the reopened investigation would have to simmer on the back burner. The state of the evidence did not justify throwing major resources at . . . what? This trail was cold, and the detectives were largely walking over grass that had already been tramped down.

From the spring of 1986 onward, Torbin, Watson, and Schwab kept the investigation alive, but barely so. Arlene Montgomery changed her phone number and had to be tracked down again with the help of Punxsutawney police.

Bill Krueger said he couldn't take a polygraph exam because his boss wouldn't give him time off work. That had to be straightened out.

No one knew where Debbie and Amy Slutzker had gotten to. Altoona police and Teresa Rocco, the missing person's specialist at Pittsburgh Police, provided a number of leads. By August, the county police detectives still didn't know where the remnants of Slutzker's family were.

Even Slutzker had dipped below the detectives' radar.

In late March 1987, the best they knew was that Slutzker supposedly operated a business off Route 30 in Forest Hills and had been issued a traffic citation there two years earlier.

And what were they going to ask Slutzker if they found him? "Did you do it? Tell the truth now. Pretty please."

The investigation slipped into a coma, where it remained for the next three and a half years.

BOOK TWO

1976–1990

Slow Train Coming

John Mudd Jr. grew up with a quick mind and a tendency to bore easily. Perhaps that's why he employed his fists so often when his intellect was idle.

He spent his boyhood and youth in Bloomfield, a busy, unpretentious neighborhood that lent much to the ethnic, rough-and-tumble character of Pittsburgh.

John and his cousin Phil Perri could hardly have been closer if they'd been birth brothers. They played T-ball, street ball, Little League ball, and football for Immaculate Conception, where John played middle linebacker and returned kicks. They played street hockey together. John also was active in organized hockey in Mount Lebanon and Bridgeville for years.

John got good grades during his elementary school years and developed a healthy sense of duty to the community. When he was an early teen, John and his cousin, Crystal, would sing Christmas carols, collect donations, and buy doughnuts and cookies for the residents of St. Joseph's nursing home.

For the infirm residents who couldn't eat such treats, they'd buy trinkets.

They often visited St. Joseph's on other holidays too, sometimes just walking up and down the halls, saying hello, talking to the residents, and sitting at lunch with them.

John's uncle, Phil Perri, who was more father than uncle, had a camp near Butler, where John and his cousin got their kicks by buzzing around on snowmobiles and quad runners.

The boys learned to hunt and fish together. On John's first time deer hunting, he bagged a buck at 7:15 as soon as it was light enough to start shooting.

Mr. Perri's parents lived on the first floor of the family's home. John knew the couple as his grandparents.

Young Mudd had a voracious appetite for technical detail. He satisfied it by tearing apart anything and everything electronic or mechanical, radio-controlled cars, tape recorders, anything, even if it was brand-new, just to see what made it work and whether he could get it back together.

As he got older, he transferred his curiosity to automobile engines and reached a point where he could strip and reassemble them almost blindfolded.

But by the time Mudd was sixteen, his physical abilities, his temperament, and the pack he ran with at Central Catholic High School proved to be a troublesome combination.

He started swinging his fists almost as often as he swung a baseball bat. His baseball days pretty much ended after one season in Pony League because he was too testy on the field.

He developed a reputation at school as a legitimate

badass. Other kids would cringe at the mention of his name, and just about everyone gave Mudd a wide berth.

John spent three years in high school but didn't make it out of tenth grade, bouncing from school to school. He went to Schenley and Oliver high schools. He tried Peabody, but only for a day because the administrators there wouldn't let him enroll.

The day he quit high school was the day he enrolled at the Conley trade school. It was only a stopping point on the way to the navy.

He'd decided to follow in the steps of his father, who'd enlisted at age seventeen and served as a gunner's mate on the cruiser USS *Springfield*.

John Mudd Sr. had gone from his birthplace, 5337 Broad Street, East Liberty, to navy training at Great Lakes, Illinois, in 1964. His father had been a traffic cop in Pittsburgh who died when John Sr. was a boy. The story was that the elder Mudd let a doctor remove a cyst from the back of his neck, the incision became infected, and the infection killed him.

After the navy, John Mudd Sr. took up truck driving, local and over-the-road. John Jr. remembered riding with his dad.

After collecting his GED at Conley's, John Jr. found himself training at Great Lakes in February, which is the wrong place at the wrong time of year for asthma sufferers. Two weeks before boot camp graduation, the navy pushed him toward the door. John appealed, but was sent home with an honorable discharge and a blank page where Plan B should have been in his career manual.

He had a series of part-time jobs, including cement finishing, selling cars, and bouncing rowdy drunks. He became a volunteer fireman. He applied at least half a dozen times for a paid job with the Pittsburgh fire department but watched from the sidelines as the department hired a number of women and minorities to make up for years of racial imbalance.

In late summer 1989, John Mudd Jr. began dating Kimberly Ann Altman. She was an attractive young woman who had enough of the rebel in her to appreciate the wild streak in him and enough tenderness and love to dissipate the hostility he carried for so many years.

They became inseparable. John stopped fighting. He seemed to be more relaxed about the world around him, not so tightly wound all the time.

In early October 1990, John Mudd and Kim Altman began living together. Her uncle had a place at 1110 James Street on Pittsburgh's Northside. The young lovers had the place to themselves.

As a housewarming present of sorts, his aunt Peggy gave him the flag that had covered his father's coffin.

November 23, 1990

The flag was about the only tangible memento John Mudd Jr. had of his father.

The flag was impressive.

It was big enough to have draped the coffin, big enough for John to wrap himself in.

The flag had heft. The material was strong and well sewn.

The cloth was smooth to the touch.

The flag smelled old and important.

The white stars were striking in their field of deep, shimmering blue. The bars of white and red were satiny and bold.

John had no particular reason for choosing this day to decide what to do with the flag. He knew that he didn't want to hide it in a drawer for another fifteen years. The thought occurred to him to display it.

He hung it on the wall of the dining room.

The flag dominated the room, and, framed by the archway to the living room and by the doorway to the entrance hall, it commanded attention.

No one who came through the front door could miss the flag.

There it was, he thought. The funeral shroud. The symbol of his good and innocent father, his murdered father.

John left the house and drove north on McKnight Road, cut west on Three Degree Road, turned right, and followed Route 19 to the pizza shop in Pine Plaza where he worked.

It was Friday, and Kim's brother, Joe, stopped to say hello and see if John wanted to do anything that evening. The two had been friends for as long as John and Kim had been dating.

"You wanna go all-night bowling?"

"Yeah. Sounds okay to me. Who's that?" said John, looking at the stranger hanging back at the door.

"Steve. Steve Spinola, a friend. We were just up the dry cleaner's talking to Kim. She's up for going bowling."

"I'm not done for a while, and Kim's not done till

nine," John said. He was addressing Joe but looking at Steve.

"Well, we're gonna hang out with Kim. Come on over when you're done, and we'll go do something till she's done."

Joe turned and walked away. Steve gave Mudd a look as if to say "Nice to meet you. See you later," and the two left for Don Royal Cleaners only a few storefronts away.

John was uneasy. That guy must be the Steve who's been hitting on Kim, pestering her at work for dates, he thought.

John begged off work early, saying his back was acting up. Kim had his medicine. He'd say he came over because he needed it.

Joe and Steve were in the back room of the dry cleaning shop talking to Kim when John arrived. He kept the real reason for the visit to himself.

An American flag, cleaned and wrapped, was in plain view among other items waiting for customers to pick them up.

John told Kim what he'd done with his flag.

"You ought to have it cleaned," she said. "You know, it's been a while. There's no charge. They don't charge you to clean an American flag."

"What's the flag for?" said Steve.

John explained.

"Wow. I'd like to see that. We ought to go over to your place, you know, if it's okay and everything."

"Sure," Mudd said.

It was decided then. They would go to John and Kim's place before heading out to the lanes. In the meantime, Joe, Steve, and John left to shoot pool and kill time while Kim finished her shift.

In the car, John was still up tight about Steve. He finally spoke up. The drift of his comment was that Steve shouldn't hit on Kim if he knows what's good for him.

"This is a different Steve. He's not the one," Joe explained.

John seemed to accept the explanation, and the three of them got along well after that. They shot pool long enough to be fifteen minutes late getting back to the cleaners for Kim.

They drove to the James Street house on the Northside and piled inside. Someone brought out a deck of cards, and they all played poker.

A sense of well-being came over John. He felt comfortable, secure, and very much in love with Kim. Maybe the resolution of the misunderstanding about Steve had something to do with it. Maybe the scene itself—four happy people enjoying a card game in the dining room of the house John and Kim shared—evoked a sense of family and harmony in John. Whatever it was, it bubbled out of him in the form of a marriage proposal to Kim.

She, of course, was thrilled. She accepted on the spot. From then on, the card game and the Trivial Pursuit that followed were merely something to do to occupy her hands while her thoughts and her conversation explored the many wonderful aspects of marriage.

When it got close to midnight, John and Joe got up from the dining room table to stretch. They wandered into the living room.

Kim had given absolutely no thought to what it was like for Joe and Steve to listen to her effervesce about her marriage plans, so she was totally unaware of the effect she was having when, in the absence of Joe and John, she picked up the theme again and concentrated all of her giddy joy on Steve. As a relative stranger to Kim and John, as a guy and as a sixteen-year-old who probably had never thought of marriage as something desirable, Steve Spinola did not share her happiness. He couldn't even appreciate it. In fact, he found her prattle to be annoying. To express himself on the issue, he chose three rather unartful mono-syllables.

"Oh, fuck you!"

November 24, 1990, 2:10 A.M.

"Y'ello," Ron Gratz said into the telephone, only half awake.

"Detective. This is Bill Wymard in the radio room."

"Un-huh. What's up?"

"Detective, I just got a call from a guy who says he's got important new information about the murder of his brother some years back. The caller's name is James Mudd. Says his brother was shot in 1975. Something just happened with the caller's nephew. He wants to talk."

Gratz got a pen and pad and started taking notes. Nothing Wymard said made much sense, but at least Gratz had a name and a phone number. He shook off the remnants of sleep and dialed.

James Mudd threw a lot of information at Gratz over the phone. Most of it wasn't well connected, but all he had to do was convince the detective that something important had happened; he succeeded at that.

John Mudd Jr. was acting very strangely.

Something inside his mind, some tightly wound bundle of emotions, anxieties, sights, and sounds that had been stuffed into a corner of his psyche, had come loose with results equivalent to all the hoops on a barrel of warm beer bursting at the same time.

The unbundling occurred in a moment, as if a lone, rusted chain had finally failed and a reservoir of mental energy had flung open the floodgates and come roaring out. As though a fully wound mainspring in an old timepiece had lost its moorings and leaped forth, hurling out its coils in one agitated act of twanging and jiggling.

The past had leaped to life. A darkened stage was suddenly lit. John Mudd Jr., the five-year-old, sprang from the shadows into the spotlight, costumed as John Mudd Jr., the twenty-year-old. The lines of dialogue were the climactic scene of a drama that had been suspended, unresolved, fifteen years earlier.

The boy's knowledge of what happened at 1515 Marlboro Street in Wilkinsburg on the night of December 28, 1975, had suddenly found voice and expression in the man.

To those who witnessed it, the noises, the words, and the emotions that erupted from John at the James Street house that night were eerie, awesome, and frightening, almost otherworldly. Between sobs, tears, and twisted, emotion-racked facial expressions that reflected the fragmentary images flashing before his mind's eye, he described the memory. In doing so, John spoke with the voice of a child, a high-pitched whine. It seemed as if he'd actually transmuted into the five-year-old who had absorbed the fearful experience of John Mudd's violent murder.

Kim, Steve, and Joe watched and listened in slack-jawed amazement as John's psyche purged itself. The Mudd relatives were called and immediately came to the house. The job of notifying the police fell to James, John's uncle.

The entirety of the event was more than James Mudd could assimilate, so he did his best to patch the details together and relate them to Gratz.

A number of the details he provided over the phone would later be disputed by other witnesses. Nonetheless, James Mudd accomplished his most important mission. He convinced the authorities that new information had surfaced, sufficient to revive the murder investigation.

The essence of what James Mudd told Gratz was that John remembered a man being in his house the night of the murder and that the man was Steven Slutzker.

The rest of what James reported was either jumbled with his own recollections or was largely background information not essential to the homicide investigation that was about to gain a full head of steam.

For example, James told Gratz that, in John's recollection, the man kissed his mother.

James also said he couldn't remember the names of all the detectives who worked on the case previously, but the investigation had been led by a detective he remembered as "Fanelli" who was by then working in security at Divine Providence Hospital.

He said the investigation had been reopened several years earlier, and in that phase attention seemed to focus on Arlene Mudd.

James Mudd told Gratz the family questioned John Jr. soon after the murder and even went so far as to have him hypnotized to learn what he might have witnessed. Nothing came out of those attempts.

It occurred to Gratz to rouse himself and conduct interviews that night at the James Street house, but he thought it would be better to wait until after daybreak. It was a very good call. John was in no shape to grant a meaningful interview with detectives. Besides, the investigators would need a little time to orient themselves with the case file.

At 8:30 that morning, Gratz called Detective Regis Kelly at the county police homicide office and turned in a report on his conversation with James Mudd. With that phone call, the investigation of the murder of John Lawrence Mudd finally fell into the hands of the man who had the determination and startling new evidence sufficient to bring the case to court.

Regis Kelly does not give up easily. If he has a kindred spirit in the animal world, it probably would be a lean and hungry mutt, streetwise, battle-scarred, indefatigable, and totally unfamiliar with the word "quit."

During nearly two decades of service with the Allegheny County Police, Regis Kelly built a reputation as one of the hardest-working detectives in western Pennsylvania.

He's the kind of guy few women want to date, at least for very long. Not that Kelly isn't attractive. It's just that he's a cop who is driven. His passion for his job is such that he has repeatedly sacrificed his personal life; he'd been divorced once and lost a series of girlfriends who, once they found themselves attracted to him, wanted him to be around. Instead, he's almost always on the job, and when he's not, chances are he's thinking about it. Sometimes Kelly can't avoid the job even when he tries, like the time he was shot in the head at Three Rivers Stadium.

He was enjoying himself at a ballgame when a trouble-maker started mouthing off to Kelly's friend while Kelly was away getting snacks. The guy pulled a gun when Kelly returned, then ran out of the stadium. Kelly chased him and was ambushed when the man stepped from behind a concrete column and fired. Kelly remained conscious and returned fire despite having lead fragments in his head. If Kelly had been using something other than a 9 mm pistol, the gunman probably would have gotten what he so richly deserved, a body full of fatally shredded organs. Instead, the high-powered slugs zipped right through him without causing fatal injuries. Bullets like those will mushroom and tear things up when they hit bone or dense tissue. But if they don't strike something hard, they're in and out without much fuss. If you don't hit the head or the heart, trying to kill someone with a 9 mm is like stabbing him with a hat pin.

Only several years later, Kelly had the pleasure of running into the gunman on the street. He marveled to himself that a would-be cop killer could be sentenced to such a ridiculously short term.

The outcome of the prosecution could have soured a lot of people, even a veteran detective, on the criminal justice system. Kelly took it in stride.

By the same token, a lot of cops would have played the head injury to the hilt. They would have claimed that headaches or seizures caused by the remaining bullet fragments made them unable to work. They would have taken a disability pension and coasted through life with a can of beer in one hand and the TV remote control in the other. They would have been within their rights to do so.

Instead, Kelly was back in his shoulder holster and his impeccably tailored clothing—he was so fastidious about his clothes that he often ironed creases into his blue jeans

—as soon as his doctors would let him. And, despite the risks associated with working a high-stress job while carrying the souvenirs from the stadium shootout, the detective drove himself as hard as ever, as if an eighty-hour work week was an end in itself.

■ ■ ■

Kelly was working alone on the Saturday morning when Gratz phoned him to report what had happened the night before. Kelly checked in with his boss, Sergeant David Schwab. Schwab told Kelly to pull the file, then joined him in the office, where the two spent most of the morning going over the records. They drove away from the West Penn Building at the foot of Ross Street shortly before noon, headed for James Street on the Northside.

Earlybird Christmas shoppers had brought some bustle to downtown Pittsburgh on what would otherwise have been a very quiet Saturday morning. Even so, traffic was light. Kelly and Schwab had a clear shot over the six-lane, double-decked Fort Duquesne Bridge to the north shore of the Allegheny River. From there they wound their way into the red brick heart of the Northside and arrived at 11:55 A.M. at the house where John Mudd and Kim Altman lived.

They eased into the situation by listening to James Mudd run through the high points. He recalled the warning of John's counselor, Peg Gillick, who had said in the mid-1970s that the boy's memory of his father's killing might one day come flooding back to him.

Then it was John's turn to talk. He was seated at the kitchen table with Kelly and Schwab. The detectives analyzed his words, scanned his expressions, and noted his body language. John's uncles James and Terry were at his side.

Mudd was shaken but in control as he set the stage with the details about the people who were present and the activities of the evening. He said the evening turned on the remark Steve made to Kim, accusing her of "fucking up" or something like that.

John said he felt himself go into a rage. He rushed at Steve and threw him from his chair in the dining room to the floor. As he held Steve pinned to the floor, he looked up at the flag on the wall. Then he began crying, and the memory came flooding back.

By now, John was sobbing. Tears streamed down his face. His thick arms shook as he told Kelly and Schwab how he got up from the floor, walked out of the dining room, and went into the living room. Kim had followed him and listened as he rattled off descriptions of the things he was remembering. As he relived the recollection for Kelly and Schwab, Mudd spoke in a voice that still had something of the high-pitched character of a child's.

Terry and James confirmed that after they arrived at the house, they too heard their nephew repeating the recollection in a voice that sounded young, as John's had before it changed.

In the memory that John Mudd Jr. described to Kelly and Schwab that Saturday, he and his mother and father had been sitting on the couch in the living room, watching television. John had his Superman blanket. The lights went out. His father got up from the couch and said he would check the fuses. John heard his father open the basement door and heard him walking down the steps. Then he heard seven loud noises. A guy came up and went past him and out the front door. The man was a white male, about John's height, five-foot-ten or eleven.

He was skinny and had short dark hair. John couldn't recall exactly what happened, but the next thing he remembered was seeing his dad at the bottom of the steps. He was able to see down the steps because the light was on in the fish tank in the kitchen.

His father was lying on his side on the basement floor.

John remembered being back on the couch and seeing his mother on the telephone. He was still on the couch when his uncle Jimmy arrived. John was taken by a man he didn't know to a house where his mother was. He asked his mother what was going on, and she didn't answer. Then he asked the man who had taken him to the house. The man picked him up and told him his father had died.

Kelly asked John if he could remember anything more about the man he saw in his house right after he heard the seven noises.

John said the man was wearing jeans and a sweater whose color he could not remember. His shoes looked like loafers. John added that he could remember being in a sleeping bag that evening and that the bag opened into what he called his Superman blanket.

Details about the Mudds' home had also returned.

He remembered that you could walk through the front door, turn right, and climb a couple steps to a landing, from which led a staircase to the second floor. There were three rooms up there.

The aquarium in the kitchen contained goldfish. The tank was on the wall opposite the basement steps. The steps were wooden with open spaces between them. A wall faced you at the bottom of the steps, and the cellar was to the right.

He remembered the cellar door leading to the backyard, where there was a wooded hill and a garage with holes in its roof. His father had warned him not to go near the garage, but John did anyway and fell through the roof.

The front yard had a narrow concrete walkway on either side of which was grass.

John recalled the time their neighbor Steve came over and asked him to go around to the backyard and get Steve's dog, a German shepherd. He found the dog playing in the yard, brought him to the front, and walked into the living room to see Steve apparently trying to kiss his mother. When Steve saw John watching, he released Arlene and left the house.

John remembered that Steve had a daughter, although he could not remember her name. He used to play with her. She was always bigger than he.

The man who went past him that night was the same man he'd seen in the house trying to kiss his mother. Of that he was "100 percent sure."

John said he never returned to 1515 Marlboro Street after that night. That's right, Terry Mudd said. The family never took John back to the house. In fact, family members never talked about his father's death or the details surrounding it in John's presence.

■ ■ ■

Kelly promised John and his family that the new information would be brought to the attention of the district attorney. It was. W. Christopher Conrad, one of Bob Colville's most trusted deputies, took the call from the county police homicide squad the next week.

Conrad listened impassively to the pertinent details and agreed that an investigation was warranted.

When he hung up the phone, he turned around in his seat and looked at the young woman who was in the room with him. Kim Clark was not necessarily a rarity as a female assistant district attorney in Allegheny County, but neither was she the most experienced prosecutor in the department. But there she was, and here this was, an unusual case to be sure.

As far as anyone could tell in late November 1990, the Mudd case was pretty much yesterday's news. The original investigation had yielded little. The authorities had disguised their embarrassment over losing the homicide charge as amazement that Stanley Stein, the coroner's solicitor, could have ruled as he did. The additional information collected during the 1980s after Harvey Vogel stepped forward showed that there was more to the case than the first set of investigators had come up with.

The new development wasn't exactly a prosecutor's dream come true either. The event that occurred on the Northside on the night of November 23–24 was not easily understood by psychologists, let alone detectives, prosecutors, or your run-of-the-mill jurors. To the extent that nonspecialists could understand mental phenomena like Mudd's recall, they associated them with posttraumatic stress disorder. That malady, in turn, was mentioned most often in connection with the dysfunctional lives of a few veterans of the war in Vietnam.

As such, the new evidence would be highly vulnerable to attack from the defense and going to a jury with John Mudd's flashback recollection would be a high-risk move. High-profile prosecutors such as Conrad knew instinctively that convictions, long careers, promotions, pay raises, and, above all else, good publicity for themselves and their bosses were not the most likely outcomes of high-risk maneuvers.

The words were never spoken, but in essence, the third

incarnation of the John Mudd murder case had, in the eyes of people who knew how to judge these things, all the markings of a piece of shit. Kim Clark was just the woman to handle it.

Whether she saw the case that way or not, Clark didn't flinch. After all, young prosecutors rarely get to pick their first murder cases.

Building the Case

Shortly after interviewing Mudd, the detectives contacted Dr. Alan Pass, a forensic psychologist whom the department sometimes consulted on the psychological aspects of criminal cases.

Pass said that Mudd's restored memory seemed to fit perfectly within posttraumatic stress syndrome. Before that diagnosis could be made with certainty, however, several possibilities had to be eliminated. One was that during the fifteen intervening years someone had planted a scenario of the murder and a description of Steven Slutzker in the young man's mind.

Pass said he and the investigators would have to carefully review whatever records existed of the counseling John Jr. had received as a boy.

On January 3, 1991, Sergeant Schwab assigned Lee Torbin to get John Mudd Jr.'s signature on a county police release form. It authorized the Allegheny County Children and Youth Services and Catholic Social Services to release the records of the psychological counseling he received as a child. The Catholic agency insisted that Mudd sign its own release form. That signing occurred on January 22.

But while he was in the homicide detectives' offices with Kelly and Torbin that day, John revealed a growing paranoia about his role in the case.

"Does Steve Slutzker know what's going on?"

"He has no idea that we've begun to investigate him again," Kelly said.

Mudd said he'd been living in fear ever since having the recollection. He was having nightmares and wanted to stay home all the time and couldn't bring himself to go into the basement of his house. He rattled on about the possibility that Slutzker knew he'd been targeted by Mudd's flashback.

The detectives repeatedly assured John that Slutzker was in the dark and that there was nothing to worry about. John seemed satisfied with their assurances and parted a calmer but still concerned young man.

Kelly and Torbin finally had enough paperwork and signatures to satisfy the record keepers at Catholic Social Services in the Bank Tower on Fourth Avenue downtown. They got a look at Mudd's case file on January 31 and saw that John had undergone counseling from early 1976 until late 1978, although they also found notes dated January 1981.

They saw a bounty of significant information about John Jr. and immediately recognized the need for Dr. Pass to review the records.

The release form, however, was not enough to satisfy the attorney representing the Catholic agency. It would take a court order or search warrant, which the detectives obtained from Judge Robert Dauer on February 4.

Copies of the typed and handwritten notes of the boy's counseling sessions were turned over to Pass.

Meanwhile, armed with more releases, on February 11

Kelly and Torbin examined records kept in Bloomfield at the offices of Allegheny County Children and Youth Services. The agency became involved in John Jr.'s case from January 7, 1976, on a referral from Maureen Perri. Service was terminated on December 12, 1977, after the boy was placed with the Perri family by Judge Tamilia.

The file contained little that the detectives considered significant regarding the mental state of John Mudd Jr. as a boy, but it contained several notes that they found interesting.

The file noted that both Arlene Mudd and a Wilkinsburg police officer, believed to be Patrolman Mangano, claimed that John Jr. was asleep during the killing and up until the time he was removed from his home.

■ ■ ■

The next afternoon, Tuesday, February 12, Kelly drove up the Monongahela River to Homestead, exited Eighth Avenue and climbed the steep hill that led to Lincoln Place.

The sun was low in the winter sky when he pulled up in front of 1062 Lindberg Avenue, the home of John Jr.'s uncle Terry and aunt Donna.

Kelly's mission was to find out how much influence might have been exerted over the boy's memory by conversations the Mudd family members must have had about the murder. He was hoping the answer would be "none," but hope isn't admissible in court, so he had to find out for sure.

As good investigators often do, Kelly took an oblique angle on the issue that interested him most. He asked Terrence Mudd first to describe the day of the murder and his relationship with his brother and his sister-in-law, Arlene.

Terry said that on the day of the murder, he, Donna, and their daughter, Doreen, who was four at the time, started their outing with a stop at his mother's home in East Liberty. Around dinnertime, they arrived at the home of his sister, Maureen Perri. Throughout most of the evening, Doreen, Johnny, and little Phil Perri played on the third floor.

"How were your brother John and Arlene getting along that evening?"

"Well, there weren't any arguments during the evening, if that's what you mean," Terry said.

"Were they drinking? Was there any alcohol consumed that night?"

"I don't believe that they were drinking, but I remember that Arlene stayed off to herself most of the evening, and she was continually asking what time it was."

Terry said he went outside with John, Arlene, and Johnny to say good-bye to them when they left Maureen's. Soon after that, Terry and his family headed back to their home. He and Donna skipped the 11 o'clock news and were in bed soon after they got home.

The first of Arlene's two phone calls came a short time later.

"She was hysterical. Before she could get more than a few words out, the call was cut off. I was having trouble with the phone, so I tried to call her back but her line was busy. Right after I hung up, the phone rang, and it was Arlene again.

"She was hysterical. She said Johnny had been shot and was lying at the bottom of the cellar steps."

Terry dressed and drove to his brother's house. The

trip took longer than normal because of the snow and ice on the roads. After explaining to the police who he was, Terry entered the living room and saw his brother, Jimmy, there with an expression that told him instantly that their brother was dead.

Having warmed up Terry Mudd, Kelly got to the heart of the matter. "Did you ever discuss the night of the murder or your suspicions as to Arlene possibly being involved or whether Steve Slutzker was the killer in front of your nephew?"

Terry said that to the best of his recollection he had not.

Jimmy Mudd, his wife, Kathleen, and the Mudds' sister, Nora, were living in Mary Mudd's home at the time of the murder, he said. The other Mudd sister, Patty, might also have been living there, and their uncle, Johnny O'Conner, was a frequent visitor. Terry and Donna made it a habit to be at the house with Doreen on Sundays.

Terry said he couldn't recall ever hearing the case discussed in front of John Jr., but he conceded that it is possible the boy overheard the adults talking.

"It was accidental if he did," Mudd said. That was largely because Mary Mudd had given orders to shield the boy from such talk.

When John Jr. grew older, Terry took care to avoid the subject during his frequent conversations with his nephew. "Johnny would call me sometimes and he would want to know about his father, but he would want to know what his father and I did when we were boys."

Terry said John Jr. never asked him about the night of the murder. On a few occasions, Terry asked John Jr. what he remembered about his father. The boy would speak about riding in his dad's truck and other things they did together, but never about his father's death.

Terry also said "Arlene is strange. She would do things then brag about them. Like the time she walked into Sears and stole a shelf that would go on a wall above the toilet. She thought it was a big joke, and she talked about it. It was a pretty big box too, maybe three foot by two. She used to brag about the fact that she just picked it up and walked right out of the store."

On the evening of the recollection, Doreen, who was eighteen by then, took John's call sometime around midnight.

"Doreen didn't recognize his voice at first," Terry said. The voice on the other end of the line was sobbing heavily. "She was about to hang up because she thought it was a prank phone call when Johnny finally got his name out. She handed the phone to me, and I talked to John. He was sobbing and talking in a strange kind of voice. When he mentioned something about his dad, I just told him I'd be right over."

Terry arrived at the James Street house at the same time his brother, Jimmy, did. The two entered together and found their sister, Maureen, comforting their nephew.

John was crying and talking. He wasn't talking in sentences but in snippets of narrative. The experience moved Terry Mudd to tears.

Days later, Terry played cards with John Jr., but the young man seemed to not want to talk about the recollection, "so I didn't push it," he told Kelly.

The detective told Mudd that investigators were able to find only one other case where a flashback recollection had led to a successful prosecution. It was the case that sprang back to life in 1989 in San Mateo County, California, when Eileen Lipsker looked into the eyes of her red-haired, five-year-old daughter Jessica and suddenly remembered the time when, at age eight, she'd claimed to have looked into the eyes of her playmate, Susan Nason, a few minutes after Eileen's father had raped Susan in the back of his van and an instant before he supposedly smashed Susan's brains out with a rock.

"Do you recall that incident being reported in the newspaper?" Kelly asked Terry Mudd.

"I read the paper from front to back all the time, and I did read about that."

Terry said he didn't think about the Nason case until Saturday, November 24, as he listened to Kelly and Schwab interviewing John Jr. Terry said he never talked to his nephew about the California case and doubted whether John Jr. ever heard about it. "Johnny never reads the newspaper and never watches the news. He has very little interest in it."

When it was Donna's turn to answer Kelly's questions, she gave much the same information until the detective asked her to describe the relationship between Arlene and John Sr.

"I'm aware of two particular incidents that I've never told anybody about," Mrs. Mudd said.

The first occurred close to Christmas 1975. John Sr. and Arlene had come over to the house and while they were visiting, Arlene suggested that she and Donna go shopping. Donna couldn't recall which store they went to, but she clearly remembered that the two of them had agreed on the store before they left the house.

Inside the store, Arlene told Donna she would be back in a short time and left her sister-in-law in one of the aisles. Donna finished her shopping, waited for Arlene, and then began looking for her.

"I walked around the corner of one aisle and saw

Arlene and Steven Slutzker in the aisle, and they were kissing. I saw Arlene say something to Steve."

Arlene was surprised when she realized Donna was watching. "She asked me not to say anything."

Donna said she agreed to keep Arlene's dirty little secret.

The other incident occurred late in December 1975. John Sr. came over, and he and Terry left to buy tickets for the New Year's celebration at Roman Garden's, a night spot on Route 51 south of Pittsburgh.

John and Terry were gone for around two hours, during which Arlene called Donna five or six times asking if the men were back yet.

"I never said anything, but from the sound of her voice —she sounded very anxious—I thought that Arlene was with Steve Slutzker. She called so many times that I finally told her I would let her know when they got back."

■ ■ ■

By late February 1991, Dr. Pass had read John Jr.'s counseling records and familiarized himself with the history of the case. It was time for Pass to interview Mudd.

The purpose of the interview was twofold: The investigators wanted to solidify as many new facts as they could, and Pass wanted to assess Mudd's recall to see whether it was consistent with posttraumatic stress syndrome.

At Pass's request, Torbin and Kelly invited Maureen Perri to be there. The doctor thought it a good idea to have someone present as a calming influence on John. In midafternoon on February 28, the two detectives, the doctor, Mrs. Perri, and John Mudd sat down at a conference table on the seventh floor of the West Penn Building.

Everyone stole glances at the Lanier tape recorder that hummed quietly in front of Torbin.

Maureen sat close to her nephew. She said nothing throughout the questioning, but held his arm and rubbed it gently when the retelling reduced him once again to crying and sobbing. The strongest emotions surfaced as he described the scenes he remembered from the night of the murder.

He also told his version of the events the night of his recollection.

"I don't remember exactly what I heard this kid say to my girlfriend, but I remember jumping over my couch. I grabbed the chair. I hit the kid with the chair, knocked him to the ground. I was over top of him, and I was shakin', but I wanted to kill the kid. I hit him approximately three times and just didn't want to stop. Then I walked away from him. I walked out into the hallway. As I got to the hallway, I just started crying and I started rememberin' everything. It came back all at one time, real fast. I didn't really catch anything.

"I sat down, and as I sat I closed my eyes and was tryin' to relax, and then I seen everything, which I just told you comin' to me, slow, and I got to take a good look at everything. And that's when I called my aunt Maureen, my uncle Jimmy, and my uncle Terry to come over, 'cause I thought I needed help 'cause it was scarin' me. I didn't know what was happening, and now, after it happened, I can't get the picture of my dad layin' there out of my head. It scares me. It taunts me, whether I'm awake or at work. I see that, that picture of him laying there."

Pass probed at length about the man John had seen come from the kitchen and speak to his mother before leaving the house. "Now this man, I believe you described him as a tall, thin man with dark hair."

"It was kind of dark in the house. It was short hair," Mudd said.

"Can you recall what he was dressed like?"

"Jeans, darker jeans on and I . . . it was a one-piece shirt or a sweater of a darker nature. It was long-sleeved. The guy's face was thin, had a bigger nose."

"Just focus on the picture that you see in your mind."

"About all I can remember is him standin' there. He was thinner, I mean, not heavy at all. Had a thin face, and his shirt was, like I said, a dark color, long-sleeved."

Mudd couldn't remember whether the man had anything in his hands, and he could not remember hearing any of the words that were exchanged, only that the man spoke.

"It was a deeper voice, 'cause even though I can't hear what they were exactly sayin', when the conversation was going on, I could distinguish his voice. It was deeper."

"He spoke to my mother first, then my mother said something back to him, and he said something, and that's when he left."

"Now," said Pass, "when this conversation was taking place, where was the man? Where was your mother, and where were you?"

"On the couch. My mother was sitting next to me, on my left. And the man was standing, facing the couch where we were at, in the middle of the living room floor."

"Do you recall anything of your mother's reaction when this conversation was taking place?"

"No reaction, really," Mudd said. "She didn't get off the couch. There was no hysterics. There was no cryin'. There was just words being exchanged."

"As he was leaving through the front door, can you recall where your mother was?"

"Getting off the couch to close the front door. I remember her closing the front door after he exited.

"She came back and sat on the end of the couch. She didn't say nothin' to me."

"Do you recall saying anything to her?"

"I remember asking what's going on, with no reply."

"She did not answer you?"

"No."

"Do you remember where she went or what she did?"

"I don't remember her getting off the couch."

"And the next thing you remember is what?"

"Just being on a different couch in a different house," John said, later contradicting himself in answer to a question by Torbin.

"At some point after Steve left is when you found yourself looking down the basement stairs, right?"

"Yes," Mudd said.

Torbin also picked up on an inconsistency in Mudd's description of his father's body.

"I'm a little bit confused," the detective said. "Can you tell me what direction his feet would have been pointing in?"

"It seems to me that one of them was under the step almost. And the other one would have been facing towards the back of the cellar, or the wall of the cellar."

"Am I understanding you right, that essentially his feet were toward the stairs?"

"Yes," Mudd said.

In fact, John Mudd Sr. had lain with his head, not his feet, against the bottom of the cellar steps.

Torbin also questioned John Jr. about the time when he saw the man trying to kiss his mother, and this time a new detail surfaced.

"When I come back into the house, I remember him

comin' over. He bent down, and he said, 'Thanks,' and he walked out the door, got his dog, and walked across the street."

Mudd also told Torbin he remembered being at the man's house.

"We were over having lunch there, with his daughter. He had bar stools, 'cause I remember sitting up."

"And where were these bar stools?" Torbin asked.

"Well, when I went in his house, we used the back door. We went in . . . 'cause I asked where his kitchen was. By his back door. And you went inside, the way they were set up was to the right of you. That's where the kitchen was.

"And there was a counter space there. And it had bar stools on the outer . . . outside of it is where we sat. On the bar stools."

"And were you at this man's house more than once?" Pass said.

"I don't remember any other time."

"Can you tell us who you were at this man's house with?"

"His daughter."

"And do you remember his daughter's name? Or what his daughter looked like?"

"Kind of pudgy, longer hair, like a darker blond, almost a brown, straight hair."

"Can you recall her name?"

"The name Kathy is staying in my head for his daughter's name."

Mudd remembered that the man's house was directly across the street from his own, but the only outside feature of the house that he remembered was its lack of a back porch.

"There was no porch in the back?" Pass said.

"No, just the back door was there."

Kelly asked him about the flag that hung on the dining room wall at the house he shared with Kim.

"That's the flag off my dad's coffin. I've been waitin' to be old enough, as my family or whoever would say, to get that. And it wasn't longer than a week before this that I got the flag off of my aunt. It hung on the wall. And that night, that's what I used when no one was there to be with me. I went over. I stood next to the flag, and I was holdin' it and leanin' against it. It was like a good luck charm, I guess, or like my blanket that's goin' to keep me safe. That was hangin' on the wall where me and this kid, Steve, had our fight. He was . . . when I was beatin' on him, he was leanin' . . . the flag was touching the radiator. He was leanin' against the flag and the radiator."

Pass took Mudd's thoughts back to the family gathering the day his father was killed. John couldn't remember where the gathering was, who was there, or specifically how his parents were getting along. One thing stood out in his memory, however.

"It was fun to be there."

"And why is that?"

"Everybody was having a good time, laughing. I was playing."

Pass asked the question that Torbin and Kelly must have been mulling over to themselves.

"Okay," the doctor said. "John, you mentioned that this man that you had seen the night that your father was killed looked familiar to you because you had seen him in the house before. Is that correct?"

"Yes."

"Then you mentioned his name."

"Yes."

"And what is that name?"

"Steve Slutzker."

"John, how can you be . . . I'm sorry. What makes you as sure as you seem to be that this was one and the same man?"

"I know I'm sure because when I asked, or when I talk to someone now present, and I bring up the girl I used to play with across the street and this and that . . . I was told what her father's name was, and it's the same man that was in the house that evening."

"All right, but at the time that this occurred, you didn't know his name, is that right?"

"Correct," Mudd said.

Pass pressed on to the heart of the matter. "After all this had happened, at some point in time, do you recall ever talking to your mother about this?"

"No, I don't remember ever talking to my mother again."

"Okay. And who would have been, if anyone, the person you can recall talking with about this after it happened?"

"I just remember in grade school, I seen a . . . I don't know what she was, a counselor, I don't know. But it was in my early years in grade school. I remember just going to her office, and I don't even really remember talking to her about this. I remember going and playing with blocks and coloring and that with her. I never remember talking with her about this incident."

"And from that point forward, up until just recently when you started to remember all these things, do you remember talking with anybody about this night?"

"No."

"Okay. Good."

"Nobody would talk to me about it."

"So, when all this came to your memory, it was suddenly?"

"Yes."

"No one told you about these things beforehand?"

"No."

"And you did not go over any of these things with the woman who you described as a counselor?"

"Not to my knowledge."

The interview lasted for about an hour. When it was over, Kelly took the tapes to the district attorney's investigative branch office in Penn Liberty Plaza and had two copies made. He gave one copy to the prosecutor, Clark, and kept one for the work file in the county detectives' homicide section. The original would be preserved for evidence in court.

■ ■ ■

As winter faded toward spring in 1991, the central issue was the credibility of John Mudd Jr.

If his story was to be believed, then it would represent significant new evidence worthy of filing homicide charges. If the recollection held up to scrutiny, then it certainly would blow apart Slutzker's alibi. There was no way he could have been walking out the front door of the dead man's home shortly before midnight if he was also sleeping off a drunk at a home on Grandview Avenue in McKeesport.

At the very least, the recollection made Arlene look like a liar. At most, it pointed to her as a participant in the murder. And John Jr.'s recollection didn't make Janet and Patrick O'Dea look like upstanding citizens, not that many people would have mistaken them for that in any case.

But the district attorney's staff and the detectives had

to ask themselves whether John Mudd Jr. was telling the truth. Was he lying? Could he be that skillful, that talented to pull off such a convincing charade?

Maybe Mudd's sudden recall was fabricated and he didn't even realize it. Could his mind have created an incriminating tapestry by unconsciously weaving together strands of his own legitimate memories, snippets of conversation he'd overheard among his relatives, and possibly even details of the case that quite likely circulated among his cousins, neighbors, and schoolmates?

The Mudd family members would have been justified in harboring bitterness and resentment sufficient to keep their tongues wagging for years. The crime was unsolved, and John Mudd Sr. unavenged. Slutzker served a relatively short sentence, and the authorities never laid a glove on Arlene.

Mary Mudd's civil suit against Wilkinsburg had gone nowhere. Civil suits weren't the golden egg they seem to be today, but even in the late 1970s and early 1980s it was common knowledge that litigation of that sort often paid off. The family hadn't received a dime.

It's conceivable that the sons, daughters, and in-laws of Mary Mudd obeyed her orders not to discuss the murder in front of John Jr. But what are the chances that no word of it was uttered during all the occasions when John Jr. was within earshot? Could any family be so disciplined as to not talk about it during all of those Sunday gatherings at the matriarch's home? Aren't boys and girls naturally inclined to sneak about every once in a while and eavesdrop on the after-dinner conversations of their elders, the grown-up talk that so fascinates children even when it is truly mundane?

Aside from those considerations, would a jury give much credence to the recollection even if it were demonstrated to be authentic? Clark knew she would be asking a lot of a panel of ordinary men and women to send a man to prison or the electric chair based on a vision, a sudden recollection of fifteen-year-old events first witnessed by a five-year-old boy.

Clark and her superiors in the DA's office could assess the chances of success in court based on the evidence in hand. They could devise a strategy to make best use of the information they had to work with. But to a certain degree, they had to rely on the judgment of others.

One was Pass. He'd found passages in the counseling records that would be exploited quickly by the defense in a trial. They included the assessment that John Jr. would make an unreliable witness even if he could recall what he'd seen and heard the night of the murder. Another weak point was the boy's vow that when he grew up, he was going to kill Steve.

But in the main, Pass had to conclude that despite some weaknesses in Mudd's story and his counseling records, his recollection appeared to be authentic.

Then there were the gut instincts of the detectives. While they had no psychology degrees, the investigators often were reliable judges of character and credibility. Usually they could smell bullshit a mile away, and to them, Mudd's statements had a fresh, wholesome scent about them.

Kelly, for one, had learned just about all he needed to know during his first interview with John Jr.

"He was exactly like someone who was traumatized, who'd witnessed something violent," Kelly told the others working on the case. "As he started to go through the story he started to talk faster. The reason I found it believable was the manner in which he was telling it. His hands were trembling. He had tears streaming down his face.

He was very excited. Talking very fast. Jumping back and forth. It was to me, obviously not a created story. If it was a created story, then he deserved an Academy Award, because I've heard a lot of bullshit from a lot of good bullshitters. I tell you, this story is something you'd get off a legitimate witness telling what he'd just seen. I found it to be pretty amazing, really."

Others may have dressed up their language in describing Mudd's credibility, but the people calling the shots in the prosecution agreed with Kelly's assessment.

As a result, Kelly and Torbin soon sat down at the typewriter and pecked out an affidavit in support of criminal complaints charging Steven Slutzker with criminal homicide and criminal conspiracy to commit homicide. They typed another set of documents supporting the same charges against Arlene Dudas, also known as Arlene Mudd, aka Arlene Montgomery.

Allegheny County coroner Dr. Joshua Perper issued the warrants on April 9.

Detectives Henry Watson and Tom Wolfson arrested Arlene at a quarter after noon the same day at the Ames department store in Punxsutawney. She'd lived in the borough for five or six years with Charles Stewart, whom Arlene described as her fiancé. She'd been working at Ames for the previous five months as a cashier for $4.25 an hour.

Chief Ronald Krolick of the Punxsutawney Police Department accompanied them to the borough's police station, where Arlene listened to her Miranda rights and called her parents.

An hour later, she stood before Magistrate George Miller in Brookville for her initial appearance. Six minutes after that, Arlene slumped into the backseat of the detectives' car for the two-hour ride back to Pittsburgh.

In the city, she was arraigned at the coroner's office, photographed, and offered the opportunity to apply for bail. By 7:30 P.M., Arlene was an overnight guest at the Allegheny County Jail.

Slutzker was arrested the next day on the same charges, criminal homicide and conspiracy to commit homicide. Things went much more smoothly for him because arrangements had been made through his attorney, Charles Scarlata, to surrender at the detectives' offices in the West Penn Building.

He arrived at the West Penn Building a few minutes after 1 P.M. Detectives Herb Foote and Mike Cunningham had him processed and in jail two hours later.

Kelly and Torbin didn't have the satisfaction of arresting Slutzker and Montgomery. They were halfway across the continent.

Houston, Texas, April 9, 1991

"Get them the fuck outta here!"

The voice came from a shabby town house on Leader Street in Houston.

Janet O'Dea was bellowing from her living room, where her big, mushy ass, in a conspiracy with gravity, was crushing the springs of a sofa.

"Stop right there! You're going to talk to these men."

The command came from Doug Bacon. The Houston homicide detective had escorted Kelly and Torbin to the O'Deas' home and introduced them when Patrick O'Dea answered the door. O'Dea remembered Kelly from his previous trip to Houston to interview the former McKeesport couple.

"Come on, Pat. Let's you and me go into the other room," Kelly said to the banty rooster.

Bacon stayed with Torbin while he interviewed Janet.

Kelly wanted to get Pat away from Janet in the hope that Pat would screw up. It didn't take long. As usual, Kelly backed into the issues of greatest interest. He first got Pat O'Dea to talk about himself. "What are you doing with yourself these days, Pat?"

O'Dea said he was working as a maintenance man at Cambridge Properties on Faninn Street. He'd been there around five months. Before that he was self-employed but largely associated with a builder.

Not that anyone gave a shit, but Patrick revealed that he'd married Janet in Roanoke, Virginia, seventeen years earlier. They divorced in 1980 and remarried in 1988.

Once he had Pat's jaw warmed up, Kelly asked him about Slutzker and the night of the killing.

O'Dea recited the story much as he'd told it previously, except that this time, he acknowledged the possibility that Slutzker could have left during the evening and returned. O'Dea said he would not have noticed if Slutzker had left and returned because "I was drunker than shit" and had passed out.

The next thing O'Dea remembered was waking up in his bed to voices in the living room. He stumbled out of the bedroom and recognized Wilkinsburg police Lieutenant Irwin Krueger among the officers who'd come to talk to Slutzker.

While Pat O'Dea was giving up as much as Kelly reasonably could have hoped to get, Janet was angrily responding to Torbin's questions.

She explained that she couldn't recall ever hearing Slutzker talk about Arlene or John Mudd.

"He definitely never talked to me about killing anyone," Janet said just before bursting into a tirade. She motherfucked everyone involved in her arrest, imprisonment, and subsequent acquittal on the charges brought against her in 1976 "for nothing, for that fucking Billy Krueger telling lies about me."

Unlike her husband, Janet remained certain that Slutzker stayed in their home the entire night with the exception of the hour he was gone early in the evening. Steve came back from that short trip with alcohol on his breath. He drank more after he returned, got drunk, and flopped on the O'Deas' bed.

"Krueger and this Jerry what's-his-face came over and then left. I remember that it was fairly late when Krueger and Jerry left because I think that me and Pat went to bed a little bit later. That's how I know Steve was still there."

Janet couldn't remember whether it was she or Pat who roused Steve and sent him to the couch in the living room, but regardless, "He was still there in the morning when the police came, and that's all I know," she said, her anger rising again.

"Why do you people keep harassing me about this case? Pat and I had nothing to do with what happened."

"We're not convinced of that," Lee Torbin said.

"They proved Krueger was a damn liar because I was acquitted, that little shit, and the phone calls weren't made or received by me. How could you think I was involved in Mudd's death when the only two things that could link me to it were proven not to be true?"

"Was your car at your house all that night?" Torbin asked.

"I never let anyone use that car because that car was very special to me."

Janet's mouth was still for a moment while her brain churned. "Why? Did someone say they saw my car at Mudd's house that night?"

It was Torbin's turn to be silent.

"That's it! That's it, isn't it? Someone saw my car there."

Torbin and Bacon watched O'Dea. She stared into the distance.

"Well, I guess it's possible that Steve could have gotten out of the house without me seeing him, but I doubt that. He could have taken Pat's keys from the dining room table. That's where he always laid them . . . then snuck out of the house and come back without me knowing it. Pat and I were drinking that night, so something like that could have happened."

"Did Steve borrow your car?"

"No," Janet snapped. "I never let anybody borrow that car.

"That's all I know. If someone saw my car there it was because Steve must have found Pat's keys, snuck out of the house, and come back without either of us knowing about it."

"Did either you or Pat maybe drive Steve to Wilkins-burg?"

"Absolutely not," she snapped.

"Why would your ex-husband, Harvey Vogel, tell us in July 1985 that you told him you'd done exactly that?"

"He's a goddamned liar, that's what he is. Harvey Vogel is a low form of life. He's not worth a shit, and you can't believe a fucking word he says."

Janet was just finishing her tirade against Vogel when Kelly and Pat O'Dea entered the room. Torbin and Kelly then explained that there was new evidence linking them to Mudd's murder.

"That's a bunch of bullshit," Janet blurted out.

"What kind of evidence?" Pat asked.

"My car was seen at Mudd's place that night," Janet explained.

"That's not all," Torbin said.

He and Kelly explained about John Mudd Jr.'s flashback and how the new eyewitness account, coupled with evidence from the original investigation and the details uncovered after Vogel stepped out of the woodwork in 1985, had led to charges being filed against Slutzker and Montgomery.

"So you see, it was impossible for Slutzker to have been at your house and the scene at the same time."

For once, Janet agreed.

"The only possible explanation is that he found Pat's keys on the table, snuck out of the house, and returned before we knew he was gone," she said.

"That's right," Pat said.

The wet dream of every homicide detective is that people like Janet and Pat O'Dea break down in tears and confess every detail of their suspected involvement in the crime. Short of that, however, Kelly and Torbin were getting what they wanted: a major crack in the alibi. Now it was time, they figured, to pull their trump card and see how far the O'Deas would go.

"We want to advise you that the district attorney's office has authorized us to offer you immunity from prosecution in this case if you are totally truthful," Kelly said.

Janet's nostrils flared and the blood rose in her cheeks. "We don't need any goddamned immunity from anything because we haven't done anything, and I've already been found not guilty."

"That's true. You were found not guilty," Torbin said. "But the charge wasn't criminal homicide. If any charges are filed against you based on the new evidence, it will be criminal homicide."

Janet continued hurling angry rebuttals at her accusers.

"Come on, Janet, calm down. Let's listen to what they have to say. What do you mean?" Pat asked, turning to the detectives.

"All right. Let me lay this out as plainly as I can," said Kelly. "Evidence exists that one or both of you possibly supplied the gun Stephen Slutzker used and that he may possibly have used your car to get back and forth from Wilkinsburg."

The visitors now had the O'Deas' undivided attention.

"If that evidence is true, both of you could be charged with the actual crime as opposed to merely conspiracy. The DA's office has authorized us to offer you immunity in exchange for your truthful cooperation. We're making that offer to you here today. Once we leave Houston, that offer will be withdrawn, and it will not be offered to you again."

"But I have told you the truth as best I can remember it, so help me God," Pat said.

Then the O'Deas sat in silence for a moment. Torbin, Kelly, and Bacon just watched and waited for the next words to be spoken.

"Listen, how 'bout you give us a little time to talk about this and think it over? Give us the night to talk it over?" Pat said.

The detectives agreed. They would return the next day for the O'Deas' response.

■ ■ ■

The *Pittsburgh Press* was the city's afternoon newspaper.

The first edition hit the streets in late morning, so reporter Mike Hasch's story on April 10 about the arrest of Arlene Montgomery and the warrant outstanding for Steven Slutzker was hot news for the noon broadcasts.

Sandy Catone was one of the many people who heard the news that day. Most just clucked their tongues, if they paid attention at all. To the twenty-nine-year-old Mrs. Catone, this was news you could use. She picked up the telephone and called the Allegheny County Police homicide branch. She had information about the Mudd case, but she didn't want to deliver it over the telephone.

Sergeant Schwab dispatched Detectives Gorny and Thomas Glenn to meet Catone, as she requested, at 5:30 P.M. at the McDonald's on Penn Avenue in Wilkinsburg.

As the detectives sat in their car in the restaurant parking lot, Catone talked to them through the driver's open window.

"Back in 1983 or '84, I rented an apartment from Steve at 1712 Brinton Avenue. That's in North Braddock. I never bothered with him because, to tell you the truth, I just didn't care to be in his company at all.

"Anyway, the way he told me about the shooting is that one night he had some sort of a gathering of friends at his apartment. His was upstairs from mine. Apparently they were harassing him or something. So, he comes down to my place, and he's talking to me about what's going on upstairs, and he says, 'Who do they think they're messing with? Don't they know that I shot and killed a man a few years ago in Wilkinsburg? He was a neighbor of mine. I shot him because he was sleeping with my wife. I got away with it because they said it was a crime of passion.' "

"Did he ever mention Arlene Mudd as being involved?" one of the detectives said.

"All he ever mentioned was that he shot a man for having an affair with his wife."

Gorny and Glenn thanked Catone for coming forward with her story, then they drove back to town to write their report to Schwab.

About an hour later and 1,200 miles to the southwest, Kelly and Torbin were back in touch with the O'Deas.

"Janet and I stayed up all night practically trying to remember everything that happened the Sunday night that this thing occurred," Patrick said. "We tried, but we couldn't remember anything more than what we've already told you. I wish we could have, but we couldn't. We've been as truthful as we can. There's really nothing more to say."

"Pat, do you and Janet fully understand the offer of immunity?" Torbin asked.

"We don't see where we've done anything wrong, so we don't see how immunity applies to us."

"But you do understand the offer?"

"Uh-huh. Yes, we do."

"Do you understand that once we leave Houston, the offer is withdrawn?"

"Yeah. We understand that, too."

"Okay, then."

"If anything does come to mind, if there's something we maybe are forgetting, can I reach you later?"

"You can call anytime, Pat," Torbin said, thinking that he wasn't going to hold his breath waiting for that telephone call.

Kelly and Torbin left Houston and traveled to San Antonio to interview Harvey Vogel's daughter Clare Dugan. She had moved there sometime after being interviewed in 1986.

San Antonio homicide Detective Tom Fulcher saved the two visiting lawmen the trouble of finding their own way to the cash register that Clare operated at a gas station. They walked through the door at 4 o'clock in the afternoon on April 11. She agreed to go with them to Fulcher's office for an interview.

Clare was now thirty years old. The detectives were asking her to recall details of events that occurred when she was fifteen. To help her overcome the gap, they had her read their report of her 1986 interview. Clare looked up from the last page and said she could remember nothing beyond what she had said five years earlier. Then Ms. Dugan proceeded to serve up a potentially important new detail.

She said she was certain that someone borrowed her mother's Monte Carlo the night before the police arrived to talk to Slutzker. She wasn't certain that it was a Sunday night, but she was sure that the car was borrowed the night before the police came.

"It was highly unusual for my mother to let anyone use that car, and as far as I know, no one ever borrowed it before that night," she said. "My mother treated that car better than her own children."

Another detail made her certain that someone had borrowed the car. The next morning, she heard one of the policemen remark that the hood of the car must have been warm during the night because there was no snow on the hood, and everything around the car was blanketed with fresh snow.

Clare said she could not remember seeing Slutzker in the house that night. However, she might not have recognized him if she had seen him.

She was much more certain that Amy Slutzker had not been in the O'Dea home that night.

"There's no way my mother or Pat were baby-sitting anybody that night. If anyone brought a young child over to the house, and that was rare, I'd have to watch them. There's no way my mother would let any child interfere with her drinking and partying, and that's all she and Pat did when they got home from work every day.

"I don't ever remember baby-sitting a child named Amy, and I probably would remember that because I was the oldest one, and I had a lot of jobs to do around the house. I would have remembered having to baby-sit someone else's kid on top of all that."

Clare also said she was certain that her mother and Pat were present when one or the other of them talked about Mudd's death and how the gun used to kill him was thrown off the Homestead High-Level Bridge.

The detectives also showed Clare a report of the interview that Torbin and Watson conducted with Billy Krueger in February 1986. She said she could not remember talking to Krueger at the Wilkinsburg Street fair and she doubted that she ever told him that Slutzker killed Mudd.

"I was never allowed out of the house to attend anything like a street fair, so I can't see how I could have seen Billy at one. I assume most street fairs are in the summer, and I wasn't living at home any more in the summer of 1976. My first son was born in March of '76, and three or four months later we left my mother's house and never returned. I just don't see how the conversation could have taken place, but I can't say for certain that it did or it didn't."

From San Antonio, Kelly and Torbin jetted eastward to St. Petersburg, Florida, to interview Mike and Donna Pezzano. Their story hadn't changed over the years, but they were concerned about the possibility that Slutzker might try to silence them.

Donna told the detectives of her suspicion that Slutzker had started the fire that destroyed their house in Connellsville.

Mike said Slutzker had threatened to get even with him for testifying against him in 1976.

The Pezzanos were within two years of paying off the loan when the house burned on February 8, 1980. They'd seen Slutzker in the neighborhood right around the time of the blaze. Firemen said the cause was electrical. The couple moved to Florida soon after the fire.

"So, while I was losing my home and moving down here and living on four- and five-dollar-an-hour jobs, he was still out making big bucks. He bought an old church and converted it into a house," Mike said.

Torbin and Kelly were still digesting their dinner that Friday when Watson and Wolfson pulled up in front of 816 Sally Street, in White Oak, a tree-lined bedroom community neighboring McKeesport.

Dorothea Vantrick, Clare Dugan's childhood friend, had agreed to tell what she knew about the O'Deas.

Vantrick recalled the two occasions in the spring of 1976, the time she saw Janet waving a gun around only a few feet from the crib containing Clare's newborn son, and only a few weeks later when she recalled Janet saying that the gun was thrown from a bridge.

Vantrick also filled the detectives in on the indignities Janet inflicted on Clare and the beatings Janet occasionally administered to the other children in the family.

"Mrs. O'Dea was a rotten person," Dorothea concluded.

■ ■ ■

On Tuesday afternoon, April 16, Judge·Robert Dauer held a hearing on attorney David Lichtenstein's motion to set bond for Arlene Montgomery. Dauer agreed that she could be free on $15,000 property bond. Her parents were glad to post their property, and their little girl walked out of the jailhouse late that afternoon.

After the hearing, someone mentioned to Detective Torbin that Slutzker had been freed on the 11th, the day after his arrest. Torbin realized immediately that the principal witnesses and local police had to be notified that Slutzker was on the loose. The detective was surprised that no one else had thought of making those calls while he and Kelly were touring the South.

The conditions of Slutzker's bail prohibited him from having any contact with the Mudd family or other witnesses. His release created a "potentially dangerous situation," and Torbin so informed police in Pittsburgh and St. Petersburg, Florida.

■ ■ ■

In the weeks and months after John Mudd's sudden recall, Kimberly Altman moved out of the house they shared on James Street and moved back in with her parents in Glenshaw. She also changed jobs twice, leaving Don Royal Cleaners for Z&H Uniforms in North Hills Village, then leaving there to help prepare a storefront a block from Allegheny General Hospital on the Northside to open as Salvatore's pizza parlor. The owners were going to employ both Kim and John.

That's where Kelly caught up with Kim on the afternoon of April 18, a Thursday.

She told him everything he wanted to know about the events of November 23 and the early hours of the twenty-fourth. Her brother, Joe, was living at home at the time. She'd known Steve Spinola for years because his aunt lived next door to the Altmans' and he was Joe's friend.

Kim recalled that when John started to cry and become hysterical, she told Joe and Steve to go upstairs. She followed John down the hallway and joined him in the living room.

"He told me he was afraid of losing me and how every time he got close to someone he lost them. He mentioned his father and his grandmother."

She said that when John got Maureen Perri on the phone he told her, "You're my real mother, not Arlene."

He babbled in that high-pitched voice and cried about remembering his father, the night he died, and all the images that were returning to him.

Maureen must have told John to put Kim on because he handed the phone to her. Mrs. Perri told Kim to keep him as calm as possible until she arrived.

Maureen got there in about fifteen minutes, and John's uncles were not far behind.

John described the position of his father's body at the bottom of the steps, and "when his uncle Jimmy told Johnny that that was exactly how his father's body had been found, Johnny was mad and asked them why they'd never told him any of this."

James Mudd explained the family's rationale for shielding John from details of the murder. He told his nephew that a psychologist had told the family that memories of the event might all come back to him one day.

"In the past, did Johnny ever tell you anything about recalling the events of the night the murder occurred?" Kelly asked.

"No, he didn't," Kim said.

"What did he tell you about his father?"

"He told me that his father was murdered when Johnny was five and he mentioned that he thought a fellow named Steve did it."

Kim told Kelly that there might have been a couple of times when John mentioned Steve as his father's killer. She said he also told her that his mother abandoned him and that he had no desire to see her again.

She told Kelly that John never mentioned anything about Arlene's possible involvement in the crime.

The interview with Miss Altman lasted for about half an hour. Late that evening, Kelly was in the Altman home interviewing Joe, whose parents were at his side.

The session with the Altmans revealed little that Kelly hadn't already heard, and the bits of new information they did reveal were irrelevant: Mr. and Mrs. Altman didn't know about Mudd's recall until they read about it in the papers; on one of the few occasions when the father had seen John Mudd, they argued about how Altman was treating his daughter, but that John's behavior the night of the recall went beyond anything he'd ever witnessed in the young man.

A few days after questioning Kim and Joe Altman, Kelly learned from Steve Spinola that John's recollection was so vivid as to be uncanny.

"Was it like he was telling a story?" Kelly asked.

"No. He would just blurt out sentences, like seeing his

father at the bottom of the steps in a pool of blood. Then he would go over the fact that his mother was having an affair with the neighbor, that he saw the neighbor kissing her and that he heard loud noises after his father went to the basement.

"It sounded like he was actually there, seeing it as it happened," Spinola said. "It all seemed so clear, the way John was talking about seeing these things, that I could almost see them myself."

Spinola said he heard Mudd talk repeatedly about not being able to find his mother. After that, he talked about his mother being outside. Spinola had been in a second-floor bedroom where a radio was on. Even so, he could hear Mudd downstairs, talking on the telephone, telling someone " 'I love you, Mommy, you, not her.' "

John Mudd Jr. had been present when Kelly questioned Kim at the pizza parlor. During the interview John said he'd seen a navy-blue Chevy Beretta with Ohio license plates drive past the shop a dozen times. The driver also stopped the car for a while across the street from the shop. All of this happened between noon and 1 P.M.

John described the driver as a tall thin man with brown hair and a large nose.

The day after Kelly interviewed Kim Altman, the assistant district attorney, Kim Clark, along with Kelly and Torbin, interviewed John Jr. Again, he told them about the car circling the pizza shop. He'd also learned that a car that looked a lot like the one at the pizza shop cruised the Mudd home on Broad Street in East Liberty and that family members had been receiving strange phone calls ever since the arrests of Steve and Arlene. The caller was a man, who sometimes asked if John Mudd Jr. lived there.

John's uncle Jimmy described the car on Broad Street

as a dark-blue Chevy Corsica with Ohio tags and a rental car company sticker on one bumper.

Torbin notified the Anonymous Call Bureau of Bell of Pennsylvania, where an agent said line traps would be put on two of the Mudd family phones immediately.

Kelly gave Pittsburgh police a description of the car and the driver and explained why the information was important.

If Slutzker was the person cruising Salvatore's and calling the Mudd family, it meant two things. First, it meant he probably could be put back in jail for violating the conditions of his release on bond. Even though the caller may have done nothing more sinister than ask if this is the home of John Mudd Jr., the court would construe such a question coming from the man accused of murdering John's father as intimidation or harassment of the victim and his family. For Kelly, putting Slutzker back in the can would be one of the small pleasures en route to a murder conviction. But that would have its price, which was the other ramification of John Jr.'s news about the blue Chevy and the phone calls. Someone would have to verify the information with phone calls and legwork. Then there would be a hearing to revoke Slutzker's bond. All that would take time, how much Kelly could only guess. Problem was, not much time was left before the coroner's inquest, where Clark would get an opportunity to do what Nickoloff had failed to do in 1976.

The inquest was scheduled for April 23, a Tuesday, and Clark was still in the market for evidence to tie Arlene more closely to the murder. Without that kind of evidence, for example someone who heard Arlene admit her involvement, the case against her was significantly weaker than the case against Slutzker.

Kelly learned about the blue Chevy on the eighteenth.

John told Clark about the car and the phone calls on the nineteenth, which was the Friday before the inquest. That's why Kelly spent Sunday evening, the twenty-first, interviewing Steve Spinola, then driving forty minutes south from Glenshaw to Boston.

It was almost 11 P.M. when he arrived at 1917 Drake Street, the home of William Montgomery, Arlene's second, third, and by then ex-husband.

"You know, I was hoping that was all over," Montgomery said. "That woman caused me quite a bit of humiliation six years ago when she ran off with my best friend. Then I read in the paper that she's arrested for the murder of John Mudd, and once again she's bringing me humiliation.

"But, yeah, I'll talk to you about her, but I'm telling you, I'm not testifying in court to any of this."

With that, the two men settled into the interview.

Montgomery said he and the widow Mudd began dating before the soil had settled on John Mudd Sr.'s grave. They met on Valentine's Day 1976 in a bar. Montgomery remembered it as the Panther Room on Route 51, which is a commuters' nightmare, an unsightly, cluttered stretch of undivided, four-lane highway on the backside of Pittsburgh's Mount Washington.

Montgomery said Arlene was easily influenced. They were married the following May and during the ensuing nine years they argued quite a bit, divorced, remarried, and divorced again.

"Looking back on it, it was probably more of a sexual relationship than anything," Montgomery said.

In the mid-1980s, Montgomery's friend moved in with him and Arlene in Boston, a small community built on the narrow southern shore of the Youghiogheny River. The friend brought his wife, who was terminally ill with cancer, and their two children. Before long, Arlene ran off with the friend, leaving the dying woman and her children with Montgomery.

Eight months later, the cuckolded Bill Montgomery asked the woman to find another place to live because her kids were getting into trouble.

To that point in the interview, Montgomery hadn't done anything to enhance Arlene's reputation, but he hadn't helped the prosecution's case against her either.

The best Montgomery could do was to say several times that "She gave me the impression that Steve Slutzker had done it." He said he never pressed her for details about John Mudd's murder because he didn't want to know.

Montgomery said Arlene was afraid of Slutzker. He said she was gullible and that, given a little time, a person could get her to do just about anything.

"For example, she had a girlfriend who she hung around with who was having an affair. She convinced Arlene this was the thing to do, so Arlene then went out and had an affair."

On his midnight drive back to Pittsburgh, Kelly considered what a disappointment the interview had been. Montgomery had an appalling story to tell, good for headshaking and clucking at the water cooler, but it wasn't much in the way of useful evidence in court.

The next day at the office, Kelly's attention was yanked back to the blue Chevy and the mysterious caller when Sergeant Schwab told him what John Mudd had just reported. A man fitting Slutzker's description had been in the pizza shop. His looks and quirky behavior were enough to make the prosecution's star witness nearly wet his pants. Mudd was so rattled that the shop owners sent him home.

Kelly reached John by phone at his home, heard the pertinent details, grabbed a photo of Slutzker, and headed for the Northside.

Carole Yakelis, manager of the shop and sister of the owner, said without hesitation that the man in the photo was the same one who had been in the shop shortly after noon that day. The only difference is that the man who entered the store wore glasses.

He was wearing a white shirt and tie under a trench coat. He was accompanied by a husky, good-looking man in a suit. They took a table in the back of the room. They ordered a twelve-cut pizza and two glasses of water and told their waitress, "This is for John." They watched the kitchen while they waited.

After the pizza arrived, they complained to the waitress that there was a hair on it. Yakelis looked and, yes, there was a hair on the pizza, but it was black. No one else in the pizza shop had black hair besides Slutzker's companion.

Yakelis couldn't figure out what kind of game the two were playing. She apologized and ordered another pizza. Before it was done, Slutzker was at the cash register saying he wanted to pay because they had to leave. He said his friend was a doctor from New York who had to perform surgery at Allegheny General Hospital.

Yakelis didn't stop to wonder how often the AGH surgeons went out for pizza right before operating.

"Well, wait. I'll make him a sandwich. I don't want him to perform surgery on an empty stomach," she said.

"We gotta go," said Slutzker, who had an obvious case of the jitters. He paid, and the two were gone, except they didn't cross the street and walk toward the hospital. Instead, they ran in the opposite direction.

"I think that's the man who killed my father," John

said. He walked outside, stood on the corner, and stared in the direction the men had fled.

The other employees helped John calm down when he came inside. One of them offered to work past his quitting time so that Mudd could punch out and go home. Yakelis initialed his time card at 1:30 P.M.

The employee who worked the rest of John's shift, Michael Vinezeale, also identified Slutzker from the photograph.

Kelly drove back to his office through the thickening late-afternoon traffic. He assembled eight mug shots, including Slutzker's, and nudged through rush-hour congestion to the Mudd home on Broad Street to meet John. He immediately identified Slutzker as the "surgeon's" companion and as the driver who had cruised the pizza shop,

While Kelly was there, John's aunt, Pat Hill, gave him the log she kept showing that from April 16 through 3:04 P.M. that afternoon, the family had received thirteen phone calls, either from the man who originally asked whether John Mudd Jr. lived there or from someone who hung up without speaking. Four of the calls came between midnight and dawn.

Torbin, in the meantime, set the wheels in motion to arrest Slutzker. He contacted the Allegheny County Bail Agency, which sent a representative to Judge Terrance O'Brien. The judge revoked bail and issued a bench warrant, which was carried to the county sheriff's office.

Torbin and Kelly then tried to locate Slutzker but couldn't. They turned to Charles Scarlata, who said he would try to arrange for his client to surrender. That happened at 10 P.M. at the West Penn Building. A half hour and two trips to the men's room later, Slutzker was across town in the county jail.

The time and energy spent putting Slutzker back behind bars didn't advance the case one inch, but at least there was no doubt about where to find the chief defendant for the coroner's inquest the next morning.

The Second Inquest

Fifteen years and three months after he'd beaten a homicide charge at a coroner's inquest, Steve Slutzker was back in the same venue to face the same charge. This time, he was joined by his former lover, Arlene Mudd Montgomery.

Who knows what thoughts went through Arlene's mind as she sat at the defense table.

Her hair was clean. It shined with a brushed luster. It cascaded down past her shoulders, ending in an easy curl. Her bangs were done up in a small crop of curls that tumbled over her brow and combined with her makeup and soft, sad eyes to give her face an innocent, feminine appeal.

When her son testified against her—especially when the court remarked on the confusion about whom John meant by "mother"—Arlene repeatedly dabbed tears from her eyes and cheeks and wiped her nose dry. As she sat there, leaning into her hankie, her right hand poised above the bright paisley cuff of her long-sleeve dress, Arlene was, at age thirty-seven, a picture of maternal tragedy. She seemed an innocent whose dreamy naïveté had corrupted her judgment, whose weakness of character had left her incapable of taking command of her life. Her fear and gullibility deluded her into thinking that, by running, she could maintain a tolerable distance between her present and her past, never fully understanding that the two are inseparable, a continuum, an evolving whole whose continuity now rudely confronted her in the judgmental presence of her only child, her former in-laws, attorneys, newspaper reporters and photographers, the black-robed coroner's solicitor, and soon, quite possibly, a judge and jury with power to send her to prison for a long time.

Slutzker presented a very different picture. A veteran of the defense table, he wore a nearly impenetrable expression, much as he had during his prosecution in 1976.

Back then he'd listened intently to the proceedings. Whatever points he had failed to grasp on his own about why the homicide charge failed, attorney David Rothman had explained to him. Slutzker appreciated, no doubt, that this was a whole new ballgame.

He hadn't wanted to go to jail in 1976, but the eleven and a half month sentence he served had to be chalked up as a victory, considering what was at stake for him.

One can almost imagine his reasoning as he sat at his second inquest.

He'd served his sentence. He'd paid his debt. So much time had passed since Mudd was killed that Slutzker, now forty, may have believed that his personal ledger was balanced and he didn't deserve to be punished any further. Wasn't the world a better place without Jack Mudd? That was the premise behind the job Slutzker offered to Pezzano and Hairston. The beatings and abuse stopped for Arlene. Young John Mudd was raised by decent people who cared about him and worked hard to steer the boy right. Hadn't everything worked out for the better? Why couldn't the world just leave Steven Slutzker alone? Well, if he had to go to trial, at least he had one of the best criminal defense attorneys in the city.

By experience, reputation, and fees, Chuck Scarlata

was a heavy hitter in the specialty of criminal law. Besides being a former county and federal prosecutor and one of the better-known names in the profession in Allegheny County, he had served as a judge on the county bench. He was appointed to fill a vacancy created when a Common Pleas Court Judge moved up to a state appeals court. Scarlata then lost the election for a full term. But having once walked on the hallowed ground of judicial service, he still enjoyed the distinction of being addressed as "Judge Scarlata" by other attorneys and by other judges. That was more than an ego trip. It was useful leverage, if only psychological, in the courtroom. Imagine being a young prosecutor in a case where the judge addresses your adversary as "Judge Scarlata."

Arlene was represented by David Lichtenstein, a competent and experienced criminal attorney but one who cast a less brilliant light than Scarlata's.

Deputy Coroner Arthur Gilkes Jr. called the inquest to order. The show was under way.

The star was the first witness to take the stand. Clark was just beginning a line of questioning about what John Mudd Jr. remembered from the day his father died when Lichtenstein interrupted. If the prosecutor was going to probe Mudd's memory of events fifteen years earlier, then the defense wanted a chance to argue whether the young man was competent to talk about those things.

Everyone knew that challenge was coming, and there it was. The first volley had been fired in a battle that would be fought in exhausting detail before the case ran its course.

Clark didn't want to get mired in that debate right off the bat. She backed off the line of questioning. She switched to questions about Mudd's recollection of the events on November 23–24.

Mudd said that when he heard Spinola make the remark to Kim, he leaped over the couch in the living room and charged.

He recounted the flashback memory for Clark, then she turned him over to the defense for cross-examination.

Under questioning by Lichtenstein, Mudd could not remember how long after his father's death his counseling began, who counseled him, or what the counseling consisted of at Immaculate Conception school in Bloomfield.

"The only thing I remember is going there and playing games. That's all."

Gilkes asked if Mudd knew why he was in counseling.

"I believe it was because they were making appointments to see my mother, but she never showed up when I was there. It wasn't really counseling."

"Did you ever discuss with any of the adults what happened on this particular night in your family, any of the adults in your family?" Lichtenstein asked.

"No."

"You've never had any discussions with them?"

"No."

"The adults in your family never had any conversation with you explaining what happened on this particular night?"

"Never."

"Did you ever inquire about it? Did you ever ask anybody about it?"

"I don't know."

Mudd then told Scarlata he didn't remember whether he ever saw his mother again after the murder.

He did remember moving from his grandmother's home to the Perris', but didn't remember how long he lived with Mary Mudd.

He knew that his father had three brothers and three sisters.

"I have a close relationship with my whole family," he said.

"Now, in connection with the close relationship that you have with the Mudd family, would it be fair to say that from time to time you have Sunday dinners together?" Scarlata asked.

"No."

"Is the Mudd family close to one another?"

"Yes."

"So, that on occasion they would visit one another at the house that you were residing in?"

"Yes."

"And they would have conversations about various and sundry matters, isn't that correct?"

"I can't answer that. I don't know."

"You never overheard them talking about sports events?"

"No."

"You never heard them talking about things of interest in the community?"

"I don't remember."

"And as I understand your testimony, you never heard them talking about your father's death? Is that correct?"

"I was told that my father was killed."

"Did they ever talk to you about their suspicions as to who may have perpetrated that murder?"

"No."

"Did you ever ask anything beyond the fact that your father was killed?"

"I don't remember."

Mudd told Lichtenstein that he had no relationship to speak of with his maternal grandparents.

"Do you talk to them upon some occasions?"

"Upon some occasions."

"Do you visit them upon some occasions?"

"Once."

"Have you ever had any discussions about the night your father died?"

"No, I haven't."

Scarlata questioned Mudd further. "On the twenty-fourth, were you interviewed by the police?"

"Yes, I was."

"When?"

"In the morning."

"They didn't come that night?"

"No."

"Who notified the police?"

"I believe it was my uncle, James."

"Who came to the house that late night?"

"My aunt, Maureen Perri, and my uncle, Terry Mudd."

"Can you describe your parents' house for me?"

"The house sat, in the yard beside it was a slope. If you would walk in the front door, you would be in the living room. To the left of you was a staircase leading upstairs.

"If you would walk through the living room along the left-hand side wall, you would walk into the archway into the kitchen. Once in the kitchen you would go over to your right-hand side to the corner and that's the basement door."

"When your father went to take care of the lights, what did he say when he got up?"

"He told me not to worry, he would take care of it."

"You were there with your mother?"

"Yes."

"About what time was this? Do you know?"

"No, I don't."

"How did you get from the couch to the top of the cellar steps?"

"I don't remember."

"How long after you heard the loud noises was it before you went to the top of the cellar steps?"

"I remember that. Immediately after hearing the noises."

"But you don't know how you got there?"

"No, sir."

"What did your mother do when the loud noises occurred?"

"I don't know, sir."

"When you say you were in somebody's arms or somebody's hands, would it be fair to assume you were talking about your mother?"

"Yes."

"You don't know how you got into her arms?"

"No."

"When you were looking down at your father, did you say anything?"

"Not that I remember."

"Did she say anything?"

"Not that I remember."

"Can you clarify for me, please, the position of your father's body? As you're looking down the steps, was he perpendicular to the steps?"

"He was laying with the steps."

"I'm sorry."

"His head was facing the wall and his feet were facing me."

"So, he was parallel to the steps then?"

"Yes."

"Was he on his back or on his stomach?"

"On his stomach but also on his side."

"Do you recall which side?"

"Left side."

"Had the television come back on?"

"I don't remember."

"The next thing you remember is being back on the couch with your mother?"

"Yes."

"Was your mother trying to comfort you?"

"No."

"Had she screamed or made any noise whatsoever?"

"No."

"Did you see her go to call the police or do anything like that?"

"No."

"How long was it before this man appeared in the living room?"

"Right after I was back on the couch."

"But you don't know how long that was from the time you were at the head of the steps?"

"No."

"On one occasion prior to that you saw him apparently trying to kiss your mother?"

"Yes."

"Was your mother resisting?"

"Yes."

"Or cooperating?"

"Resisting."

"Did that make you angry?"

"I don't know."

"Now, how big was the living room?"

"I can't estimate that."

"When you were in the living room with your parents on some other occasions, you would be able to hear what they were saying, the same as you could hear what I'm saying now; isn't that correct?"

"I don't know."

"When your mother would call you for dinner from the kitchen, would you be able to hear her?"

"I don't remember."

"Would it be fair to say, Mr. Mudd, you have no recollection then of those kinds of events?"

"Yes."

"Now, when this man came into the living room, you heard him talk to your mother?"

"I saw him."

"You saw him but you didn't hear him saying anything?"

"I couldn't understand what it was."

"Then you heard something said, but you just didn't understand what it was?"

"Yes."

"And is that because he was too far away from you?"

"I don't know."

"And you heard your mother respond; correct?"

"Yes."

"How long did they converse?"

"Short; maybe a minute or two. . . . I never understood what they said."

"What did she do after that?"

"I remember her sitting back on the couch."

"Did she comfort you at that point?"

"Not that I know."

"You did know, did you not, Mr. Mudd, that Mr. Slutzker was arrested back at that time in connection with this case?"

"No, I didn't."

"No member of your family ever told you that some-one had been arrested for your father's murder?"

"No."

"And you never told anybody about seeing Mr. Slutz-ker in the room that night?"

"No."

"Were you there when the police arrived to investigate the murder that evening?"

"I don't remember."

"And you don't know what house you were taken to?"

"No, sir."

"Your first recollection of what happened to you was when you were with your grandmother?"

"Yes."

"Do you remember whether you saw your mother at any time after that evening?"

"I don't remember."

"Do you remember being in court at all in connection with who would have custody of you?"

"No."

"Did anyone ever tell you how it is you ended up away from your mother and ended up in the custody of your grandmother and aunt?"

"No."

"Did you ever wonder what happened to your mother and why you weren't with your mother and father?"

"Yes."

"Did you talk to your aunts and uncles, grandmother about what happened to Mom?"

"No."

"Did they ever tell you that it was in your best interest that you not be with her?"

"I don't remember."

"Then you wouldn't remember if they told you why it was in your best interest that you not be with her?"

"I don't remember."

Under questioning by Lichtenstein, Mudd said he could not remember what television program was on that night, what his mother was wearing, who carried him to the neighbor's house, or when he last saw his mother prior to being in the courtroom that day.

He said he received a picture of his mother some time within the previous ten years, but he did not remember who gave it to him.

Mudd also did not remember what was on television in the living room of his apartment when he and Joe Altman sat on the couch moments before the recall.

"What do you do now, John?"

"I'm a pizza maker."

"A what?"

"A pizza maker."

"Do you remember where you work?"

"Salvatore's."

"How long have you worked for them?"

"I worked for Salvatore himself for about six months."

"Where did you work before that?"

"Corleone's Pizza."

"Have you always been a pizza maker?"

"No."

"What did you do before that?"

"Automotive detailing."

"Where did you work?"

Clark objected on relevancy, but Gilkes overruled her.

"Where did you work before as a detailer?"

"Numerous places."

"Do you remember who your employer was when you worked as a detailer?"

"There were numerous employers."

"Who was the last one?"

"National Car Detail in South Side."

"Do you remember who the company was that you worked for before that?"

"No."

"You don't, therefore, remember who your employer was, who your boss was, do you?"

"No."

"If I asked you a continuous series of these questions as to where you worked before and who your employer was, you don't remember those either?"

"I know where I worked, I just don't remember what order they were in."

Lichtenstein was making Mudd look like not such a smart guy, and that's exactly what he wanted to do. He switched from Mudd's foggy recollection of the jobs he'd held to the visions he claimed he saw on November 23–24.

"From the night this occurred . . . until November, did you ever at any time ever see Mr. Slutzker in your mind?"

"No."

"Did you ever see your mother?"

"No."

"Did you ever see these events at all?"

"No, I haven't."

Lichtenstein was having things his way, too much so, and Prosecutor Clark realized it. "What events?" she interjected.

Gilkes intervened to set the time frame, then Lichtenstein continued. "Did you ever see that picture before?"

"No, sir."

"Did you ever see any portion of that picture?"

"No, sir."

"Did you ever see your living room? Do you remember the living room?" he said, asking two questions.

"No, sir," Mudd, responding to one.

"You were never in the house after that night?"

"I don't know, sir."

"You don't remember?"

"No."

"Did you attend the funeral?"

"I don't remember."

"Was there a service? Did you attend the service? You don't remember that either?"

"I don't remember."

Lichtenstein jousted with Mudd over whether he'd used the word "murdered" to describe what he understood of his father's death.

"And when did you first understand that he was murdered?"

"The night this happened."

"So, that the night it happened you understood that he was murdered, right?"

"Well, I knew from my family that he was killed."

"Okay. Now, from what family did you know that he was killed? Which person?"

"I don't remember. . . . I knew that my father was killed because I knew I didn't have a father."

"You knew he was killed because you didn't have a father and you also knew because family members told you?"

"Right."

"I would like to know, again, what family members told you that?"

"I'm going to tell you again I don't know."

Mudd did remember calling Arlene in the mid-1980s.

"Do you remember telling her that your father was killed and you hoped that nothing happens to her?"

"No."

"You don't remember that?"

"No."

"Do you remember telling her anything about the fact that your father was murdered?"

"No."

"You don't remember that?"

"No."

"Is it possible that you had such a conversation?"

"I don't know."

Mudd said he had no recollection of ever talking to police before November 1990 about the things that happened on December 28, 1975.

He said he never saw any photographs of the position of his father's body at the bottom of the steps or of the living room.

He said his grandmother gave him a picture of his father. The picture came from a case that also contained a letter from the President.

He couldn't remember ever hearing his relatives talk about Arlene.

Mudd said he had seen mental images of the scene of the killing many times since the flashback.

After Lichtenstein, Gilkes asked Mudd whether he'd been back to visit the house at 1515 Marlboro. He had not been back and had no desire to go back.

Gilkes also had Mudd review his memory of the position of the body and reestablished that the first place he saw Slutzker the night of the murder was "coming out of the doorway leading from the kitchen to the living room."

"Okay. During the period from 1975 to November of

1990, it sounds as if you've had very little contact with your natural mother."

"Yes, very little."

Mudd went on to say that he didn't remember corresponding with or meeting Arlene, and he never knew why.

Lichtenstein then reaffirmed Mudd's earlier statement that the seven noises he heard sounded like someone slapping a pillow.

When Mudd said the back door to the house was the door in the basement, Gilkes asked, "How would you know?"

"Because I remember the woods in back of my house."

Mudd said he did not graduate from high school. He repeated ninth grade at least once and thought that he took his GED exam following his third attempt to pass ninth grade.

"You recall that you attended only as high as ninth grade?"

"Yes."

"And you indicated to the coroner that for fifteen years you never inquired of the people with whom you lived what happened on that night? Is that what you're saying?"

"I don't remember inquiring about it."

"Is it possible that you did?"

"I don't know."

"Did your father's family ever indicate to you that you were not allowed to see your mother?"

"No."

"Did they ever indicate to you you weren't allowed to talk to her?"

"No."

"Now, when you called her, how did you get her number?"

"Her parents, my grandparents."

Scarlata tried to box Mudd in by asking if there was anything else he remembered about his house in Wilkinsburg and the night of his father's death.

Clark objected to the questions being open-ended.

Gilkes agreed, but sympathized with Scarlata on the question of Mudd's selective memory.

"There are lots of things he doesn't remember," Scarlata said.

"There certainly are," said Gilkes.

Clark next wanted to put Pezzano on the stand, but Scarlata objected that Pezzano's knowledge was confined to the crime of solicitation. "The Commonwealth's burden is to prove a prima facie case that a crime occurred and that my client participated in that. They don't need to introduce this evidence to prove intent. The solicitation did not culminate in this crime being consummated. They are two separate, independent, unrelated events," the defense attorney said.

Gilkes withheld ruling on the defense objections and allowed Clark to question Pezzano.

Pezzano was just about to get on the stand when Scarlata made a motion to have Mudd sequestered. He wanted the young man kept out of earshot of the other testimony. The move was unusual. Once a witness has testified, as Mudd already had, it is normal to let him hear what others had to say.

"I would ask the court to sequester even witnesses who have previously testified, especially Mr. Mudd, who has demonstrated a remarkable ability to remember things and forget things, and not have him risk further visionary experiences by listening to the testimony of additional witnesses," Scarlata said.

Clark jumped in.

"Your Honor, first of all, Mr. Mudd's testimony was about what happened on December 28, 1975, the date that his father was killed. Mr. Pezzano's testimony has nothing to do with that date because he was not present there, and we're not alleging that he was present there. It's what happened a week or some days before the killing of John Mudd Sr., and, therefore, there's no way that his testimony can be prejudiced or influenced by the testimony of Mr. Pezzano."

While she had the floor, Clark had something else to get off her chest. "Additionally, your Honor, I would object to the use of the term 'visionary' or 'visions' or 'visionary experience.'

"They're not visions. It's Mr. Mudd's present recollection of what happened on December 28, things that he presently remembers. I would object to that term."

Gilkes wasn't inclined to weigh in on exactly what was going on inside John Mudd Jr.'s head, but he agreed with Clark and denied the motion to sequester witnesses after they'd testified.

Pezzano, now forty-eight, took the stand.

His testimony was essentially the same as in 1976, except that his memory of a few minor details was blurred by the intervening years.

He told Clark that after his phone conversation with Slutzker on December 19, 1975, he met with Slutzker in the latter's home on the twentieth or twenty-first and made plans that called for Pezzano to make a second trip to Wilkinsburg on December 23. But Pezzano said he left Slutzker's home on the twentieth or twenty-first, went to the state police, and never followed through with the plan for December 23.

At the 1976 inquest, Pezzano told John Nickoloff that, after speaking to Slutzker on December 19, 1975, the two next spoke by phone, not in person. In that phone call, Pezzano said, Slutzker stated that "Mudd was abusing his wife, beating his wife up. He wouldn't give her any household money. He beat up on his kid, and he was in love with her and they had to get rid of him to get married."

Pezzano had also switched gears in describing Slutzker's state of mind at their meeting in Slutzker's house on December 30, 1976. In his sworn statement, Pezzano said, "Steve was to me, nervous." But on the witness stand at the 1976 inquest, Pezzano described Slutzker as seeming just the opposite. "Steve was pretty cool," he said. "Calm. . . . It was just like you haven't seen somebody for a long time, 'Glad to see you.' That's it."

At the second inquest, Clark never asked Pezzano to describe Slutzker's attitude at their December 30, 1975, meeting.

After Gilkes dismissed Pezzano from the witness stand, he swore in Donna Mudd, Terry's wife. Clark wanted Donna's testimony about Arlene's meeting with Slutzker in the toy store, but she almost missed getting a key detail on the record.

"Well, I went to an aisle, and I walked up the aisle, and I saw her with Steve Slutzker. They were hugging. And when she looked at me, she gave him a kiss and told him to go, and he left," she said.

Donna said she approached Arlene. " 'That was Steve, but could you please not say anything to Johnny,' " she quoted Arlene as saying.

Lichtenstein picked away at the many aspects of the shopping trip that Donna couldn't remember, including whose idea it was to go shopping, what they bought, and where the store was located.

It wasn't until Lichtenstein and Scarlata had finished their cross-examination that it occurred to Clark to ask a crucial question: "Do you recall, Mrs. Mudd, who picked the store?"

"She did," Donna Mudd said.

Until that tidbit was on the record, it had to be presumed that the meeting between Arlene and Slutzker was a chance encounter.

Clark also had Donna testify about a pact the Mudd family made not to talk about the murder around young John, although the prosecutor had a rough time phrasing the question properly.

"Now, Johnny has described the Mudd family as kind of a close family. Would you agree with that?" Clark asked.

"Yes, they are."

"And do the brothers and sisters and spouses and nieces and nephews spend time together visiting each other and socializing?"

"Yes."

"Has the subject of John Mudd Sr.'s death ever come up among the brothers and sisters?"

Montgomery's attorney, David Lichtenstein, objected.

Clark didn't catch on. "I'd ask what the basis and what the . . ."

"The basis," Lichtenstein explained, "is she would not be humanly able to know whether the subject came up among people. If you want to limit it to the time when she was present, then of course she can answer it."

"I'll rephrase the question," the prosecutor said.

After a bit more difficulty with the questioning, Gilkes allowed Mrs. Mudd to answer. She said there was an agreement among family members not to talk about the murder around John Jr.

When Scarlata's turn came to question Mrs. Mudd, he ripped into her about the particulars of the pact—When was it made? Who was there? Whose idea was it? Where was John at the time? Did anyone talk to John about the murder before the pact was made? Did anyone break the agreement after it was made?—none of which Donna could answer with much beyond "I don't know."

It also came out that Donna Mudd had not told police or detectives during the original investigation that she'd seen Arlene kissing Slutzker in the toy store only days before the murder.

Donna said she told her brother-in-law Jimmy Mudd after the murder, but she didn't tell her husband, Terry, until she told the police in early 1991.

"Did it occur to you that it might be something the police may be interested in knowing about?" Scarlata asked.

"No, it didn't. It just occurred to me now that I should say something."

Perhaps if the original investigating team had interviewed Donna Mudd, her intriguing observation in the toy store might have found its way into the 1976 prosecution. She was never questioned back then, however.

Clark rested the prosecution's case after Donna Mudd stepped off the witness stand. Then it was time for final arguments.

Scarlata got right to the point. "I would suggest that the only evidence that the Commonwealth has directly related to the matter before the court is the testimony of John Mudd Jr. His memory is very selective, and if you couple that with the fact that the memory is one that was rekindled or reawakened after fifteen years of domancy, the inherently preposterous nature of the story is enough for this court to dismiss the charges against Mr. Slutzker."

Mudd "never told his mother what happened, never told his grandmother what happened, never told his aunts or uncles what happened. The logical conclusion that one would reach is that that is precisely what someone would do and that the failure to do that and to sit on that information and evidence for fifteen years speaks to the fact that it is born of fantasy."

Lichtenstein adopted all that Scarlata said and added another thought about Donna Mudd. "I think it is incredible that sixteen years later she testifies to something that she neglected or willfully withheld from everyone else."

Perhaps more important to Arlene's interests, Lichtenstein also argued that Clark was using hearsay from Pezzano to prove that Arlene was involved in a conspiracy with Slutzker to kill John Mudd Sr. Lichtenstein recalled Pezzano testifying that Slutzker told him Arlene "was in on it."

In emphasizing Pezzano's testimony, Lichtenstein seemed to be trying to run the old misdirection play, and Clark quickly called him on it.

It was her own son's testimony, much more so than Pezzano's, that put Arlene in the conspiracy, the prosecutor said.

"It's not just her mere presence at the scene . . . but it's what she did after she heard the shots and after Mr. Slutzker came up from that cellar and came into the living room," Clark said. "She sat and had a conversation with him.

"This is a woman who hears seven noises that apparently are shots . . . and does not cry out, does not immediately run out, does not call the police, goes and sits on the couch, has a conversation with a man that comes up from the basement, that man that the evidence, at least circumstantially, shows was in some type of love or romantic relationship with her."

Clark was scoring points, and Lichtenstein could see defeat staring him in the face.

"Your Honor," he jumped in. "Ms. Clark should have called herself to testify. She's reciting testimony as having been put into evidence that, in fact, never occurred.

"Young John never said how he got back to the sofa. He sees that he was up high, so he believes that he's being held by somebody. He doesn't know who held him.

"Ms. Clark testified that Mr. Slutzker came up from the basement. There is no evidence as to where he came from. There is no evidence as to whether he might lay in wait. . . .

"Now, young John doesn't know whether they sat there for two minutes or ten minutes. He doesn't have any idea as to whether or not, in fact, his mother called the police. In fact, he has no evidence of whether she may have called Mr. Slutzker for some help."

Another interesting interpretation of the evidence. But Lichtenstein failed to mention that Arlene told police Slutzker wasn't there that night. He forgot to mention that Slutzker claimed he was in McKeesport all that night.

Gilkes wasn't buying it.

"Okay. I'm going to disregard the solicitation evidence. However, I am going to rule that the Commonwealth has presented a prima facie case based upon the fact that the evidence presented by John Mudd puts both the accused at the scene with the opportunity to commit the crime."

Next Gilkes said something that left the impression that Clark had met the burden of proving a prima facie case but that she'd done so by the skin of her teeth.

"It is my conclusion that the Commonwealth has met its burden, but it also is interesting to me that in many cases I get deluged with details. But there's a lot of salient facts which are available which were not presented," he said.

With that swipe at the prosecution's performance, Arlene and Steve were ordained to travel together for at least a while longer on the road of life, with a detour toward a murder trial.

■ ■ ■

One of those who still addressed Chuck Scarlata as "judge" was Allegheny County Judge Robert Dauer.

It was with a sinking feeling, then, that Regis Kelly sat in Judge Dauer's courtroom the day after the inquest and listened to Dauer call Slutzker's attorney "Judge Scarlata" throughout a hearing on a defense motion to reinstate bail.

Kelly and Lee Torbin had spent enough time chasing down the details of Slutzker's antics in the precious days leading up to the inquest. They didn't relish the idea of doing more of the same. They would have plenty of other things to do, including helping Clark prepare for trial and the pretrial gyrations that Scarlata was likely to put them through.

Since it was Scarlata's motion that brought them all together, he started off. Slutzker couldn't have been at Salvatore's pizza parlor on April 22 between 12:50 and 1:15 P.M. because he was in the prothonotary's (chief clerk's) office in the county courthouse downtown. He filed papers in an unrelated matter. Court employees logged Slutzker's papers at 1:26 P.M. and witnessed Slutzker's signature.

There was no confusion in their minds about the visit because Slutzker wore a navy uniform, Scarlata said. Slutzker, it turned out, was a volunteer tour guide on the decommissioned World War II submarine *Requin,* which is moored on the north shore of the Allegheny River.

Things were getting complicated. Dauer called a recess and sent for Slutzker to be brought from the jail. Kelly headed for the Northside to bring in Carole Yakelis from the pizza shop. On the way, he asked that detectives be dispatched to the submarine to ask about Slutzker.

With the pizza shop manager in his car, Kelly keyed his microphone and asked the radio room to log his time and position. It was 2:54 P.M. as he pulled away from the shop at the corner of James Street and North Avenue. He slipped onto the lower deck of the Fort Duquesne Bridge to cross the Allegheny River, exited the throughway onto Grant Street, drove three blocks, and turned right into the shadow of the courthouse. It was 2:59 P.M., five minutes after he started the trip.

As Kelly and Yakelis parked and made their way back to Dauer's courtroom, Detective Charles Lenz was on his way to the Carnegie Science Center. He learned from submarine coordinator Tom Flaherty that yes, Slutzker was a volunteer guide. He'd led three tours that morning and left around 12:15 to 12:30 P.M., which left plenty of time to cover the ten blocks or so between the *Requin* and Salvatore's.

When the hearing resumed, three employees of the prothonotary's office identified Slutzker as the man in the sailor suit whose document was stamped 1:26 P.M., April 22. Likewise, Yakelis said she was positive Slutzker was in her restaurant between 12:50 and 1:10 to 1:15 P.M. the same day.

Scarlata threw a monkey wrench into Kelly's theory that Slutzker could easily have left Salvatore's when Yakelis said he did, zipped across the river, and been in the prothonotary's office by 1:26.

Slutzker, the attorney said, left the submarine, went to the Southside, got on a Port Authority bus and rode it to the courthouse.

"Well, Judge Scarlata," Dauer said.

To Kelly's amazement, Judge Dauer denied Scarlata's motion and ordered Slutzker back to jail for having violated the terms of his bail. But Scarlata wasn't the type to give up. He petitioned for another hearing on the matter, claiming new evidence.

At 4 P.M. April 29, the Monday after their first appearance before Dauer, the parties sat in his courtroom once again. Scarlata had with him a Port Authority Transit bus driver named Bernard Jones, who was prepared to testify that he remembered Slutzker, in Navy blues, riding bus No. 1102 as Jones drove it from Carson Street on the Southside to Fifth Avenue beside the courthouse.

But, Dauer was tied up, so the hearing was postponed.

Good, Kelly thought. The delay would allow time for him to interview the driver. That, however, turned out to be no easy task.

The next day, Kelly learned that the PAT dispatching office did not have a home phone number or address on file for Jones. "He's a very secretive guy. He even gets his mail delivered to the garage," a dispatcher told him.

PAT was able to come up with a birth date. From that, Kelly ran down the man's operator's information through the state Bureau of Motor Vehicles and obtained an address, the license number of his personal vehicle, and its description, a 1986 Ford. When he rapped on the door of Apartment 11, 1400 Maple Drive, however, Kelly got no answer.

He moved a few steps to the side and kept knocking. This time, he raised a neighbor who said Bernard Jones had moved away a year earlier. The neighbor occasionally saw Jones in the Prospect Park area, along Skyline Drive.

Kelly took a drive. He spotted the Ford parked in the driveway of a home where a woman answered the door and said her husband was upstairs. Kelly found Bernard Jones sleeping on the floor of the living room, where he interviewed him.

Yes, he remembered the sailor suit and the guy with the big nose who wore it. He got on Jones's bus either at Eighteenth and Carson at 1:15 to 1:16 that day or near the Tenth Street Bridge at 1:21 P.M. He stepped off the bus at the corner of Fifth and Grant, beside the courthouse, where the bus is scheduled to arrive at 1:27 P.M.

That story was enough to change Dauer's mind, and he so informed "Judge Scarlata" at a hearing May 1. Slutzker was freed that day. So were the restraints on John Mudd's paranoia and anxiety.

It wasn't long before John quit Salvatore's. He had developed a habit of showing up late and leaving early. Even worse, he was starting to give customers a hard time. The owner and the manager overlooked as much as they could and forgave the rest, up to a point. They couldn't run their small business with unreliable employees, and John Mudd Jr. simply wasn't going to be a slave to a time clock. Mudd, who didn't have a reputation for sticking with one job for very long anyway, wouldn't budge on the matter, so he quit.

There was talk of a movie about the case. John was telling people that Republic Pictures offered what to him was a very large sum of money for the rights to his story and his services as technical consultant on a film. So, without benefit of a steady job, he went automobile shopping.

Maybe John wanted someone to stop him, maybe he was following the desires of Kelly and Torbin to do nothing out of the ordinary without their knowledge, but for some reason he called Kelly from Northview Motors, a dealership on McKnight Road just north of the city.

"I'm with a salesman, and I'm going to buy two cars," Mudd said.

"You with the salesman right now?"

"Yeah."

"Put him on the phone," Kelly told Mudd. He then gave the salesman orders. "Listen, I don't want you selling this kid any cars unless he talks to us."

"Oh, no, no, no. . . ."

That was the end of the episode . . . for a short time.

Not long after that, Kelly received a frantic phone call from the pizza parlor. John Mudd had just left the shop after a loud argument over money. He wanted a paycheck. The manager told Kelly that Mudd had screamed at her and threatened to beat her if she didn't pay him. He said he had a gun.

Kelly hustled across the river. This incident had to be diffused or the ground could open up under the prosecution's star witness. Yakelis was still distraught when he arrived. She was grabbing her chest and downing nitroglycerin tablets as he talked to her.

If there was a silver lining in the incident, it was that the owner wasn't there when Mudd was carrying on. Otherwise, very likely the next bench warrant issued in the case would have been for John Mudd.

Kelly got the woman calmed down with a promise that he would take care of young Mr. Mudd. The next day, he and Torbin staked out Northview Motors. Sure enough, John drove onto the lot and parked behind the building. They watched him enter the showroom and take up a position as a salesman, as though he worked for the dealership.

The two detectives yanked him out of the showroom and walked him to his car. There they read Mudd the riot act. They reminded him of the many accommodations his employers at the pizza shop had made for him. Without hesitation, Yakelis had cooperated with the detectives, setting aside her work to grant interviews and leave the shop in the middle of the day to testify. All this had been done in the middle of trying to establish a new business. And for their many kindnesses, what do they get? Belligerence and threats from the person they helped.

"Oh, I'm just losing it," Mudd said somewhat sheepishly. "Slutzker's driving me crazy."

He let up on his friends at Salvatore's, and he soon abandoned his career in auto sales.

"Thank You, Officer Brendlinger"

Considering all the things that the homicide department had done in building the case against Slutzker, Regis Kelly's short excursion to Pittsburgh's suburbs in the near East Hills on May 30 was about as routine as they come.

In typical fashion, Kelly was working at night. It was around dusk when he and Detective McCarthy arrived at the Edgewood police station. They went there to interview Sergeant Dominic LaBella.

No compelling reason existed for interviewing LaBella. The case file surely contained every word LaBella had ever uttered and every thought that had ever entered his mind about the Mudd murder . . . or so one might think.

The LaBella interview was the kind of thing that some people do half unconsciously, out of instinct, habit, or perhaps something else. The motivation might have been what psychologists call operant conditioning, the thing that allowed Russian physiologist Ivan Pavlov to do his trick with the dogs: reward a creature every once in a while for a particular kind of behavior and it will repeat the behavior again and again in anticipation of the reward. Good cops, reporters, researchers, and conscientious people in all walks of life have experienced this. It's why they go back and interview witnesses for the second and third times, double- and triple-check important facts, review laboratory findings that seem incontrovertible, and question common assumptions.

Late in his conversation with LaBella, Kelly got his reward. The sergeant recounted the remarkable conversation he had with Tim Brendlinger, his partner the night of the Mudd murder, on their ride back to the station from the Mudd home at 1515 Marlboro Street.

Two nights later, shortly after sunset on Saturday, June 1, Kelly interviewed Brendlinger, thus becoming the first investigator to take an interest in the Edgewood officer's account of the scene outside the Mudd home in the minutes following Arlene's distressed call to the police.

Brendlinger told Kelly he was sure that he told Wilkinsburg police at the crime scene the night of the murder that he'd seen Arlene, holding her son, talking to a man as they stood on the sidewalk across the street from her home.

Brendlinger also told Kelly that a day or two after Mudd's death, he saw a photo of Slutzker in a newspaper and recognized him as the man he'd seen talking to Arlene Mudd.

"There's no doubt in my mind. It was him," he told Kelly. Brendlinger said he told Wilkinsburg police that he recognized Slutzker from the newspaper photo, but, he added, "At that time Wilkinsburg handled their own investigations and they didn't particularly care for other po-

lice departments making suggestions." Wilkinsburg's re-
ponse was to tell Brendlinger that the department "knew
who did it" and that "everything was taken care of."

The significance of Brendlinger's statement leaped out
at Kelly, his boss, Sergeant Schwab, Kim Clark, and every
other person associated with the prosecution's case. It also
became painfully apparent to Chuck Scarlata when on
June 12 he received copies of the report Kelly typed after
interviewing the Edgewood officers.

Three days later, Slutzker's attorney filed a motion with
Judge Dauer to suppress the revelations from LaBella and
Brendlinger. He wanted the court to bar the officers'
statements from ever reaching the ears of a jury. Scarlata
argued that Brendlinger had seen only one photograph of
Slutzker in the newspaper. To be valid, his motion went
on, a photo identification had to be made from an array of
pictures. In addition, he argued, sixteen years had passed
since the night Brendlinger claimed to have seen Arlene
talking to Slutzker. For both those reasons, Brendlinger's
identification of the defendant was invalid.

Dauer had no intention of ruling on the motion immediately, if ever. Protocol required that the decision be left
to the trial judge, and that person hadn't been selected
yet.

Scarlata's recognition of the devastating potential of
the new evidence may have been reflected in the fact that
he formally attacked Brendlinger's statement even before
he attacked John Mudd's recalled memory. Granted, considerable research was required to prepare the motion to
suppress Mudd's testimony due to the psychological and
legal complexities of the flashback. But it seemed clear to
everyone involved that if an upstanding, credible witness
—a police officer no less—could offer eyewitness testimony putting Slutzker on Marlboro Street minutes after

the killing, and not just on Marlboro Street but also conversing with Arlene Mudd, then it would become much less critical that a jury believe John Jr.

The shape and nature of the trial were coming into focus. By mid-June, Clark and Scarlata now could see the ground on which the contest would be fought.

With one major exception, the summer passed uneventfully for the case. John Mudd kept his nose clean. Clark had the key elements of her case assembled. She knew that the refining, the tweaking, could be done when the trial was closer at hand. Scarlata used the warm months to assemble experts who could throw the considerable weight of their credentials and experience against the competence and credibility of Mudd's flashback recollection.

The exception was the petition for a writ of habeas corpus on behalf of Arlene Montgomery, aka Arlene Mudd. David Lichtenstein, her attorney, filed it in the middle of June. He argued that despite the outcome of the coroner's inquest, the prosecution had failed to establish that Arlene knew that Slutzker was in her basement the night of the murder or that she participated in the murder or the murder plan.

In essence, Lichtenstein was asking the court to force the prosecution to present evidence that Arlene was part of the crime, or set Arlene free.

On the homicide charge, the Commonwealth had to show that Arlene "intentionally, knowingly, recklessly, or negligently caused Mudd's death," his petition said. On the conspiracy charge, the prosecution had to show that Arlene agreed with Slutzker that they would murder Mudd or that she would aid him in murdering her husband.

She may very well have done one or both of those

things, but the world may never know because Clark didn't offer evidence of that kind at the coroner's inquest.

While Pezzano had testified that Slutzker told him "Arlene Mudd was in with him on this," the defense objection as to the admissibility of that claim was never ruled upon, Lichtenstein said.

In the absence of evidence showing that Arlene caused her husband's death or entered an agreement with Slutzker, the only things on the record possibly linking her to the crime were her association with Slutzker and her suspected knowledge after the fact. Those two elements amount to nothing more than "surmise and conjecture that a conspiratorial relationship existed," he said.

In a four-page opinion issued July 23, Judge Dauer agreed with Lichtenstein that the prosecution had not established a prima facie case.

The evidence may show that, because of her silence during police questioning and because she spoke with Slutzker immediately after the murder and calmly opened the door for him when he left, Arlene was an accessory to the crime after it occurred.

"But even then, it may be that the defendant told Slutzker she was outraged and shocked by what he had done; and he may have responded, 'Keep your mouth shut and open the door or I'll kill you,'" Dauer said.

The judge dismissed the charges against Arlene. Only Slutzker remained as a defendant.

Pregame Warm-up

The case went on the criminal court calendar for the fall. Jeffrey Manning would be the judge. Scarlata launched his frontal assault on Mudd's flashback recollection on October 22.

In a motion to declare John Mudd Jr. incompetent to testify, the defense argued that the professionals who treated Mudd as a boy stated specifically that he was "too young to be relied upon as a witness to the murder, even if he does eventually state that he knows who killed his father. "John Mudd Jr. has heard so many adults talk and speculate as to who may have committed the murder that certainly fantasy and fact are not clear to this young child."

Scarlata argued that Mudd's memory would be no better in the fall of 1991 than it was in the spring of 1976 when he entered counseling.

In addition, the defense claimed that Mudd underwent hypnosis, which "tarnished his ability to accurately recount the events."

Manning took the motion under advisement.

In the days leading up to the trial, Mudd, who, with Kim, had moved forty-five minutes north of Pittsburgh to New Kensington, was once again feeling the pressure building. If someone wanted to rattle him further, shattering the bathroom window of his second-floor residence was one good way to do it. When it happened, John's thoughts gravitated toward a gunshot as opposed to a stone.

The county police radio dispatcher rousted Kelly at 12:30 A.M. Saturday, October 26. The dispatcher said New Kensington police were already talking to John and Kim at their place on Fifth Avenue. The young couple did not intend to stay in the house that night.

"Tell them I'm on my way up there," Kelly said.

Before he got into his car, Kelly called the North Braddock Police Department, explained his suspicions, and asked that borough officers check 1712 Brinton Avenue to see if Slutzker was at home.

When he got to Mudd's home in New Kensington, Kelly found glass on the floor of the bathroom and a bent slat in the metal blinds covering the window. He came away convinced that it wasn't a bullet that did the damage but something bigger, perhaps a rock. Nothing was on the porch roof below the broken window, and it was too dark in the backyard to make a proper search.

John and Kim quoted their neighbor, Karen Lauden, as saying she heard someone yell from the backyard, "Karen, John, Kim, you're all dead," at the moment she heard glass breaking.

Mudd and his girlfriend, shaken but unhurt, left for his aunt's home. Kelly headed across the backyard to Lauden's house.

The neighbor confirmed that she'd heard the threat, but she couldn't figure out why the man she saw in the backyard would have called her name, too.

"I've never seen him before," the woman said.

"You sure it couldn't have been one of your friends?"

"He looked like a yuppie. Trust me, none of my friends look like that," said Lauden, a tattooed mama whose old man, "Butch," was a member of the Barbarians motorcycle gang. Butch tended bar at a biker hangout and didn't choose to associate, or have his woman associate, with yuppies.

"I wouldn't have anybody like that in my house," she said.

Lauden said the intruder was a white male, about five-foot-ten, 150 to 165 pounds. He had short hair, wore a dark jacket and a ball cap. The man ran away when he noticed her looking at him.

Word came over the radio, in the meantime, that North Braddock police spoke to a man named Bill Linsenbigler at Slutzker's house. Linsenbigler told them Slutzker wasn't there.

Kelly and the local police were helpless to do anything further. At least Mudd was in one piece, physically if not emotionally.

The Suppression Hearing
October 28, 1991

Judge Manning combined both of Scarlata's pretrial motions in one hearing, which began Monday morning, October 28.

The court heard the more sensational of the two matters first.

The thrust of Scarlata's challenge to the flashback recollection was that the testimony of the man could be no more competent than the testimony of the boy. Around that core, Scarlata spun a web of nuances, hoping to entangle the star witness.

"Miss Clark cannot show that there was any recollection existing in this young boy's mind at the time that he was five years old because she hasn't even bothered to talk to the counselor who was seeing him at that time," the defense attorney said as the hearing got under way.

John Mudd, according to his uncle, was hypnotized at or about the time he was five to five and a half years of age, maybe six years of age. Prior to that, he had no recollection, according to members of the Mudd family and according to the counselor who saw young John Mudd, Scarlata said.

"He is not to be trusted. Merely because he happens to

be twenty-one years of age now does not necessarily make him competent.

"Mr. Mudd's recollections today can be no better, and in all likelihood are far worse, than they were back when he was five years of age, and the people who saw him when he was five years of age concluded that he was not to be believed."

John Mudd Jr. was never hypnotized, Clark said, even though hypnosis is mentioned in one police report.

Scarlata insisted that Mudd had been hypnotized, that the case record showed that he had, and that therefore Mudd's "flashbulb" memory was invalid.

Whether Scarlata was deliberately corrupting the word, his refusal to dignify Mudd's experience as a flashback got under Clark's skin.

"The word is flashback, not flashbulb," she chided him.

"Flashback, flashbulb, it's the same concept," Scarlata said.

"It's not the same concept."

The bickering did not impress Judge Manning. He simply asked Clark to begin questioning the witness, which she did by eliciting Mudd's claim that he was certain he'd never been hypnotized.

Mudd also said that no one used drugs in his home the night of the recall and that he did not have any alcohol to drink. Kim may have had a beer or two, he said.

Then he described what happened after he knocked Steve Spinola to the floor.

"I picked up a chair, and I was going to beat him with the chair, and he was lying against my dad's flag that was on his casket which was hanging on the wall, and I just couldn't hit him with it. But I felt like I wanted to hurt him really bad. I said several times that I was 'going to fucking kill him.' "

Mudd said he never did strike Spinola, but dropped the chair and left the room as he started crying and seeing "perfectly clear" images from the night of the murder.

The images he saw created a mixed-up vision of different scenes from the night of his father's murder.

"I was sitting in the hallway on the steps, and then I started seeing everything again, and it was slower, and the pictures were sticking longer, and that's when the whole thing came in, like, almost order.

"It wasn't like I was getting a vision and it was staying there for a half hour and letting me look at it and pick out details. It was coming back fast, and I was seeing different things."

Almost as a matter of routine, Clark asked Mudd if he understood the difference between fantasy and truth. Of course, he said he did, but the question provided Scarlata with an opportune transition to his cross-examination.

"Now, explain to us, what is the difference between what you recall and fantasy?" Scarlata said.

"Fantasy is something you wish would happen."

"Uh-huh. And you didn't wish to hurt Steve Slutzker?"

"I don't know Steve Slutzker."

"And you didn't know him when you were five years old?"

"I knew him as a neighbor, as a guy who come to my house."

"And he came to your house for the purpose of seeing your mother, didn't he?"

"Correct."

"As a matter of fact, your mother moved out of your house and moved in with Mr. Slutzker for a period of time, didn't she?"

"I have no idea."

"You don't remember that?"

"No."

"Was your family religious?" Scarlata asked, abruptly changing the subject in a tactic intended to keep the witness off balance.

"Yes."

"When did you first remember having asked your family members what had happened to your father?"

"Three or four years ago. I was over the age of sixteen," Mudd said, perhaps forgetting that he'd testified at the coroner's inquest six months earlier that he didn't remember ever asking family members what happened to his father.

Mudd said he had no recollection of ever accusing Slutzker of having murdered his father. He couldn't remember the name of his counselor, and he said the sessions were not therapy, merely opportunities to visit his mother.

"My mother was supposed to meet me there, and she never showed up, so all I did was play when I was there."

Mudd said he had no recollection of lying to his grandmother when he was a boy or his aunt being concerned about his lying.

He said he thought about his father's death for the first time when he was around thirteen or fourteen years old. "All the thoughts were 'Why I'd had to be without my father' and 'Why he was taken away from me,' and that was it."

Mudd said none of his relatives ever asked him what he knew about his father's death, and he could not remember ever being told that Slutzker had been charged with solicitation to commit murder.

He told Scarlata that, in the vision, when he was back on the couch with his mother, Arlene was not hysterical or upset.

"She was calm, cool, and collected?"

"Yes."

"Not comforting you?"

"No."

"Actually not paying much attention to you?"

"That's a fair statement."

Mudd said he remembered seeing his mother politely usher the man out of the house after speaking with him, actually walking him to the door and holding it open for him.

In his flashback, Arlene came back in and sat down, not comforting her son or suggesting in any way that something terrible had happened. Mudd told Scarlata he had no recollection of his mother calling anyone on the telephone and no recollection of seeing any blood in the vision where he viewed his father's body.

Mudd said he didn't recall his mother attending any of the counseling sessions when he was a boy and that he never saw her in the years that followed. He said he didn't remember ever being angry at his mother for leaving him and that he never gave any thought to whether Arlene was involved in the murder.

When Scarlata finished questioning Mudd, Clark tidied up the hearing record by eliciting denials that Mudd had ever read any police reports about his father's death, looked at any pictures taken of the murder scene, or read any newspaper articles or reports of any other kind about the case.

Manning then opened a colloquy with Clark and Scarlata about a subject that went to the heart of the entire case—whether Mudd's ability to observe as a five-year-old should be recognized as something separate from his capacity to remember as a man what he had observed as a boy and to communicate that memory.

"How do we determine what he was like when he was five years old?" the judge wanted to know.

"The memory at age twenty can be no better and probably is worse than it was at age five. And if at age five he's not a truth-sayer, then what he says at age twenty is presumptively untrue," Scarlata said.

"I don't understand this as something that he thought he knew when he was five years old," Manning said. "I understood this as some type of potentially colossal event that occurred, that he observed and then repressed for some reason and then, bang, here it comes back."

"The truth of the matter is at age five, he accused Steve of doing this. It's not anything that he repressed," Scarlata countered. "He was talking about it when he was five and six years old."

Manning brushed the debate aside for the moment and allowed Clark to introduce her expert witness, Dr. Pass.

At the time, Pass was vice president of human resources for Chambers Development Company, a Pittsburgh-area company that hauled garbage and operated landfills. Before Pass joined Chambers, he'd been a staff psychologist for ten years with the Pennsylvania Department of Corrections, based at the diagnostic center at Western Penitentiary. His job at the prison was to evaluate newly committed felons.

By way of qualifications, Pass said he had a bachelor's degree in psychology from Penn State University, a master's of science in counseling from Duquesne University, and a doctorate in counseling from the University of Pittsburgh.

Pass said he was not certified as a psychologist in Pennsylvania.

Based on one interview with John Mudd Jr., a review

of Mudd's counseling records, and briefings by Detective
Kelly, Pass said Mudd showed symptoms of posttraumatic
stress disorder. One leading manifestation of the condition is repression, either partial or total, of memories of
the traumatic event.

Other symptoms include hypervigilance, exaggerated
reactions when startled, paranoia, loss of interest in important activities, and recurrent intrusive recollections of
the traumatic event.

Repression of the memory can occur immediately or
be delayed, and once pushed out of the way, memories of
the traumatic event can remain locked away for very long
periods, he said.

Pass said Mudd's flashback recollection was consistent
with the key details of the murder, including the position-
ing of the body.

The Catholic Family Services records showed that the
counselor talked about the death of John Mudd with the
intention of getting John Jr. to accept his father's death,
Pass said.

"Does he mention somebody by the name of Steven in
connection with the death of his father in these records?"
Clark asked.

"Yes, he did."

"Can the repression take place in steps, so that a person could repress the details of the event gradually?" she
asked.

"My opinion is yes."

Pass said the revival of repressed memories is sometimes triggered by a stimulus. He told of a patrolman who
saw a motorcycle rider who'd been cut in half in an accident. The officer could not remember exactly what he did
immediately after seeing the body. When he returned to
the place where the accident occurred, a motorcycle

passed, and he remembered. The flag or Spinola's first name could have been triggers for Mudd, Pass said.

"Is it possible, Doctor, that a person could remember an event, as far as the senses being able to record it in the memory, prior to that person being sufficiently educated to be able to articulate what it was he remembered?" the judge asked.

"No," said Pass. "And the reason why is because I think the literature shows that if you go back much beyond the age of five, there isn't the conceptual or cognitive awareness. The individual doesn't have that degree of cognitive or conceptual awareness to be able to associate clearly what has occurred. So, as a result, recall would be impaired."

The doctor said that a child five and a half years old would have the capacity to observe and understand what he observed.

As for the lying noted in the counseling records, Pass said the behavior is not unusual in children who've been traumatized as Mudd was. The same would be true of the behavior the boy displayed during his play sessions with his counselor: anger, hostility, and the need to feel all-powerful and protected.

"It's my opinion that within a reasonable degree of professional certainty he was and is still suffering from posttraumatic stress disorder," Pass said.

When Clark yielded to Scarlata to cross-examine, Pass said that the purpose of counseling Mudd was, ideally, "to prevent him from sealing over his emotions about Steve, for whom he showed dislike."

Scarlata read from the notes made by the woman who counseled Mudd when he was a boy: " 'Therapy now is crucial so that the whole traumatic experience is not repressed.' "

"Would it surprise you, Doctor, to learn that John has no recollection of any of those discussions with the counselor? Would that affect your diagnosis?"

"That would surprise me, yes. Would it affect the diagnosis? I don't believe so."

The counselor's notes also reflected that John had been told that Slutzker was in jail in connection with his father's murder and that he had made threats against the boy.

Scarlata chopped away at the notion that young John Mudd's mind was untrammeled by knowledge of the murder or of his family's suspicions about Steve and Arlene. Again, Scarlata read from the counselor's handwritten notes where they reported that young Mudd had expressed anger toward Slutzker.

"As a matter of fact, he told the counselor he was going to kill him when he was 21 years old, right?"

"Yes," the doctor said, acknowledging a moment later that the details brought up by Scarlata were causing him to question his diagnosis.

But Pass's doubts faded quickly. "I would still hold to the opinion," he said.

Not one to overlook an opportunity to cast suspicion away from his client, Scarlata then won Pass's agreement that the counselor's notes raised the prospect that perhaps Mrs. Mudd had something to do with this event.

Scarlata now had something he could use at the trial to lead the jurors to wonder whether the former Mrs. Mudd shouldn't be sitting at the defense table along with Slutzker.

With that, Scarlata recapped the argument he was pursuing with his line of questioning: John Mudd Jr. knew Slutzker as his mother's boyfriend, knew Slutzker had been jailed, and had heard that Slutzker had killed his father.

"Then the counselor concludes, 'Johnny is certainly too young to be relied upon as a witness to the murder, even if he does eventually state that he knows who killed his father.' That's what it says, right?"

Scarlata wasn't so much questioning Pass as using him as a blank screen on which to project the words of the counselor, words that played into his hands as Slutzker's defense attorney.

Scarlata had tried to bring his cross-examination to an artful conclusion, but Pass stood his ground, saying young Mudd's statements as a five-year-old didn't necessarily make his recollection invalid.

"Then you disagree with what the counselor said: 'He is too young to be reliable?' " Scarlata asked.

"Yes."

As he walked back to his chair, Scarlata might have been wondering whether he should have asked that last question.

After Pass was excused, Clark and Scarlata still had a considerable volume of evidence to present. It was late in the afternoon. Manning adjourned the hearing until the next day.

Dominic LaBella was the lead-off witness Friday morning. Clark put him on the stand to testify to the shocking nature of what John Mudd Jr. saw when his mother held him at the top of the basement stairs the night of the murder. While his partner was outside looking for signs of anyone leaving by the basement door in the rear of the house, LaBella stood beside Arlene as they looked at the body at the bottom of the steps.

Clark wanted to rebut the notion presented during Scarlata's cross-examination of Mudd that because Mudd didn't remember his mother being hysterical there was no trauma.

Before leaving the witness stand, the sergeant confirmed that he and Brendlinger filed no incident report because they were assisting officers, not primary investigators. In fact, the first time anyone formally asked him to describe what he witnessed that night was on May 30, 1991, when Detective Kelly called to set up their interview.

Clark also swore in James Mudd, who described his nephew as "quite radical, hysterical, crying, making odd sounds" the night of the flashback.

"The first remark he made to me was that Slutzker killed his daddy," he said, adding that he could not remember whether young Mudd had said "Slutzker" or "Steve."

He said John would describe the visions he was having, then ask if the vision was accurate. "When he would mention something, he'd ask me, 'Is that right, Uncle Jim? Is that right?' "

"Johnny sounded almost like he had gone back a little bit into his childhood, where he was speaking sometimes like a much younger man with a squeaky voice and that, you know, just kind of weird, out of it," the uncle said.

James Mudd said he never discussed the details of his brother's death with the boy prior to the flashback and knew of no other family member who did. In avoiding such conversations with John Jr., the Mudd family members were honoring Mary Mudd's orders.

"She said, 'If he wants to know, he'll ask.' "

"I believe in the beginning, right after the murder, questions were asked him not by the family as much as by the police, but I can't remember any of us ever pushing him, trying to push him into anything," James Mudd said.

The uncle told Clark that he mentioned hypnosis in his telephone conversation with Detective Gratz around 2 A.M. the night of the recall. But, he said, he never intended to suggest that John Jr. actually had been hypnotized.

"It never happened. It was suggested, and it was refused," James Mudd said. "So, that's a mistake in Gratz's report. It's very possible that I may have made a statement that Johnny looks like he's under hypnosis right now. I can't recall. I was in a charged state where I was trying to push something to make something happen."

Clark also established for the record that James Mudd told no one, not even his wife, the gruesome details of what he'd seen at the bottom of the basement steps the night of his brother's murder.

On cross-examination, Scarlata immediately began grilling the uncle about whether the family ever questioned the boy about the murder.

An argumentative exchange ensued, with Scarlata asking why Detective Gratz would write in his report that Mudd said the family questioned Johnny right after the murder.

"I do not remember telling Detective Gratz that I questioned young John in 1975, no sir. I do not remember saying that."

"Did any other family members question him?"

"No, I do not remember telling the detective that either."

"Do you remember telling Gratz that on the night when John had this recollection, when you questioned him, that he told you that the man who came up out of the basement . . . was Steven Slutzker . . . and had kissed his mother?"

"Yes, I remember that."

"On November 23 to 24, 1990, did John tell you that his mother's emotional state was calm, cool, and collected?"

"No, he did not."

Scarlata hammered at the uncle about the line in Gratz's report that had James Mudd saying apparently Johnny's memory was coming back.

"Well, how do you know that he didn't have a memory before if you never asked him about it?" Scarlata asked.

"Because he never related it to me before."

"But you never asked him about it, did you?"

"Because he never related it."

"I see. You assumed he had no memory because he never told you about it?"

"Yes, sir."

"But you never bothered to ask him whether he had a memory?"

"Sir, none of us ever asked the boy about it. I've told you that four times already."

"I would assume, Mr. Mudd, that you harbor a belief as to who was responsible for your brother's murder, don't you?"

"No, sir. I don't harbor a belief."

"You don't have any suspicions or ideas?"

"I have my own ideas, yes, sir."

"But none of those conversations ever occurred in the presence of John?"

"Not a one."

"And did your mother have a belief similar to yours about someone who might have participated in this?"

"Yes, sir."

"You all felt, didn't you, that Arlene had something to do with it?"

"Yes, sir."

"John's mother?"

"Yes, sir."

"And Steve had something to do with it?"

"Yes, sir."

"Do you remember telling the police that the young boy could never recall or discuss what happened the day of his father's death?"

"Which he never was able to do. He had never discussed it with us and we never discussed it with him."

"That conclusion . . . is reached because he never said anything, and you never asked him anything?"

"Yes, sir."

Scarlata immediately put Gratz on the stand to build upon his theory that members of the Mudd family discussed or attempted to discuss the murder with the boy. Gratz was a twenty-five-year veteran of the county police who had spent the last thirteen years with the homicide squad.

Scarlata quoted from the officer's report on his conversation with James Mudd. " 'He stated that the family had first attempted to question the boy.' "

On cross-examination, Clark attempted to put a quick end to the theory.

Gratz said he resisted James Mudd's suggestions that a detective be dispatched immediately to listen to his nephew's recollection. Gratz said he wanted time for others to review the file and for "cooler heads" to prevail.

"Would it be fair to say that as he talked to you, he was rambling and babbling?" the prosecutor asked.

"I had to stop him on several occasions."

"Did you get the impression he was drunk or drugged?"

"No," Gratz said. "I had gotten out of bed. I was sound

asleep, and when I first talked to him, I got the impression that he was quite emotional, almost hysterical."

Clark finished with Gratz, but Scarlata wasn't finished with his theory. He told Manning he would call Peg Gillick, John Jr.'s counselor from Catholic Social Services, which was formerly known as Catholic Youth Services.

Manning was not overjoyed at the prospect of hearing more on the subject.

"Like I said yesterday, I built a mouse trap and snapped it on myself here," the judge said.

"You may be surprised to learn, Judge, that perhaps you haven't done that."

"Well, the further we go along with this, the more I am becoming convinced that opinions as to John Mudd's credibility, which is essentially what they are—"

"No, no," Scarlata interrupted. "It's his competency, because his competency turns on his ability to have observed back when he was five years old and then to bring that information to the courtroom today."

Manning resisted Scarlata's assertion that the most important question was whether John Mudd Jr. was competent, meaning whether he was fit to be a witness. To the judge's way of thinking, the predominant issue was whether Mudd was believable, or credible, and the job of determining whether he was credible belonged to a jury.

Scarlata yielded the floor, but he didn't surrender on the point he was trying to get across.

After a ten-minute recess, he called Alexander Levy, a psychologist with a master's degree in counseling from Pitt, a licensed practitioner in Pennsylvania, a former executive director of the drug rehabilitation program Alpha House, and a private practitioner in psychotherapy.

Levy explained that posttraumatic stress disorder is essentially the same thing that was known as shell shock in

World War II. After the Korean War it was known as battle fatigue. The longer name attached after the Vietnam War. It is seen in victims of sexual abuse and physical violence. It is brought on by extraordinary fear and extraordinary danger.

Levy said he would not consider it a terror-inducing event for a five-year-old boy to see his father lying at the bottom of the basement stairs.

"Now, if you were to couple that with the testimony . . . that he was not terrorized and in fact was very comfortable and safe, do you have an opinion as to whether or not he experienced a trauma-inducing event?"

"Yes. When people who in fact suffer from posttraumatic stress disorder remember an event related to the trauma, they remember it with terror. If he was not terrified in recounting the event then I would say it was not a terrifying experience," Levy said.

Levy then went on to say that traumatic things occurred in John Jr.'s life, including his mother moving across the street with another man, his parents' fights, the loss of his father, and moving in with his grandmother. But, Levy said, it wasn't clear that the boy experienced those events as trauma.

He said Mudd's experience was not necessarily inconsistent with posttraumatic stress disorder; it just didn't go far enough for anyone, including Pass, to make such a diagnosis, and Pass failed to rule out other conditions, such as organic mental disorders, anxiety, depression, and adjustment disorder.

"What would you have done if police called and said they wanted you to see this boy who just had this mystical recollection?"

"Objection to the term mystical," Clark interjected.

"I'm sorry, this flashback recollection."

"At a minimum, at a minimum, I would have conducted what's called a mental status examination. It's a series of requests of an individual that they engage in certain tasks to help rule out confused thinking, impaired memory, organizational disorder, disorientation to time, place or person, attention deficits, indicators of certain kinds of possible brain damage, and in all likelihood I would have conducted in addition to that a complete psychological battery, again to rule out all the possible ways of explaining this.

"The myriad possibilities that could account for some of what's going on here need to be ruled out, and they weren't."

Scarlata led Levy on a tour of the technical aspects of emotions that filter memory. Examples would be the gratitude that Mudd associated with sailing paper airplanes out through a window and his strong reaction to his counselor going away on vacation.

The prevailing professional opinion of the day, Levy said, was that occasionally a child may be mute or refuse to discuss a traumatic event, but the behavior should not be confused with an inability to remember what occurred. In younger children, distressing dreams of an event may, within several weeks, change into generalized nightmares of monsters, of rescuing others, or of threats to self or others. Young children do not have the sense that they are reliving the past. The reliving takes the form of repetitive play.

In the counseling records, "I see evidence that he is struggling with emotion, but not reliving trauma," Levy said.

For example, John Jr.'s threat to kill Steve when he reaches age twenty-one shows that the boy had a clear sense of the future, which is inconsistent with a diagnosis of posttraumatic stress disorder.

If the boy had experienced trauma and developed a stress disorder as a result, he would have unsettling recollections that would repeatedly intrude on his everyday life, or as a child he would have repeatedly engaged in play that bore themes or aspects of the trauma, Levy said.

"Do you see any evidence in any of the records you have reviewed that there existed trauma on that night sufficient to trigger posttraumatic stress disorder?"

"No, I don't. I don't see evidence that he was terrorized."

"And in the absence of terror, you can't have the phenomenon?"

"Correct. Not to say it wasn't a horrible night." But, added Levy, "It didn't satisfy the conditions of a psychic trauma."

Young Mudd was said to have experienced nightmares, but no record existed to describe the subject of the nightmares. Even the opinion expressed by Pass that the American flag was a trigger to Mudd's repressed memory was questionable, Levy said.

He said that if the boy had seen a flag on the night of the murder, then a flag could have triggered his recollection, but no one ever said that a flag was displayed in the Mudd home on December 28, 1975.

Such emotional triggers tend to be literal associations. Long after they've been freed, soldiers who were in prison camps where it was very cold may experience the nightmare of captivity when the weather turns freezing, Levy said.

Some war veterans will react out of proportion when they hear a car backfire, but they won't dive on the ground and scream for others to get down when they see a flag go by, even though flags are associated with their military experience.

Scarlata led Levy through a discussion of even deeper, more obscure details of posttraumatic stress disorder and the symptoms associated with it. As examples, the specialist cited the exaggerated startle response, where a victim of the disorder will leap out of a chair at a slight noise, and physiologic reactions. An example would be a woman who, after having been raped in an elevator, breaks into a sweat whenever she enters another elevator.

"I want to stress, posttraumatic stress disorder is really a serious, serious condition," Levy lectured. "It's a debilitating condition. People who struggle with this thing are not walking around feeling great. They're feeling terrible."

Levy said one of his colleagues knew of a woman who was being troubled by a very odd rash. She went to a hospital emergency room, where doctors said the rash appeared to be the result of spider bites. The woman said the diagnosis couldn't be correct because she hadn't been around any spiders.

It turned out, Levy said, that as a child the woman had been locked under a porch and was, in fact, bitten by spiders. The memory of the experience caused her skin to break out.

So as not to leave the impression that he was accusing Mudd of lying about his memories, Levy explained that "All of our memories are fragmentary, and humans are uncomfortable with incompleteness.

"So we tend to fill in the blanks. Where we fill them in from our fears, our desires, our fantasies, our attempts to please others, whatever we fill it in with, that's done unconsciously. It's not lying. It's called confabulation."

Scarlata was on a roll. Levy had pretty thoroughly

trashed the diagnosis made by Dr. Pass, and now it was time for Scarlata to take aim at John Mudd Jr. himself.

He got Levy to agree that memories revived through a flashback experience years later could be no better, no more accurate or trustworthy, than memory in the moments after the original event.

By the same token, Scarlata wanted to know, would long lapses of time impair memory?

"Children, unless they were sexually or physically abused over a long period of time, don't tend to repress memory in the face of trauma. So, I'm not sure how to answer your question," Levy said.

"Would one who purports to have a flashback memory who has not had a bona fide posttraumatic stress disorder have an enhancement of his or her memory?"

"I don't know what they would have. The only way we understand this kind of recall is in the context of posttraumatic stress disorder."

"And in your opinion, that's not what happened here?"

"I'm not really prepared to say it's not what happened here. I'm only saying I don't know what happened here, and there is insufficient material to form the diagnosis."

Scarlata was boring in now. "The Catholic Youth Services report, where it says that John was not to be believed—"

"Objection," Clark blurted out. "It doesn't say in there that he is not to be believed."

"Can't be relied upon. I'm paraphrasing."

The guy was crafty and always on his toes. Clark had to hand it to him for that.

"Well, I would object to the paraphrasing," she said. "This is an important issue."

Manning sustained the objection.

From there, however, Scarlata may have gotten carried

away with himself. He delved into material that would have sailed right over the heads of most jurors.

The testimony became so convoluted that Scarlata found himself asking this question of Levy: "If the opinion of the counselor that John is too young to be relied upon is accurate, would the existence of a posttraumatic stress disorder or not a posttraumatic stress disorder in the context of the flashback memory be changed by the imposition, or the adjusted position, of the flashback memory?"

Clark shook her head as if to clear the fog and objected, saying no one knew why John's counselor concluded that the boy would not make a reliable witness.

Manning didn't rule on the objection but asked Levy if he understood the question.

"Not even a little bit."

Having been brought back to earth, Scarlata recast the question: If Mudd was not a reliable witness in 1976, could he be relied on in 1991?

"The basis of her statement is that he can't differentiate fantasy and fact," Levy said of the counselor's notes. "If that's correct, his memory ten years later would be no better than it was then. Time does not tend to improve memory."

Finally, thought Scarlata, the words he wanted to hear from the expert.

Clark had no choice but to attack Levy's conclusions. She chose to do so by a route that kept her close to the basics of logic and psychology.

For starters, she got Levy to acknowledge that the aspects of posttraumatic stress disorder identified by the prevailing research are general aspects. The research did not suggest that those aspects are always present.

With one question and one answer, then, Clark

seemed to have reopened the door to the posttraumatic stress disorder diagnosis.

Then, as a matter of common sense, she challenged Levy's assertion that a five-year-old boy would not be traumatized by seeing his father lying motionless on the basement floor only moments after the father had left a happy family scene to fix the lights. After all, Levy had said the boy could have been traumatized by his mother moving across the street to live temporarily with another man.

" 'One must understand,' " Clark said, reading from Peg Gillick's counseling journal, " 'the tremendous amount of trauma that this child has been through during the past six months and the tremendous adjustments that he has had to make as well as the amount of anger and anxiety with which he is coping. And then one can easily understand his acting-out behavior.' Are you saying the therapist has misused the term?"

"I'm not really sure how the therapist is using the term 'trauma' in this particular paragraph," Levy said. "I was troubled by the use of the word because it's really not clear whether she's referring to the time of the father's death, the time prior to that, or the time since that."

Clark also established for the judge's benefit that Levy's opinions were based entirely on what he'd read and been told by people other than John Mudd Jr. Levy had not interviewed Mudd, nor had he read the statements of Mudd's friends who witnessed him having the recall.

"If I were having a flashback memory under posttraumatic stress disorder, how would I behave?" Clark asked.

"You would appear altered. The way you hold your body, the way you move your body, the sound of your voice, and the energy with which you express yourself would all seem altered."

"Would it surprise you to know that that's exactly how those people describe—"

"No. I've read that," Levy said. "Somewhere in the report, I did read that."

"Would you expect my descriptions of what I was experiencing right then and there to be so vivid that other people could almost see it or feel it themselves?"

"I would."

"Would it surprise you to know that that's how these people describe how John Mudd Jr. was when he had this recall?"

"No," Levy said, adding that when memories of this kind come back, they are accompanied by questions such as "Am I crazy? Could this have happened?"

Thank you, kind doctor, Clark thought.

"Well," she said aloud, "would it surprise you to know that after he had the recall but before he talked to Detective Kelly when his aunt, Maureen Perri, and his uncles, James and Terrence Mudd, came to his house, he did ask them questions to confirm whether or not this was real? 'Was there really a fish tank there, Uncle Jim?' 'Was the couch really on this side of the room, Uncle Terry?' 'Was the house really a red brick house?' and so forth?"

"No, that wouldn't surprise me, and it wouldn't surprise me if he would insist on being taken to the house to look at it and that he would ask those questions every day for up to a year or two. I mean, if this is what's going on, this is really, really a profound experience."

"So would it surprise you to know that after he had this recall, that he contacted one of the officers from Wilkinsburg police to ask if, in fact, he was the officer who had taken him from his house to the strange couch where he

awakened? Somebody gave him the name, one of the uncles. Would it surprise you that he contacted that police
officer to ask him questions? 'Did you take me to your
house?' and 'Did I have a blanket?' Would that surprise
you?"

"No."

"Would it surprise you that he would have a fear of
basements, going into basements, going down basement
stairs?"

"It would not surprise me."

"Would it surprise you to know that John Mudd Jr.
insists on lights being on everywhere in the house, even
sometimes during the daytime, or that he has problems
getting out of a car at night and walking in the dark from
the car to the house, that he has to sit there for a while?"

All of that is well and good, Levy said in so many
words. But behavior of that kind would have occurred
during the years between the murder and the flashback if
Mudd were truly experiencing posttraumatic stress syndrome. The fact that none of the symptoms occurred until
after he'd had the flashback was inexplicable.

Levy's statement didn't help the prosecutor's cause,
but she didn't dwell on it. Clark asked Levy a very simple
question that seemed to deflate the issue over posttraumatic stress syndrome.

"Are there any other types of disorders that can cause
repression of memory if not posttraumatic stress disorder?" she asked.

Of course there are, but repressed memory was understood only in the context of posttraumatic stress disorder,
he said.

"Sometimes people just remember stuff," Levy said.
"I'm prepared to believe that. Sometimes you'll be walk-

ing along, and there will be a little trigger, not even a traumatic repression. Gee, there it is."

Mudd's flashback might be as simple as that, even though the recollection was unnerving and compelling for him and those who saw him as the memory returned, he said.

"I'm just saying that my role here as an expert is to tell you what we know in terms of research, what's been researched, what there's an academic basis for understanding, not all the other possibilities, which you don't need a psychologist to tell you."

With that, Levy seemed to have gone a long way in legitimizing the flashback. Mudd's psychological condition may have been misdiagnosed, but that didn't mean the recollection wasn't real. That being the case, Pass's credentials and his performance as a grass-roots psychologist were no longer as important to the success or failure of the prosecution's case. Even so, Levy couldn't resist taking another swipe at Pass, and Clark couldn't resist coming to his defense one more time.

The flashback was compelling, Levy was saying. ". . . compelling to the point that Dr. Pass did not feel a need to do the rest of an examination, and I can tell you that you can bring as many psychologists and psychiatrists in here as you want. There isn't going to be anybody that says this constitutes a valid psychological evaluation."

"Well, Dr. Pass wasn't really called upon to do a psychological evaluation; do you understand that?" Clark said. "He was called upon to do the interview because John Mudd Jr. was so sensitive at that time, and the police wanted someone who might have a little more sensitivity and insight in the way to ask particular questions?"

"I do not understand that based on the introductory paragraph of that report in which it says, 'To assess John during the interview in an effort to ascertain whether or not his recall fifteen years after the event was consistent with the symptoms of posttraumatic stress disorder,'" Levy said.

Gotcha! Scarlata thought.

"And if Miss Clark maintains he wasn't called upon to do that, I'd move to strike his testimony," Scarlata said.

Once again, Manning let the two attorneys squabble.

"I believe that's all the questions I have," Clark said, hoping to end the give and take, in which she was giving more ground than she was taking.

Not being the type to drop a bone until every ounce of meat was gone, Scarlata continued. "If in fact young John was suffering from fantasies that were intertwined with his factual memory—I think that's the expression you used—what would that impact be on one's current memory?"

"It would be contaminated," Levy said, recalling Pass's words that in the absence of posttraumatic stress disorder, the accuracy of the flashback memory would be questionable.

The word "contaminated" must have had a pleasant ring in Scarlata's ear.

Manning chose that point in the testimony to ask a few questions. He first wanted to know whether a person's fear that harm would come to a loved one qualified as traumatic or whether the person had to be in fear of personal harm.

The doctor said psychic trauma generally stems from fear of harm to oneself, but if a loved one were the victim of terrible violence, then a person might experience psychic trauma even without being the target of the violence.

Levy said flashbacks were most readily understood by

mental health specialists as one of the symptoms of post-traumatic stress disorder. Flashbacks also occurred in people suffering from other mental conditions, although they were not as thoroughly studied or as well understood under those conditions.

Regardless, the examination performed by Pass was so incomplete that it was impossible for anyone to make a proper diagnosis about the cause of his flashback, Levy said.

"Before you can have a diagnosis, you need to be able to eliminate all the other things it could be. This kid could have a brain tumor," the doctor said. "You have to know you're not dealing with depression, and you have to know you're not dealing with adjustment reaction, and you have to know you're not dealing with an organic problem of some kind.

"I mean, some of this could be explained by a tumor. Some of this could be explained by a thought disorder, a mood disorder. That's got to be ruled out."

An organic brain disease or a thought disorder as in schizophrenia could have caused a hallucination that took the form of recalled memory. All of those possibilities had to be eliminated before a proper diagnosis could be made, but they weren't, Levy insisted.

■ ■ ■

When the hearing resumed Wednesday morning, October 30, Scarlata called psychologist Nancy Elman to the stand. She explained that she was licensed in Pennsylvania, a ten-year member of the faculty at the University of Pittsburgh, and a part-time private practitioner.

Pitt's counseling psychology program was new in 1983,

she said, and the first doctoral degrees were bestowed in 1986.

"Your Honor, so you can appreciate the reason for offering that testimony—"

"I assumed there was one," Manning said to the defense attorney with a note of sarcasm.

"I would pass up to you the curriculum vitae provided to me on Dr. Allan Pass, which indicates that he graduated from the counseling psychology program the year before it began at the University of Pittsburgh."

Scarlata was climbing down into the trenches to slug more mud on the qualifications of Dr. Pass.

He called Arthur J. VanCara, a clinical and consulting psychologist, licensed in Pennsylvania since 1974 and an independent practitioner since 1967. VanCara introduced himself as chairman since 1978 of the Committee on Ethical Standards and Professional Conduct with the Greater Pittsburgh Psychological Association. VanCara had been involved in licensing matters at the state level and was a member of a legislative committee that helped create Pennsylvania's first licensing law for psychologists.

"If someone were asked to assess an individual during an interview in an effort to ascertain whether or not his recall fifteen years after an event was consistent with symptoms of posttraumatic stress disorder, what would that person be doing?"

"I would say he would be practicing psychology," VanCara said.

"Is it within the bounds of propriety to represent yourself as a psychologist when you are not a psychologist?"

"No. In fact, it's illegal under the law, under the Practice Act."

"Is it appropriate to represent that one is a graduate of

Pitt in counseling psychology, when the program didn't begin until a year after he shows he graduated from it?"

"No. Under the title provision of the Psychologists' Practice Act, one is not allowed to use the terms psychologist or psychological or psychology in their title in any way. In his vitae, he uses it in several places . . . and those are all misrepresentations and would be in violation of the Practice Act."

VanCara said the ethics committee and state licensing authorities warned Pass about holding himself out as a psychologist. The warnings came after Pass participated in a prominent case in neighboring Butler County. Also, VanCara called Pass to deliver a similar warning after reading a newspaper article describing Pass as a psychologist.

Scarlata turned the witness over to Clark, who now had to salvage something of Pass's credibility.

Under her questioning, VanCara acknowledged that at the time Pass began his career in psychology, the state system allowed people with his credentials who worked in state hospitals and prisons to practice psychology and call themselves psychologists even though their formal training was limited and they did not possess all of the qualifications that were later required.

"There were no criteria in those days for entry to the career ladder of psychology," the witness said. "That has been changed in the state hospital system. I am not sure about the correctional system."

So, Pass wasn't quite the charlatan Scarlata would have everyone believe.

In fact, under a 1972 law, Pennsylvania would license a person with a master's degree to practice psychology. The law was changed to require a doctoral degree, although the revised law allowed those with only master's degrees who began in practice before 1986 to take the licensing test. The window of opportunity for taking the test under those circumstances closed in the early 1990s.

Clark wanted VanCara to acknowledge that Pass hadn't authored the newspaper article that described him as a psychologist.

"If he were pretending to be—" VanCara began in response to her question.

"Just answer my question," Clark interrupted.

"I will answer your question."

"Now, was that article in the paper authored by Allan Pass?" Clark asked.

"He had the responsibility—"

"Now, just a minute, just a minute," Manning said, losing his patience. The judge didn't seem to think that the time-consuming, contentious testimony about Pass's credentials was of much consequence to the decision he would soon be making about the admissibility of Mudd's flashback memory.

"Answer her question," he ordered VanCara.

"Not that I know of."

Finally Clark got it on the record that Pass, while at the state prison, worked under the direction of a licensed psychologist and therefore didn't need to be licensed himself.

Scarlata, however, wasn't finished hurling mud.

He asked VanCara if he'd ever heard of anybody scoring a 98 percent, as Pass claimed to have done, on the morning portion of the licensing exam, the more difficult part of the day-long test. Pass said that he didn't care to take the second half of the test, and so had no complete test results.

"No, I haven't," VanCara said.

As VanCara stepped down from the witness stand, Scarlata said he was prepared to produce test results for

Pass that "I would respectfully suggest were misrepresented to the court much the same as his qualifications were misrepresented to all of us."

After making the offer, Scarlata called Dr. Michael Moran, a specialist in neuropsychology and developmental psychology who was well known in the courts for his testimony as an expert in other cases. Manning, having grown no more patient with the bashing of Allan Pass, cut Moran off in the midst of his recitation of his credentials.

"Is that necessary? The court's quite familiar with Dr. Moran. In fact, the last time he testified here, he testified for the Commonwealth."

Moran was on the stand to state his conclusions about Mudd's mental condition. He'd reviewed Mudd's testimony at the coroner's inquest, a transcript of Mudd's interview by Pass, and the records of Mudd's therapy at Catholic Charities. Moran refused to dignify Pass by calling him "doctor" and instead referred to him as "guidance counselor Pass."

Moran said Mudd did not suffer from posttraumatic stress disorder because the boy suffered no trauma. He cited Mudd's statements that he didn't know that his father was dead and he remembered his mother being calm after the shots were fired.

"In spring of 1976, John Mudd Jr. and Arlene were evaluated by a clinical psychologist," Moran continued. "The report includes information that his childhood at home was kind of a sustained trauma and the home life was very unstable. His mother said she became pregnant in high school. She dropped out. Her father did not like her husband. The marriage was remarkable for instability and infidelity by both partners for some time.

"John Mudd Jr. was neglected in other ways. He frequently would arise while his mother was still in bed and would have to make his own breakfast. About six months prior to the incident, he . . . almost drowned because he was taking a bath alone. At age two, he was scalded severely by boiling hot water and spent ten days in an oxygen tent in the hospital. Also, his health was neglected. He needed extensive dental work. His mouth was in pretty bad shape."

All of those circumstances can be traumatic for a child, but none of them are sufficient to trigger posttraumatic stress disorder, Moran said.

He concluded that Mudd's memory for recent events was unstable and unreliable.

For example, he said, Mudd testified at the coroner's inquest that he was going to strike Spinola with the chair but decided at the last instant not to. In the taped interview with Pass, Mudd said he did strike Spinola with the chair.

"So now, if his memory is so unreliable and unstable for recent events, it calls into question the stability of his memory for events when he was age five," Moran said.

The high pitch of Mudd's voice as he described his visions could indicate nothing more than the emotionally charged nature of the experience, not necessarily posttraumatic stress disorder, he said.

Mudd's memories of his father's murder very well could be an amalgam of things he witnessed directly, things he learned by overhearing other people talk, and things conjured by his own fears and anxieties. Things suggested to him under hypnosis could have been incorporated into his memories, if he was hypnotized, as Scarlata contended.

Then there's the matter of young Mudd vowing revenge against the "Steve" whom he somehow knew had killed his father.

The comments were absolutely not consistent with posttraumatic stress disorder, Moran said.

"If it would be a posttraumatic stress disorder, then he would have repressed all of this material, and he would have shown avoidance behavior.

"One of the really outstanding symptoms of childhood posttraumatic stress disorder is a pervasive giving up on the future, not planning for the future, having no goals. So this was clearly not the case with John Mudd Jr."

True posttraumatic stress disorder symptoms would have shown themselves immediately and would have persisted throughout the years that followed the murder, he said.

Other indications appear in the record to suggest that whatever emotional turmoil may have afflicted the unfortunate boy, it wasn't textbook posttraumatic stress disorder.

"Prior to the age of seven, children don't really grasp the concept of death," Moran said. "They don't grasp the universality, the inevitability, or the finality of death.

"And in therapy, John really couldn't have been traumatized by his father's death because he didn't believe he was dead. When the therapist said 'Your father is dead,' he said 'Yes, I think he's in New York. Do you think he's in New York?' So he really didn't grasp the concept of the finality of death."

Learning in later life that one's father had been murdered years earlier would not be enough to trigger the onset of posttraumatic stress disorder, he said.

"The recall? I don't know what to make of it except that I don't think it's reliable. The flashback memory could well be bloated with contaminations such as conversations with relatives, so that I don't consider it to be reliable."

Moran then pronounced his conclusion in words that Scarlata might have authored himself. "John Mudd Jr. would not have been a reliable witness at age five. The opinion is that we know for a fact that his memory of recent events is unstable. And two, he has testified that, in effect, he regressed to age five in memory. If his memory was unstable and he would not have made a reliable witness at that time, with all the passage of years and with discussions of what happened and all, his memory now would even be more unreliable."

Then, to drive in the stake further, Scarlata had Moran expound on his knowledge of Pass's qualifications. Pass was a student of Moran's in the 1970s in a two-tiered program in developmental psychology. The first thirty credits led to a master of science degree, after which the student applied for admission to the second component. An additional 30 credits led to certification in Pennsylvania as a school psychologist. Pass completed the master's program, applied for admission to the certification program but was rejected.

Moran said he called Pass a guidance counselor because he earned a Ph.D. in 1982 at Pitt in educational guidance and counseling. In 1982, Pitt did not offer degrees in counseling psychology, which the uninitiated might infer was the degree Pass held. When Pass had recited his credentials on the witness stand, he said he had a Ph.D. from Pitt in counseling. He didn't make the distinction between educational guidance and counseling and psychological counseling.

The educational guidance counseling program prepares professionals who will work in public schools, helping young people plan their futures and deal with personal problems. Counseling psychology is a program designed to produce psychologists, and "I believe Dr.

Pass is not a licensed psychologist in the state of Pennsylvania," Moran said.

On cross-examination, Clark didn't even try to shake Moran on the significance of Pass's doctoral degree. She confined her questions to Moran's conclusions about Mudd's memory and state of mind.

As evidence that Mudd's memory of recent events was faulty, Moran had cited Mudd's conflicting statements about whether he actually hit Spinola with the chair. On the tape of the interview with Pass, he said he did hit him. But Clark was able to establish through Moran's testimony that Mudd reviewed a typed transcript of the interview and pointed out his error about the chair.

She also recalled testimony from the police that when they arrived at the Mudd home, John Jr. was screaming as Arlene held him.

Moran, however, held fast to his major conclusion. "There is no evidence of delayed onset of posttraumatic stress disorder. It seems to me that what he's claiming is that there was a resolution of a post-traumatic stress disorder when he had the flashback.

"I don't know why he was screaming at the time, as you say, when the police came and said to the mother the father was dead. If he didn't have the capacity to grasp the concept of death, why was he hysterical?" the witness asked the prosecutor.

At that moment, Clark let her guard down. She answered the question. "Well, the only way we would know that is if fifteen or sixteen years ago, we could have asked the child why he was screaming or crying. But I don't think anybody did. But screaming and crying by a child usually indicates some type of fight or discomfort. Well, crying usually indicated discomfort. Screaming indicates a little more than that. I would submit that it's an inference of some type of fright or perhaps a little bit of terror, him maybe being concerned because his mother is upset and his father is not moving on that floor. I don't know."

It was a delicious opportunity for Scarlata.

"If the court please," he said with a tone of restrained impatience. "Miss Clark is arguing with the witness."

"It sounds like a closing argument to me," Manning said.

"He asked me the question. I can't answer that. I don't know."

"That's not the normal course of business for the witness to ask you a question and you answer," the judge said.

Clark was losing control of her cross-examination. Instead of dropping the subject, she continued trying to justify herself.

"I don't know. You're more qualified to even possibly answer that than I am," she said.

If Clark wasn't going to let up, neither was Scarlata.

"Furthermore," he intoned, "I think the burden is on the Commonwealth to provide that information in a fashion other than Miss Clark's speculation."

"I'm not providing anything. I don't know," she said in a moment of petulance that immediately led to the mental equivalent of a computer locking up.

"Dr. Moran, I guess what I'm asking you, I don't know if we're quite understanding each other. I think, kind of, but not quite. It's clear, at least I would assume it's clear, from the records of the . . ."

She was babbling.

"Look, start over," Manning said. "Let's ask a question."

"I am," Clark said.

Somehow she settled herself and asked several coher-

ent questions, but none of them gained any ground
against Moran's position that Mudd suffered no trauma
worthy of a diagnosis of posttraumatic stress disorder.

On redirect examination, Scarlata wrapped up the
questioning with another exchange that couldn't have
been scripted more effectively. "Is there any reason to
believe what the boy has to say at this point?"

"Not that I can see."

"That, of course, is your judgment of his credibility,
not his competence as a witness," Manning said.

"His competency to remember accurately is clearly in
question to me. If he were competent to remember accurately, there would not be inconsistencies in his reporting
of his recollections. And yet, there clearly are inconsistencies, not only in distant memory but in recent memory,"
Moran replied.

Manning asked Moran about the case in California
where Eileen Franklin Lipsker said she experienced a
flashback that led her to testify about allegedly watching
her father kill her best friend more than twenty years
earlier.

"The child witnessed the killing of another person and
witnessed a violent act and then was threatened with the
same kind of violence by the perpetrator. That is clearly
traumatic," said Moran, who got in the final word before
they broke for lunch: In the realm of criminal evidence,
Mudd's memory couldn't hold a candle to Lipsker's.

When Manning reconvened the hearing, Scarlata announced that he had subpoenaed the state board of licen-
sure in Harrisburg and during the lunch break had spoken
with one of its representatives.

"Don't you think you've done enough damage to Dr.
Pass?" Manning asked.

Scarlata, not the least bit ashamed of his attack on the

prosecution's expert witness, said, "I would like to just frost the cake if I might."

"Or guild the lily," said Manning.

The woman with whom Scarlata had spoken could find no record of the existence of Dr. Pass and no record of him having applied or submitted an application to sit for the licensing exam, let alone any record of him scoring a 98 on the hard part.

"How far back did they go?" asked Clark.

"They went back to the beginning, the creation of the board."

"Does the memory of man run?" Manning quipped.

Clark threw in the towel on the issue. She agreed to let Scarlata enter the evidence uncontested. Manning readily approved, having already begun to think about an issue that mattered much more.

Over lunch, he'd studied a treatise on posttraumatic stress disorder. He was most interested in understanding trauma.

Manning learned that the generic meaning of the phrase encompasses all insult to the personality but does not necessarily involve a threat to life or limb. Divorce, death of a loved one, loss of a job, or bankruptcy can be considered traumatic. The term also encompasses any disruption of family life that affects the development of a child.

Among the examples cited in the writing was "seeing another person who is mutilated, dying or dead, or the victim of physical violence," the judge said.

Scarlata's next words demonstrated one of the important tools of the legal profession, an unblinking willingness to argue to the contrary, no matter how clear and persuasive are the facts and testimony presented by the opposition.

"It seems to me there is nothing inconsistent with what you just read and what the psychologists testified to," he said without blushing.

"Except no one said seeing someone dead constituted a sufficient stress," Manning answered.

"Judge, I'm not sure that says—"

Manning cut him off. He gave last call for testimony, exhibits, and motions.

Clark said she wanted to enter into the record a letter from VanCara to the state Bureau of Occupational and Professional Affairs in which he claimed Pass had misrepresented his credentials. She submitted it as evidence undermining VanCara's claim that he was not the person who initiated a state investigation of Pass's qualifications.

Scarlata said VanCara had denied filing the complaint against Pass and offered to read the letter into evidence. Clark objected. It was her evidence, and she didn't trust Scarlata to read the whole thing.

The judge spoke as a parent might to two children squabbling about who was throwing dirty looks at whom. "Why don't you just mark it, and we'll admit it, and I'll read it. At the appropriate time, he can read whatever he feels is appropriate, and you can read whatever, and everybody can go to sleep while the two of you read to everybody."

On that peevish note, the record was closed on Scarlata's motion to declare John Mudd Jr. incompetent to testify. Manning began to ruminate aloud and in that way signaled that the lamp was lit for closing arguments.

Generally the burden of demonstrating that a witness is incompetent rests with those who assert the witness is incompetent, he said. That burden is one of clear and convincing evidence. Regarding witnesses under age fourteen, the burden shifts to the proponent of the testimony, who must demonstrate three things. The witness must have the capacity to communicate, meaning the witness can understand the questions and frame intelligent answers. The witness must be conscious of the duty to tell the truth. Also, the witness must have the capacity to remember the event at issue and relate the memory.

"Mr. Mudd clearly satisfies the first two prongs of the test, that he has the capacity to communicate and the cognizance to the truth," the judge said.

The sticky issue was whether Mudd had the capacity to remember the event, whether the memory that flashed before his eyes in late November 1990 was an authentic recollection of things he'd seen and heard with his own eyes or whether it was something else.

"The truth," Scarlata offered, "is this twenty-one-year-old's mind can only be truthful, even though he believes it is, if it was true back when he was five years old. And the only way the Commonwealth, who has the burden of proving his competence—"

Manning interrupted again. "That's a major issue here because they have the burden of satisfying the court that he is competent if the court has to view him as a five-and-a-half-year-old. But if he sits here as a twenty-one-year-old, they don't have that burden. Then the burden is on your side of the case, Mr. Scarlata, to prove that he is incompetent. I want to raise that issue at the outset because it may well prevail."

Perhaps more for his own benefit than anyone else's, Manning then recited the major elements of the opposing arguments.

"Having defined the issue," Scarlata jumped in, "I move to strike the testimony of Dr. Allan Pass for a multitude of reasons. In addition to the fact that his testimony demonstrated his incompetence, his deceit further supports the conclusion that he's a charlatan. He lied about his qualifications. He lied about what he did on the—"

"Let's say he apparently embellished," the judge said, offering a generous hand to Pass before slapping Scarlata down with his other hand.

"He sat on the witness stand and said he had a 98 percent on the first part of the licensing exam . . ."

"I'm not going to strike his testimony," Manning said, "because if I strike his testimony and then I rule against you, then you have nothing to argue on appeal, do you, sir?"

If someone had to tell Scarlata how to conduct the defense case, Manning seemed perfectly willing to be that person. "You're going to argue the appropriate weight that should be given to his testimony, and that's what I'll consider, but the motion to strike his testimony is denied."

"It should be given no weight, whatsoever. Now," Scarlata said, "trying to take the matters the way you raised them . . ."

"You can take them any way you want them," Manning said.

At least Scarlata's brain didn't flame out. Maybe he'd had more experience in being pushed around by the judges before whom he argued.

"I think that the issue that we need to deal with primarily is, what are we talking about?" the defense attorney said. "Are we talking about John Mudd as a twenty-one-year-old, or are we talking about him as a five-year-old? The record here before the court only makes sense in the context of the flashbulb memory if we're talking about him as a five-year-old. The fact that he may have had a sudden recall of something does not legitimize, strengthen, or make any different the impairments or impediments which might have existed in his memory, his ability to observe, his ability to store, his ability to segregate that from fantasy, anger, and all those other emotions back when he was a five-year-old.

"So my posting is that in the first instance, the burden is on the Commonwealth. Really, what he's saying is 'I remember in my vision me as a five-year-old making these observations.' He's not saying 'I know because I remember all this stuff that happened fifteen years ago' like you might say fifteen years ago when I was in law school and such and such happened. He's saying 'I had no recollection whatsoever of this, and now I have this vision in my mind of myself as a five-year-old and in that vision, this is what I see.'"

Alex Levy had said that seeing a body was not traumatic enough to trigger posttraumatic stress disorder in Mudd. Moran had said that seeing a body could trigger trauma, but that there was no evidence it did for Mudd.

Psychology textbooks say the experience that produces posttraumatic stress disorder must be markedly distressing to almost anyone and is usually accompanied by intense fear, terror, and helplessness, none of which are in evidence, Scarlata argued.

"Markedly distressing to almost anyone, I think, is nothing more than distinguishing from the mundane," Manning said. "If it's not markedly distressing to almost anyone, then it's a meaningless event."

"But you have examples in front of you . . ."

"A dead body should be markedly distressing to almost anyone."

"May or may not be."

"Maybe not if it's the coroner or the undertaker. It may be pleasing to them."

"The question is, what constitutes markedly distressing and what was John Mudd's perception of markedly distressing?" Scarlata asked, hoping Manning would give him enough air time to deliver a complete package of thoughts.

"His ability to recall at the time it happened belies the fact that it was markedly distressing. His conversation with his psychologist at the time belies and negates the fact that it was markedly distressing. His ability to say 'I'm going to kill Steve when I get to be twenty-one' undercuts the fact that it was markedly distressing," Scarlata continued.

"The conclusions of the psychologist who examined him undercut anybody's ability to conclude that it was markedly distressing, and so does his own testimony from the witness stand in this court, in this hearing that 'I did not understand what happened to my dad when I saw him at the bottom of the stairs.'

"I asked him 'Did you know he was dead?' 'No, I didn't.' 'Did you see any blood?' 'No, I didn't.' 'Did you have any kind of a fearful reaction?' 'No, I didn't.' 'Did the man who came out of the basement threaten you?' 'No, he didn't.' 'What was your mother's reaction at the time?' 'Calm, cool, and collected.' 'The man had a conversation with your mother. Was there anything distressing about the conversation?' 'No, there wasn't.'

"And he concluded by saying 'As a matter of fact, I didn't find out my dad was dead until some time long after that and didn't find out he had been murdered until almost two years after that,' which is also inconsistent, obviously, with the psychological report, with the report that he gave to Detective Kelly the first time he interviewed him when he said he learned his dad was dead when he was on the couch of the person whose home he was taken to.

"So if you approach it from the markedly distressing issue, it just isn't that," Scarlata said.

He was on a roll.

"There are also contradictions in the record to his having experienced a posttraumatic stress disorder. The one that comes to mind and was clearly testified to by both people, yet ignored by Dr. Pass, is the foreshortened future.

"The Commonwealth has also suggested that the fact that John might have been crying when the police came indicates posttraumatic stress disorder. There are a thousand reasons why a young child might be screaming, not the least of which would be observing his mother's distress under the circumstances.

"Even if he was distressed . . . the fact that two weeks later, three weeks later, when he's seeing the psychologist undercuts the theory that that caused the repression, because he's talking about it. So if he's talking about it, it's not repressed.

"Dr. Moran said he was not competent when he was five years old."

The mention of Moran's conclusion brought Manning back to life.

"I don't see how Dr. Moran or anybody else can say whether someone was competent fifteen years ago, having never examined them or talked to them. And competence again, of course, is a legal conclusion. It falls on those three basic things that I mentioned at the outset."

"John Mudd Jr.'s troubled youth," Scarlata said, "does not mean that he meets the test necessary to document and demonstrate his competency then or now."

"No. No," the judge corrected him. "The problem is that if he were five years old, we would bring him in here, we would set him on the stand, we would ask him if he understood what the oath was, what it meant to tell the truth and a lie. That would establish that. Either he understands or he doesn't. Then we'd test his ability to communicate, and lastly he'd be asked about the events. We'd determine whether he has a recollection.

"The only way I ever know it to be done is to take the witness as the witness is at the time the witness testifies, not having someone say 'Well, he might have done it when he was five and a half, or no, he couldn't do it when he was five and a half. That, in my estimation, just has to be rank speculation no matter what Dr. Moran bases it on. It's guessing what happened fifteen years ago," Manning said.

"If that's the test that you choose to apply, it's her burden, and she hasn't satisfied it, because there's no evidence on this record in the Commonwealth's case that he's competent at age five. We can't bring him in here, Judge, as a five-year-old," Scarlata replied.

"Oh, I know, and I don't know that I can place that burden on her because I am not certain that burden is surmountable under any circumstances."

"Maybe it isn't," Scarlata said, "and maybe someone who has this kind of supposed flashback recall shouldn't be allowed to testify in this court. If that's the case, then for whatever reason, I'm sorry, but maybe a murder that was committed can't be solved."

Having listened from the sidelines, Clark finally weighed in to the debate, although in doing so she raised a diversionary issue and Manning's eyebrow with it.

"What about if at the age of five he testified, and if for some reason, after years and years and years, there was a new trial or at the age of five he was not permitted to testify because he was incompetent?" she said.

"That's precisely the case we have here," Scarlata said.

"That's the thing," the judge agreed. "If at the age of five he is incompetent, he would not be able to testify at the age of fifteen or twenty or twenty-five if the reason he was not permitted to testify at the age of five was because of any one of those three things."

"Not in a case where we're talking about a flashback memory, your Honor," Clark said. "Suppose we didn't put him on the stand when he was five because we felt he was incompetent, and now for some odd reason fifteen years later the defendant gets a new trial and now this person, even three years afterwards, is competent. It's different. We didn't put him on then because we knew—"

"You put the rope around your own neck when you say 'We determined he wasn't competent.' If you do that unilaterally, I think you're always stuck with that position," the judge said, being an equal opportunity interrupter.

"I don't know," Clark countered, her confidence returned. "Sometimes in cases, police wait to file charges because we know the witness saw something but was so young. They might wait a couple of years or a few months before they actually go back and interview that person."

"I haven't heard of that. That would be real interesting the first time that comes up," Manning said.

Oops! It may have occurred to Clark just then that she probably didn't want to be the lowly assistant district attorney who first brought such a case before this particular judge.

"Judge, the data on this record would not support a conclusion that he was competent back then, and if she's got the burden, she's got to go forward with it. That just simply didn't happen here," Scarlata said.

"What if she doesn't have the burden?" Manning asked.

"I don't believe . . ." the defense attorney began to say.

"I'll ask it this way," the judge said to Scarlata. "What if the court said you did? Why, in addition to your motion, didn't you seek to have Dr. Moran psychoanalyze Mr. Mudd?"

"I don't have the burden. Secondly, to psychoanalyze him today I'm not sure is going to tell me anything. I'd need to have him psychoanalyzed when he's five years old, and I can't do that.

"I don't know what viable data I can get from psychoanalyzing somebody who's twenty-one years old about what was his mental state when he was five years old.

"Why didn't the Commonwealth have him examined? I'll throw the question back to you," Scarlata asked.

"I assume they thought they did," the judge said.

"The last prong of the test is," Scarlata said, "the Commonwealth, I would suggest, has to establish that he's aware of what had happened, and they fail miserably in that regard also for the reason that his testimony at the coroner's inquest, at the time he was interviewed by the police, at the time he was interviewed by Dr. Pass and at the time he sat on this witness stand, is absolutely inconsistent in many of its material particulars.

"He's got the sequencing wrong consistent with a negative diagnosis of posttraumatic stress disorder. He reports on one occasion that he hit the kid with a chair. He reports to his uncle apparently that when the man came out of the basement, he kissed his mother. When he testified, that didn't happen, he didn't kiss his mother.

"I can go on with a whole litany of inconsistencies in his testimony, but all of that goes to his five-year-old, not his twenty-one-year-old, ability to have observed and recalled fifteen years later the facts in an accurate fashion not infected by fantasy, anger, fear, suggestion, or any of the other normal kinds of things that infect human memory."

"If he were five," Manning said, "we'd use his statements as a witness to determine whether or not he did observe and did remember and could recall and so state.

"The fact is that the Commonwealth elected to file this case, and they have to convince the court that he would have been able to say and give the right answers back when he was five years old. Even if I have the burden, all of the evidence that you have in front of you is consistent with the fact that he couldn't.

"While you might not strike the testimony of Dr. Pass, I would suggest it is absolutely unworthy of belief. I have never been in a courtroom and had a professional misrepresent his qualifications to a court. I have never been in a courtroom and had somebody so blatantly mischaracterize his ability to give testimony."

"His testimony may be incredible, but standing alone, I don't see how it's incompetent," the judge said.

"Unless the court is to say that he's just absolutely lying about this, and that he did have a memory or that he never had any memory, he never saw anything and he's just coming in here and lying and making that up . . ." Clark said.

"Well," Manning said, "if there's credibility to the portion of the report that says that as a young child he formulated the intention to get Steven Slutzker when he's twenty-one or kill him when he's twenty-one . . ."

"Because he murdered his dad," Clark said.

"The timing isn't all that far off," Manning said.

"But this is different than killing him, I would submit."

"Some might argue it's worse," Scarlata said.

"Well, I mean, but then . . . does that mean that he

didn't have the mental capacity to observe and understand and remember what went on when he was five years old? If that would be true and that he didn't repress anything, then I guess he did have the mental capacity to observe and remember," the prosecutor said.

It was her turn to expound.

"Now, I would submit that there is evidence of this type of trauma that would cause posttraumatic stress disorder irrespective of what anyone says about it. I would submit that seeing what he observed, which even if he only saw that body—that view, that photograph which Officer Labella testified is what they essentially saw when they all looked down the steps—that that would be markedly distressing to almost anyone. I think it would be markedly distressing to me, and I'm not a five-and-a-half-year-old.

"He could at least comprehend that something serious had happened to his father. The child, according to Sergeant Labella, was pretty hysterical. He wasn't just crying. I'm not sure five-and-a-half-year-olds have colic. He was there when his mother said 'my husband was shot. He's at the bottom of the stairs.'

"And say what you will about Dr. Pass," Clark continued.

"I'm not saying anything about Dr. Pass," Manning said.

"Well, Dr. Pass has worked eighteen years or so at the state correctional institution at Pittsburgh and as such with his educational background, he need not be licensed. He did not testify that he was licensed to practice psychology in Pennsylvania, and he worked for many years, though, in that capacity, as he was authorized by law to do.

"He was the only one who actually talked to John Mudd Jr. and saw him and heard him—"

"The basic principle," Manning said, "is that the credibility of the witness is within the sole province of the jury. Expert opinion testimony is proper only where the formation of the opinion on the subject requires knowledge, information, or skill beyond that possessed by the ordinary juror and is an encroachment on the jury's province to permit admission of expert testimony on the issue of a witness's credibility."

"That's correct," Clark said, not realizing that the judge hadn't finished his thought. "And I think these issues . . ."

". . . That, it would seem, in this case is more damaging to the defense than it is to the Commonwealth.

"I didn't view him as a five-and-a-half-year-old. That determination about whether he would have been competent at age five and a half was not made, and in my considered opinion it cannot be made. It's impossible," the judge concluded.

"It cannot," Clark said bravely.

"The question is whether the Commonwealth bears the burden of an impossibility," Manning added.

"I would submit that we do not, and I think that's the turning point. And I submit that that goes to the credibility of the witness, but not to the competency," she said.

"What we do know, Judge, is that if the Commonwealth genuinely believed it did not have the burden of proving his competence as a five-year-old, the need to call Dr. Pass vanishes," Scarlata said.

"Not necessarily. He could have been forty-five recalling things that occurred when he was thirty, fifteen years later," Clark said.

"I assume she did it in this hearing because I did not

say at the outset, and I still am not certain of, who does bear the burden in this matter. That may well be the whole issue here. It may decide the whole matter," Manning said.

With those words, the judge thanked the two attorneys and closed the discussion on Scarlata's first motion. He called for the testimony on the second motion, in which the defense wanted the court to prohibit Edgewood's Tim Brendlinger from saying he recognized Slutzker from the newspaper photograph as the man he saw talking to Arlene minutes after the murder.

Brendlinger, who by then had been with Edgewood police for nearly twenty years, took the stand and recounted the episode.

He said that when he and his partner arrived at the Mudd home he did not ask Arlene whom she had been talking to.

Brendlinger said he did not inform Wilkinsburg police, immediately but some time later in the evening he did report seeing Arlene and the man. Several days later he saw Slutzker's photograph in a newspaper and realized he was the man who had been talking to Arlene and he so informed Wilkinsburg police.

"There were street lights. It was a well-lit street."

"Are you sure?" Clark asked.

"Yes, I'm sure," Brendlinger said.

When asked to identify the man, the officer pointed at Slutzker, who had been brought to court for the purpose and sat near the door wearing a brown suit jacket and light gray or blue slacks.

Scarlata was asking what response Brendlinger got from the Wilkinsburg police when Manning interjected.

"Mr. Scarlata, I'm having some difficulty figuring out how this is a motion to suppress."

"The identification is tainted as a result of his seeing that photograph."

"He sees a photograph in a newspaper. There is no police action there to which the exclusionary rule would apply. This isn't a subject for a motion to suppress," Manning said.

The exclusionary rule is not a law but rather a rule of criminal procedure intended to deter police misconduct. Say, for example, a police officer were to drive a rape victim through a low-income housing project, pointing to one tall black man after another and asking the victim, "Is that the man?" The woman may say "Yes. That's the man who raped me." The exclusionary rule says the identification is faulty because the officer singled out one individual at a time for the victim to consider.

Scarlata argued that the same fault existed with Brendlinger's identification of Slutzker. The only problem was, Brendlinger was casually looking through the newspaper when he came across the photo. In the context of the exclusionary rule, Brendlinger just as well could have spotted Slutzker at a hot dog stand at Three Rivers Stadium.

"Is he subject to different rules than regular citizens just because he's a police officer?" Scarlata asked.

"So he's a police officer? What if he's a regular citizen? He sees a photo in a newspaper and says, 'Hey, that's the guy I saw.' That's not the subject for a motion to suppress."

"Then rule against me. The theory of the motion is—" Scarlata began.

"If a police officer had come to him," Manning said, "and handed him a photograph and said 'Is this the man you saw with Arlene Mudd,' one single photograph, there would clearly be an argument for suppression. But Brendlinger, perchance, seeing a photo of the defendant in the paper isn't a reason to suppress his testimony."

Scarlata continued defending his motion. The circumstances were suggestive enough, he said, to taint the identification.

"You certainly have the opportunity to argue that issue to the jury, but as a matter of law, I know of no theory upon which the court would suppress the evidence," the judge said, and denied the motion to suppress regarding Brendlinger.

Manning said he would rule at 9:30 a.m. the next day, October 31, on the competency of John Mudd Jr.

The next morning, before Manning began delivering his opinion, Scarlata reported a disturbing new wrinkle in the case. Clark had come to him and reported that one of the friends who'd been with Mudd during the flashback had claimed to have heard Mudd discuss the circumstances of his father's death—well before the recollection. Joe Altman was the source of the new detail.

In addition, Scarlata said, Altman's mother had been distraught over the treatment her son received from the detectives assigned to the Mudd case. Altman had raised the new information during an interview in the district attorney's office. Altman's account was a torpedo that potentially could explode the prosecution's contention that Mudd's flashback was legitimate and accurate. Upon hearing Altman's statement to Clark, one of the detectives took him from the interview room and yelled at the boy and threatened him. Mrs. Altman, who witnessed the incident, was moved to consult an attorney.

Scarlata proposed reopening the hearing record to explore the matter.

"It also might border on prosecutorial misconduct," he said.

"Everything that Mr. Scarlata has alleged here is hearsay upon hearsay upon hearsay," Clark protested.

Manning wanted to get to the heart of the matter.

"Let's strip that away," he said. "Let's forget about that for a moment, the hearsay upon hearsay, and get back to the first thing that Mr. Scarlata says, and that is that you informed him that there is a witness who will say that . . ."

"I'm not sure what the witness will say," she said with an urgency that betrayed her desire to nip this thing in the bud.

"This is what I told Mr. Scarlata," she said.

During her interview with Altman, Clark had asked him to read a transcript, prepared by Detective Kelly, of Altman's previous interview with Kelly. Altman marked several items in the transcript.

"One was Kelly's question of whether he'd ever heard John Mudd Jr. talk about his father's death before the flashback, and his answer to Detective Kelly was in fact 'no.' "

"Well, what did Altman say? Did Altman say that that was incorrect?

"No," Clark said. "He said that's what he told Detective Kelly, but now he thinks that he overheard a conversation . . ."

Manning cut her short.

"All right. I've heard enough. Where is Mr. Altman?"

"He's under subpoena, but he's not here today."

"Get him here. We'll reopen the record. We'll hear it."

After a recess, the eighteen-year-old Shaler Area High School student was sworn in and took the stand. Under questioning by Scarlata, Altman said he'd been with Mudd many times before November 23.

"I overheard some things, like he knows, he knew his father was killed and he supposedly witnessed it."

"Did he mention who did it?"

"No."

"Did he say anything beyond that about the circumstances of his father's death?"

"Nothing that I can be sure of."

"After you made that disclosure to Miss Clark, what occurred?"

"Well, we left the room, and the detective came, and we went up into another room. He was saying I changed the statement and he was like raising his voice."

"Did you change your statement?"

"I didn't change it. When he came to the house, he didn't ask any details."

"In the statement, he says you told him you could not be certain whether John ever talked about his father's death. Did you say that to him?"

"I don't recall that, but I know he said like things about his father's death. The details, I don't know."

"He also recorded that you said you could not be sure but you didn't think that he said anything about his father. Did you tell him that when he interviewed you in April, or did you tell him what you just said from the witness stand?"

"It's hard to remember. I know I knew things before, and when he came to the house, I was scared, so I don't know. Maybe that had some influence on it."

"But your recollection today as you sit on the witness stand is that you were present on one or two occasions when John did talk about the death of his father and indicated that he had witnessed that death?"

"Yes."

"Objection," Clark said. "That's not what he said. He

said John said he *supposedly* witnessed the death. There's a difference.

"Supposedly. I don't know. Maybe he heard it from his family. I'm just saying he's talked about it," Altman said.

"Did he tell you how he knew about his father's death?"

"No."

"Objection," Clark said. "His testimony is that John didn't tell him anything. He overheard the conversation."

"I understand that."

The circumstances, Clark said, were that Altman overheard Mudd talking to Kim Altman.

"Did Kim ask him any questions about what he was talking about?" Scarlata asked.

"Not that I know of. I mean, I didn't pay attention."

Clark recited several examples of the questions Kelly asked during the April interview at the Altman home.

"Yes, but he didn't take notes until I said I heard things before," the witness said.

"Are you saying that you told Detective Kelly that you heard things previously?"

"I said I heard things and like not details. I couldn't be sure of the details or anything, but I heard."

Clark refreshed Altman's memory of her interview with him in the DA's office. Detective Torbin sat in. Kelly was not present at first. When Altman dropped the news, she asked him to read the transcript of his earlier interview with Kelly, then she asked Altman to sit in the waiting room until Kelly arrived to talk to him.

"How loud was Detective Kelly's voice?" Clark asked.

"Miss Clark, that may all well be interesting, but I don't see that it's dispositive of anything that I have to decide here," Manning said.

"That's why I didn't inquire into it," Scarlata piped up.

"Mr. Scarlata made an accusation of prosecutorial misconduct, so I would like to—"

"As I see it, you've met your obligation of informing him of the potentially exculpatory information. Therefore, I see no evidence of prosecutorial misconduct."

With a sigh of relief, Clark resumed questioning Altman.

"Did Detective Kelly try to influence you to testify one way or another?"

"I don't know. I'm not a detective. He was saying like —because I didn't even want to be here for any of this, but I am, and he was saying if I change my statement, that I'm going to end up on the front page of the news."

"Well, that's not exactly what he said to you."

"That's what it was."

"Didn't he in fact tell you that this was a very serious matter and he had to be sure of what your statements were?"

"Yes."

"And that, in fact, as you said, that he knew that you were reluctant to be a witness in the case because of publicity and otherwise? Is that correct?"

"Yes."

"And did he ask you to be sure that you weren't changing your statement because maybe I wouldn't call you as a witness? Did he also tell you that? Did he ask you if that was the reason that you were changing your statement, that you thought if you changed your statement, that I would not call you as a witness?"

"No," Altman said.

"Didn't he also tell you that he assured you that I would have to tell Mr. Scarlata about the changes in your statement and therefore Mr. Scarlata would probably call you as a witness, so it wouldn't make any difference as to

what you said one way or the other, that somebody would
call you as a witness in this case?"

"No."

"You don't remember him saying that?"

"Nope."

Scarlata had only two questions. He wanted to know if
Altman changed his story out of any desire not to be involved in the case, to which the young man said no, and
whether he was telling the truth, to which he said yes.

Kim Altman took the stand.

"Did John Mudd ever talk about his father's death?"
Clark asked.

"All he ever said was that his father was killed when he
was young. That's all I can remember."

In response to a question from Scarlata, Miss Altman
said she could not remember telling Detective Kelly in an
interview that she had heard Mudd say that his father was
killed and that a man named Steve had done it. Nor did
she now remember telling Kelly that her boyfriend had
mentioned Steve in that context several times.

Clark was tempted just then to call Mudd to the stand,
but she thought better of it and called Kelly instead.

Kelly said Altman looked over the interview transcript,
took exception to the material at issue but agreed, after a
moment of hesitation, that he'd said it just that way to
Kelly.

"Did he state then, last Thursday, his recollection was
a little bit different?"

"Basically, yes."

Kelly said he asked Altman in the DA's waiting room
why he hadn't come forth during their first interview with
the things he'd heard Mudd say about his father.

"He stated that I didn't ask him specific enough questions."

"What questions did you ask him?"

"I asked him if he had ever heard John Mudd Jr. talk about his father's death before."

"That's what you asked him?"

"Yes."

"That's one of the questions that he said was not specific enough?"

"Yes."

On cross-examination, Scarlata got Kelly to acknowledge that Kim Altman had told him she'd heard Mudd say, perhaps several times, that his father had been murdered when John Jr. was five years old and that he thought a fellow named Steve had done it.

Building on the new testimony, the defense attorney argued to Manning that the prosecution's theory about the flashback was coming undone.

"The threshold question is who has the burden to prove a witness competent or incompetent," the judge said, framing the big picture much as it was before the court knew about Altman's shuckin' and jivin'.

Without saying so, Manning was waving off the Altman incident as inconsequential. The announcement of his decision was beginning.

A case titled *Rosche v. McCoy* had established that the prosecution has the burden of demonstrating that a witness under age fourteen understands the oath and its significance, has the ability to communicate, and has the mental capacity to observe the occurrence and remember it. Witnesses over age fourteen are presumed to be competent. Any party who claims otherwise has the burden of proving that the witness is not competent.

"The defense argues very persuasively that the court should impose upon the Commonwealth the burden of establishing John Mudd Jr.'s competence as a child. In that context, the Commonwealth would be required to establish John Mudd Jr.'s mental capacity at age five and a half, what he was like in fact fifteen years ago relative to his ability to communicate, understand the oath and observe and recollect. That task would be impossible."

Up to that point, the noises coming from the bench had every characteristic of a defeat for Scarlata, but then Manning gave the defense attorney reason to hope.

"Under the unique circumstances of this matter, however, the court cannot simply presume the witness to be competent. I feel compelled to apply at least part of the standard required of a child witness to a twenty-one-year-old who seeks for the first time to testify about fifteen-year-old events.

"Competency of a witness to testify, as I understand it, refers specifically to the ability of the witness—when the witness takes the oath—to testify and to articulate events that are within the witness's memory, not the witness's competence or ability at any other time."

Manning said Mudd met all three criteria established in *Rosche v. McCoy.*

"The significant question is whether the witness had the capacity to observe the occurrence fifteen years ago and the present capacity to remember what it was that occurred," the judge said.

"He would have, of necessity, had the capacity at the age of five and a half to observe. It is further clear that in this court's experience that children of five and a half years have a capacity to observe and may or may not have the ability to remember and articulate those remembrances.

"So, the defense has the unenviable and likewise impossible task of demonstrating to the court that John

Mudd Jr. did not have the capacity to observe the occurrence and recall it factually as he is recalling it now."

Manning said he was not sure whether the conflicting expert testimony shed any useful light on the central issue.

"Posttraumatic stress disorder is possible. Maybe it did, maybe it didn't occur. There is a possibility that he is telling the truth, and there is a possibility that he is not."

There's no question that a witness can be so unbelievable as to be incompetent to testify, but that was not the case with Mudd, he said.

"So, the court concludes that, while the evidence presented on these matters makes the credibility of John Mudd seriously and significantly suspect, it does not establish that he is incompetent to testify as a witness. Whether John Mudd Jr. is to be believed is a matter properly left to the good judgment of the trial jury, and for those reasons, the motion to bar his testimony as incompetent will be denied."

Scarlata, fully understanding his defeat and having no desire to beat a dead horse, asked only that Manning certify the case for immediate appeal.

Clark objected. Sixteen years had passed since the murder. Those sixteen years could grow to eighteen by the time the appeal ran its course if Manning granted Scarlata's request to suspend the case while the defense appealed over Mudd's competence.

"There's no question that this is a novel issue, but all the research that my law clerk and I have done over the past three or four days seems to fall back on the same general conclusion, and that is as I've decided this matter. It is really a matter for a jury to decide. I'm not going to certify the matter for appeal," Manning stated.

Clark had won. She'd cleared a second major hurdle on

the path toward convicting Steven Slutzker. The way was now clear to begin selecting a jury and beginning the trial.

Less than a week later, however, Clark suddenly became ill. She underwent surgery at Suburban General Hospital in Bellevue on November 1. Three days after that, her boss, Christopher Conrad, informed Manning that Clark would need at least thirty days to recover. He asked for a forty-five-day postponement. Scarlata had no objection. Manning set the trial date for January 13, 1992.

The Black Lady and the Bar Stool

Belinda Smith must have thought it a bit strange that the bar stools in her home would be of such interest to the authorities that two county detectives would haul one of them away and snap five Polaroid photos of her kitchen and the stool.

But these weren't just any bar stools, and hers wasn't just any kitchen. Smith lived at 1516 Marlboro Street in Wilkinsburg, the house that Steven Slutzker had sold to her in August 1977.

This was the house where Mudd remembered having lunch with the older neighbor girl, where he remembered sitting with her on tall stools and eating sandwiches.

When Regis Kelly and Detective Gary Tallent arrived at Smith's door on November 7, they were searching for artifacts of the world in 1975 as John Mudd Jr. had remembered it, artifacts that might help convince a jury that Mudd's recollection was real and not a fantasy conjured up just to pin a murder charge on Slutzker.

"Personally, I liked Steve Slutzker," Smith told them.

That made Smith something of a rarity on Marlboro Street in 1977.

"Most of his neighbors didn't like him. They had problems with him," she said. "To be honest, I know for a fact that he had at least four or five offers for this place that were better than mine. I had told him that I really couldn't afford to pay him what the house was worth, but I really liked it."

Lucky for this Postal Service worker, money wasn't the driving force in Steve Slutzker's life at the time.

"So he said, 'Well, give me a bid,' which I did, and like I said, it was lower than the others, but he accepted it. Not only that, but he offered to pay my closing costs.

"See, the neighborhood was all white back then, and I was the first black to move in. Slutzker wanted to get back at his neighbors, that's why he sold it to me. He told me that."

To their credit, the people who lived on Marlboro Street weren't the bigots Slutzker took them for. Smith got a house on the cheap, and she got a home to boot.

Now, about the kitchen and these stools, the detectives said.

After buying the house, Smith replaced the windows, the soffit and fascia, and had a covered patio built off the kitchen door in place of a small concrete slab.

"I understand Steve was supposed to be an electrician," she said. "Well, he must have been some electrician because when I was having work done on the house I had an electrician come in and check the wiring. He told me that whoever wired this place took a lot of shortcuts."

So the wiring was new as well.

"What about the kitchen?" Tallent asked.

The kitchen was exactly the same as when Slutzker had owned the house. The countertop was the same, and the stove and refrigerator were the ones he left. In fact, they were in the same places where he left them. Even the wallpaper and the floor covering were the same.

Great, the detectives thought. This is perfect.

"The only thing I've changed in this kitchen is the stools," she said, nodding toward the three backless wooden stools with black upholstered seats.

Shit.

"What type of stools were at the counter when you purchased the house?" Kelly said.

"They had white vinyl seat covers, and they had plastic backs. I still have one of the old stools in the basement."

The one remaining old stool left with Kelly and Tallent, but not before it had its picture taken.

The two detectives and the prosecutors who sent them in search of bar stools weren't the only people interested in 1516 Marlboro Street in the weeks leading up to the murder trial.

About a week before the visit by Kelly and Tallent, Slutzker visited. It was the first time Smith had seen him since they had closed the deal on the house.

He wanted to know if she could remember whether the streetlight outside 1517 Marlboro was there when she moved in.

"I don't recall if that was there or not," she told him.

And without inquiring how Smith was getting along with her neighbors, he was gone.

At the same time, she noticed two men in suits and ties standing across the street under the light he'd asked about.

Slutzker left before Smith could think to ask about the letters that had stirred her curiosity after she bought the house.

When he moved out, Slutzker gave her the number of a post office box in Greensburg, where his brother Norman lived. She was to forward any mail for him there.

Among the mail that arrived for him were letters addressed to "Slutzker Electric" in envelopes that were otherwise unmarked except for an unfamiliar logo in the corner where a return address normally would be.

Smith worked at the post office on Pittsburgh's Northside, so she checked the logo and found it was a symbol used by the postal service in Cuba.

The letters came frequently. She dutifully sent them on to Greensburg, but when they started coming back from there, she marked them "return to sender" and launched them toward destinations unknown.

The Trial, Day One

Slutzker's trial opened on January 14, a day later than scheduled. The first order of business was a routine matter. Scarlata wanted all the witnesses sequestered, meaning they could not be in the courtroom to hear other testimony.

In a case that would live or die on recollections about events fifteen years earlier, the defense didn't want any witness to be influenced by the memories of the others. If he could help it, Scarlata wasn't going to let a fact or two from one person ricochet through the minds of the others, freeing details that otherwise might remain hidden in the shadows of vague recollection.

Manning agreed to Scarlata's request. The witnesses would have to wait in the hallway until called to the stand.

That done, Scarlata had bigger fish to fry.

As a matter of law, jurors generally are not allowed to hear evidence of a defendant's past crimes. A man accused of rape, for example, can sit through his trial comfortable in the knowledge that the prosecutor may not tell the jury he's already been convicted of raping other women.

Pennsylvania law and rulings by judges around the country, however, have carved out some exceptions to the general rule. Two exceptions are when the past crimes shed light on the defendant's intention or motive to commit the crime of which he's now accused.

Clark reasoned that Slutzker's 1976 conviction on a charge of trying to hire someone to kill John Mudd Sr. cast a beam or two in that direction.

Scarlata knew that Clark planned to call the two men whom Slutzker had tried to hire to pull the trigger. If allowed, it could be devastating testimony, and he wanted to prevent it.

Manning appreciated the importance of the testimony to the prosecution's case, but he needed time to think. He asked Clark not to mention Slutzker's previous conviction when she outlined her case to the jury in her opening statement. Opening arguments by the prosecution and defense would take at least half a day. That would give him time to reason his way through the matter and rule before the witnesses were called.

Clark resisted the judge's suggestion. Too much was at stake for her case. Besides, she'd have to rewrite her opening statement. Plus, there was always the matter of the taxpayers' money. Mike Pezzano and Steve Hairston, the two men who had torpedoed Slutzker at the 1976 solicitation trial and were prepared to testify again, had been brought to Pittsburgh from out of state. They were being housed and fed at further expense to the taxpayers and with considerable inconvenience to themselves. Detectives had spent time interviewing them, and the prosecution team had spent time working that evidence into the Commonwealth's case.

Suddenly Clark faced the prospect of losing two big guns. Pezzano and Hairston wouldn't be testifying about long-lost memories that had returned in a flash. No leap of faith would be required by the jury to believe them.

When someone you know offers you money to kill his lover's husband, details of the conversation, the time, and the setting tend to take permanent residence in your mind. The memories stick, and in the telling make for compelling testimony.

"It is very crucial evidence in this case, and I don't want to open without it," Clark told Manning.

The prosecutor seemed peeved. Why hadn't Scarlata raised the issue earlier? The jurors had already been interviewed and selected and were in the courthouse at that very moment. Witnesses were lined up in the hallway, ready to go.

"Quite frankly," she said, "I wish this was a matter that had been brought up some time prior to today."

Manning, who had guided Clark's arguments back to the point several times during the suppression hearing, was showing no sympathy now for her complaint about what could have been or should have been.

"So do I," he said. "But that doesn't change the fact that it's here."

Well, if Manning wasn't going to let her give her opening argument as written or let her put Pezzano and Hairston on the witness stand, then Clark was determined to raise the stakes.

"Both witnesses are from out of state. The Commonwealth has gone to a lot of expense, and if the court's not going to allow it, I would prefer not to start the trial," she said, promising an appeal if Manning barred her witnesses from testifying.

She hadn't finished speaking before Scarlata recognized the opportunity opening up before him. "Your Honor, in that regard, technically, the obligation on me is not to raise it until such time as the witness gets on the stand."

Was Scarlatta offering an olive branch?

No. It was more like bait.

Scarlata was willing to hold his objection until Clark's witnesses were about to testify. The prosecutor could deliver her opening remarks, complete with their references to the testimony from the two would-be hit men. Scarlata would let her start down the path she'd chosen, then at a later time he could ask the judge to pull the rug out from under her.

If Manning permitted the witnesses to testify, Scarlata might appear to the jury as a feisty defense attorney protecting his client's rights. But if the judge barred the testimony, Scarlata would have succeeded in blowing two of Clark's best witnesses out of the tub and raising doubts in the jurors' minds about the integrity of the state's case.

"That's absolutely correct," the judge said. "You have a right to challenge other-crimes evidence before the trial begins. But then again, you're not required to, and you can still object to it later."

Even so, Scarlata's proposal went unfulfilled. Manning told his tipstaff to inform the jurors that they would not be needed in the courtroom until 2:30 P.M.

"I'll hear you both on this issue," he told Clark and Scarlata.

The prosecutor explained that she wanted to put Pezzano and Hairston on the stand not to prejudice the jury with knowledge that Slutzker had already been proven a criminal for soliciting murder, but to show Slutzker's intent to have Mudd murdered.

"We are alleging an intentional killing, and we are required to show the defendant's intent," she said. "I would argue that his intent was shown clearly nine days prior to the murder at the time he solicited Mr. Pezzano and Mr. Hairston to commit this murder. It's very relevant, and I would submit that it is crucial to our case."

That caught Manning's attention. He absolutely would not allow Clark to tell the jurors about Slutzker's conviction for solicitation to commit murder, but he left the door open on the possibility that the jurors could be told that Slutzker had tried to hire a killer.

"It is not crucial to the case even though it is a damaging piece of evidence from my perspective," Scarlata said. "If the jury believes John Mudd, then Slutzker's intent is not an issue because his intent is implicit in Mudd's testimony. Intent vanishes as a real meaningful issue in the case."

When the opposing attorneys had no more say, Manning ruled in favor of Clark regarding Pezzano.

"The evidence is clear evidence of intent and is inextricably part of the factual scenario that led to the death of the victim," he said.

Hairston, however, was not allowed to testify because only Pezzano's testimony led to a conviction at Slutzker's 1976 solicitation trial. Slutzker had been acquitted on the count of solicitation associated with Hairston's testimony.

Manning ordered that the jury be brought to the courtroom and sworn. It was the middle of the afternoon. He introduced himself and the other parties, explained the charges and the five possible verdicts, not guilty or guilty of first-degree murder, third-degree murder, voluntary manslaughter or involuntary manslaughter. Second-degree murder was not among the possible verdicts because it applies only to killings committed in the course of another felony, as when a bank robber kills a guard or teller.

Three times in explaining the concepts of trial by jury, Manning told the members of the panel that they were the sole judges of the facts. He told them that the word "verdict" comes from *verdicto*, which is Latin for "to speak the truth."

He explained their two obligations as jurors. The first is to sift the essential facts from the evidence, to find the truth, to determine what actually happened at the important times and places. The second is to apply the law to the facts they found.

He told them how they would go about fulfilling their obligations.

In applying the law, the jurors must rely on him to explain the law. In finding the facts, however, "You may follow your common sense and your knowledge of everyday life as each of you has experienced it. You may draw reasonable inferences from the facts."

Perhaps a few of the jurors appreciated the significance of his words. Here was the essence of English and American justice, trial by a jury of one's peers. Jurors can't be expected to know the law. It is too complex to be carried in the hip pocket of everyday people. So, judges explain the law to jurors.

But determining the facts and applying the law, now that's where the mystery and the majesty comes in. The precision, complexity, subtlety, and imposing formality of the court system are surrendered to people from all walks of life, people whose experience with the law goes not much farther than parking tickets and income taxes. The management consultant who cheats on his wife and his taxes, the Spanish teacher who obeys all the rules because life intimidates her, the tavern owner who knows people who collect gambling debts and carry unregistered handguns, the humble widow barely able to hang on to her rundown home in a declining neighborhood, and the cute teller who quietly puts up with the leering, sexually suggestive behavior of her lazy, cowardly bank branch manager—all of them bring their personal beliefs, prejudices, fears, pet peeves, and illusions with them to the jury box. Within the private, unspoken thoughts of the jurors as they listen and watch the proceedings, the credibility of witnesses is measured and the importance of physical evidence is determined. Then, in the sanctuary of the jury room, they deliberate. They combine the evidence with the formless, pliant mass of their subjective thinking and knead the mixture until the facts of the case emerge, then they knead some more until they arrive at justice in the form of a verdict.

■ ■ ■

As prescribed by the rules of procedure, the prosecution was first to deliver its opening argument to the jury. Clark did well for the first one or two minutes. Then, when she first referred to Slutzker, she said he was a primary suspect immediately after the killing but "has remained uncharged and unconvicted of this crime."

Her words rang like a gong in the ears of Manning and Scarlata. Such a statement by Clark or any other witness would not be admissible as evidence and was probably better left unsaid during the opening.

But there it was, hanging out. Clark continued without interruption.

John Mudd was the first of the prosecution witnesses she mentioned to the jury, but she told the members of the panel that "the Commonwealth is not hanging its hat entirely" upon his testimony.

"The only thing that he does for this case is that he

reopens the investigation. There was always a case present against Steven Slutzker. It just never came together and never got prosecuted," she said. "There was a case there at that time, and there is a case here now."

The words "thank you" were barely out of Clark's mouth when Scarlata asked for permission to approach the bench.

"Your Honor, I would ask the court to declare a mistrial based upon the comments of Miss Clark in her opening. To say that Mr. Slutzker was a suspect . . . is entirely inappropriate."

"I winced when she said that as well," Manning said. "But I'm not certain that it's of any significance, and I'll happily instruct the jury and give them a cautionary instruction if you desire me to."

The suppression hearing had been an ordeal. To declare a mistrial now would be to sacrifice all the time spent in getting to trial. Manning was kind in explaining how Clark probably got herself in trouble. Yet still, his remarks had a cutting quality.

"My impression was that she got wrapped up in what she was talking about, and it sort of slid in there as one would expect a prosecutor would not necessarily intentionally slide it in, but it just came out because that's what she was thinking about."

It is faint praise, indeed, to be thought of as a person who can't prevent her thoughts from slipping out during her opening remarks. The opening is second only to the closing as the most important words that a trial attorney will utter directly to members of the jury. For that reason, most litigators craft their jury statements with great care.

"The test is not whether it was intentional or unintentional," Scarlata responded. "The test is whether it was inappropriate."

In fact, the prosecution's intentions are an important test in situations like that one. If, for example, a prosecutor sees that his or her case is going to the dogs and the defendant is likely to be acquitted, it is not unheard of for the prosecutor to do or say something to cause a mistrial and thereby get the chance to start over with a new jury. If the judge declares a mistrial in the belief that the objectionable comment was intentional, then the defendant is freed as if the verdict was "not guilty." If the offense is clearly unintentional, then the remedy is to dismiss the jury and pick a new one.

"It's marginally inappropriate," Manning said. "I don't think it's mistrial material."

Manning cautioned the jurors not to attach any significance to the prosecutor's remark. Clark had dodged a bullet.

Scarlata chose to deliver his opening immediately rather than wait until the prosecution had entered all of its evidence. He attacked Clark's contention that John Mudd Jr. was not the linchpin of the prosecution's case. Scarlata told the jurors that the notion was "curious."

"He is essential to the Commonwealth's case," he said. "The reason Miss Clark spent a good deal of time talking to you about John Mudd Jr.'s testimony not being that important is because of its infirmities."

He suggested that the jurors' common sense and collective wisdom would be put to good use in judging whether Mudd was worthy of belief.

The highlight of Scarlata's opening was his not-so-subtle attempt to turn the spotlight of suspicion on Arlene Mudd Montgomery.

"You'll have to listen to the witnesses both for the defense and for the prosecution and also assess things that aren't introduced in this case, because there are things that you're not going to hear about, that you may say 'Well, why wasn't there any evidence having to do with that aspect?'

"I told you there were two people present at the time of the incident. There are things that are absent from that initial investigation relative to Mrs. Mudd as to whether or not she might have been a suspect in this case and whether or not she had a motive to kill Mr. Mudd Sr."

Scarlata told the jurors he was confident that they would feel compelled to find Slutzker not guilty.

Clark put Mudd on first. He testified at length and in detail about his recollection.

"It was almost like watching a slide show" in his head, "like I was there," Mudd told the jurors. The noises he heard coming from the basement sounded as if someone were slapping a pillow close to his ear. The man who came out of the kitchen was a "taller fellow, slim, had blue jeans on and a darker pair of shoes, short dark hair."

The man in the vision wasn't known to Mudd by name, but in describing the flashback scenes during his first interview with Regis Kelly, with some of the Mudd family members present, someone mentioned Steve Slutzker. Mudd later identified Slutzker from a photo array.

"That's him, right there," he said, thrusting his finger in the direction of the defendant.

Mudd broke down and cried when he described the reaction he got from his family when, as a boy, he asked questions about his father's death.

"I'd wonder why it had to be my dad, and, you know, why they'd taken him away from me, and I'd get upset and I'd cry and I couldn't sleep, and that's when I'd confront someone. I would never get nothing but a hug, and they'd say 'That's okay, John. You still have the rest of your family,' and, thank God, I do."

Scarlata tried, through his objections, to cast doubt on the integrity of Mudd's flashback recollection. He asked early on whether Mudd was "telling us what he recalls he recalled in November or what he now recalls happened?"

Manning played into the objection. "Well, I'm not sure where we are. Are we in November of '90 or back in 1975?" the judge asked Clark.

"Right now, I'm still in November 1990."

Later, Clark asked Mudd, "Are you sure in your mind that this is a memory of what happened back in 1975?"

Scarlata objected and Clark withdrew the question.

By 3:35 P.M., Clark was only midway through questioning Mudd. Manning called it a day. The trial resumed on January 16 because Manning had a prior commitment for the entire day of the fifteenth.

Manning was delighted to find all of the jurors, witnesses, and attorneys in court Thursday morning, considering that winter weather had slammed into Pittsburgh during the night and the Parkway, the only major east–west route through the city, was a snarled mess.

In light of the flap that occurred with Joe Altman during the suppression hearing, Clark made a point of having Mudd deny to the jurors that he'd ever mentioned Steven Slutzker to his girlfriend, Kim, prior to the recollection.

On cross-examination, Scarlata went right to work attacking Mudd's ability to distinguish between the flashback recollection of the murder and memories he'd always had of events when he was five years old.

"How I'm capable? I don't know. I'm not a psychiatrist," Mudd said. The difference, he said after making the wisecrack, is that in the flashback, Mudd saw himself as well as the others. The memories that had survived through the years weren't so much like a slide show.

But under a series of complex and confusing questions

by Scarlata, Mudd ended up agreeing that the two kinds of memories were "one and the same."

Scarlata also succeeded in tripping Mudd on a number of details as when he said Steve Spinola was standing, not sitting, when Mudd attacked him the night of the recall. A few minutes later, Mudd said his only memory of the house at 1515 Marlboro is what came back to him in November 1990. Yet he'd previously said he remembered playing in his backyard and falling through the roof of the dilapidated garage. Mudd had told Kelly he had pinned Spinola to the floor after knocking him off the chair. He told Scarlata from the witness stand that he stood over Spinola, straddling him with his legs. Mudd had testified previously that he could hear his mother talking to Slutzker in the living room after the shooting but could not distinguish the words they were saying. He testified at the trial that there were no voices at all in the flashback visions.

Under questioning by Clark, Kim Altman quoted Mudd as saying "Steve" the night of the recall when he described the man who came out of the kitchen. "He said 'Steve' a couple of times."

The young woman also said that before the recollection she never heard her boyfriend mention that he thought a man named Steve had killed his father—just the opposite of what she had told Regis Kelly.

She told Scarlata on cross-examination that she didn't remember making the statement to the detective. She also claimed she couldn't remember whether Mudd had struck Spinola with the chair.

Spinola, from the witness stand, remembered Mudd standing over him when "He kind of picked up the chair but really didn't do anything with it. That's when he broke down, and he started saying 'I killed him. I can't believe what I did. He's lying there. I killed him.' He just kept going on and on saying that over and over, then he said, 'He's lying there like my father was at the bottom of the steps.'"

After scampering up the stairs to get away from Mudd, Spinola heard Mudd going on about Arlene.

"He's saying he hates her. 'I hate my mom. She had him killed. She's such a bitch.'"

Spinola told Scarlata that contrary to previous testimony, he didn't remember Mudd coming over the couch and through the archway between the living room and dining room. Spinola said Mudd came another way, through the hall, to attack him.

Of more satisfaction to Scarlata, however, was Spinola's testimony that early on November 24, during the period immediately after the flashback, Mudd had explained that "I just happened to be the wrong Steve.

"He said that it was just a bad night for him because everything had to do with a Steve. He said that the one that was harassing his girlfriend was Steve. He said that the one that killed his father was named Steve, and I just showed up being named Steve."

"So, this conversation took place before the police arrived?"

"Yes."

Joe Altman gave his version of the night of the recall. Then Cynthia DeMann came to the witness stand. She'd been a neighbor of the Mudds' on Marlboro Street. She was also an insomniac—and a defense attorney's worst nightmare under the circumstances.

DeMann had told the original investigators that she heard the gunshots and that she saw Arlene outside with a man. What she hadn't said at the time was that she recognized the man as Steven Slutzker.

Scarlata's cross-examination pointed out that DeMann never identified Slutzker in her original statement to police. He didn't ask her why she withheld that information, but she answered him anyway. "I was frightened at the time," she said.

Knowing, or at least able to guess, what she would say if he asked her why she was frightened, Scarlata sat down, and Manning excused the witness.

Pezzano followed DeMann to the witness stand and came within a breath of telling the jurors—inappropriate and prejudicially—that he knew Slutzker well enough to believe that he was capable of committing the murder. It was knowledge that Scarlata took pains to keep away from the jury. On the other hand, Scarlata used Pezzano's knowledge of the Mudd-Slutzker love affair to paint John Mudd Sr. as a bad actor, a wife-beater and child-beater, a junkie and a drug dealer who may have owed money to someone over a drug deal.

With Pezzano's testimony complete, Manning adjourned early. The courtroom cleared out. Clark returned to her office, where a phone message was waiting for her. It was from a Lieutenant Horton of the Logan Township police department near Altoona, two counties east of Pittsburgh. The message was marked "urgent." She almost missed seeing the slip of paper on her desk.

When they finally connected, Horton reported that he'd received a call from Amy Slutzker. The young woman, it seems, had received a visit late Wednesday from her father and his new wife. They had tried to refresh Amy's recollection that she and her father had spent the night of the murder at the O'Deas' house in McKeesport.

Amy had told them she didn't remember anything of the sort. What she didn't tell her father and stepmother is that she remembered other things about that night, things that would detonate another depth charge in Steve Slutzker's bathtub.

Amy was coming forth to report that at age six she routinely slept in her father's bed, and on December 28, 1975, she remembered lying awake in bed and pretending to sleep as her father got up, went to the dresser, removed a gun, and left the room.

Some time later, she heard loud bangs from outside. She next remembered sirens and flashing red lights. Scared, she searched the house for him. He came through the front door, somewhat surprised to see her up.

There were other details.

First thing Friday morning, January 17, Clark presented the news to Manning in open court but before the jury was brought in.

Manning's gut reaction was encompassed by two words: "Holy shit!" Scarlata tried hard not to turn white. This was a bolt from the blue. He wasn't even prepared to explain what the hell his client was doing in Blair County that week.

Thinking on his feet, Scarlata pointed out that Slutzker had an alibi in the statements of Janet and Patrick O'Dea. "So, the overture, such as it was, is consistent with that, if nothing else."

"That's a matter of interpretation," said a skeptical Clark.

Manning immediately saw the implications. It was one thing if Slutzker's visit was a legitimate attempt to obtain an alibi witness. If, on the other hand, the trip was an attempt to obtain perjured testimony or fabricate a defense, then the jury would be allowed to consider the incident as consciousness of guilt on Slutzker's part.

From Slutzker's point of view, the effect on the jurors could be devastating.

Manning granted the defense attorney a fifteen-minute break to try to get his bearings. He was in not much better shape after the break.

"Your Honor, about the only thing I can tell the court is that at this point, I am absolutely unprepared to deal with this information." Scarlata wanted at least the three-day weekend, including the Martin Luther King holiday on Monday, to patch together a strategy.

If that were to be the case, Clark wanted Manning to order Slutzker to stay away from his daughter.

"Amy Slutzker is very much afraid for her safety," Clark said, elaborating on the reasons why the young woman should be. First of all, she remembered her father holding a gun to her mother's head as he forced her out of the house in 1975. He told her he would kill her if she sought custody of Amy. Debbie Slutzker, battling cancer in 1991, warned Amy not to come forward because she knew Steve to be a dangerous man. Then there were the incidents at the pizza parlor and at Mudd's house in New Kensington.

Over the arguments of the defense attorney, Manning ordered Slutzker not to leave Allegheny County until further notified, and to "neither do nor cause to be done nor permit to be done on your behalf any act involving the intimidation of witnesses or victims or retaliation against witnesses."

In the meantime, the Amy Slutzker bombshell would be withheld from the jurors. The court would take the matter up on Tuesday.

For the rest of the half-day session, Clark proceeded with other witnesses. Former state trooper Donald Mates told of receiving Pezzano's warning about a murder plot.

Tim Brendlinger identified Slutzker as the man he saw talking to Arlene under the streetlight in that snow-white landscape on Marlboro Street. Jim Finello and Joe Dugan testified about details at the murder scene. Terry Mudd described his nephew's emotional state the night of the recall and the Mudd family's concerted efforts to shield the boy, throughout his youth, from details of his father's death.

The prosecution's case was building to a powerful crescendo. The defense would have to make some equally powerful music to pull the jurors back to Slutzker's side. In cross-examining the prosecution witnesses, Scarlata used his best aggressive voice and most skeptical tone to draw out minor inconsistencies in the testimony. He did a good job regarding Mudd's recollection about the position of his father's body and whether blood was visible from the top of the basement steps. Finello said the drawing of the Mudd home that John Mudd Jr. testified about was all screwed up. The layout was very different from what Mudd remembered.

Scarlata failed, however, in an attempt to get Finello to testify that it would have been highly unlikely if not impossible for anyone to have heard gunshots from across the street through closed windows, especially shots that Mudd had described as someone slapping a pillow. Finello wouldn't know that unless he had conducted an experiment, a fact that Clark persuasively pointed out to Manning.

The judge released the jury around midday with stern instructions to keep their lips zippered and their ears tuned out to any aspect of the case.

Come dawn Tuesday, western Pennsylvania was nearly invisible under a heavy blanket of new snow. Highway travel was a nightmare for anybody who absolutely had to be somewhere on time. Clark wasn't going to let the weather stand in her way. She arranged for a state police helicopter to give Amy Slutzker the first flight of her life. The chopper landed at the Washington, Pennsylvania, barracks, from which troopers raced north on Interstate 79 to the Allegheny County Courthouse in a blur of blue-and-white police cruiser trailing vortexes of white snow.

Standing in front of the judge's bench on Tuesday morning, January 21, Scarlata made a desperate attempt to force the prosecution to qualify Amy Slutzker as a six-year-old witness. He raised the same arguments as he did against Mudd during the suppression hearing, only this time he did not have hour after hour of esoteric testimony from psychologists with which to pad his argument. For that, Manning and Clark might have been immensely grateful, not that they feared the outcome would be any different but for the time that such arduous testimony would take.

Scarlata also did not have the benefit of a flashback recollection on Amy's part. He tried to establish one nonetheless. He argued that according to the information he had from Slutzker and his wife, Joyce, Amy at one time had no recollection of events on the night of the murder.

Ah yes, Clark argued, but that's only because she was withholding from them details that she's always carried in her memory.

Manning was consistent in disposing of the issue. He had Clark put Miss Slutzker under oath for the purposes of demonstrating her competence as a witness. The judge was not going to abide either attorney delving into the substance of her testimony. All he wanted to see was her ability to differentiate a lie from the truth, to have a memory of certain events, and to communicate that memory.

The young woman, pretty, plump, the twenty-two-year-old mother of four children, demonstrated precisely that.

Scarlata succeeded in showing that Amy had forgotten a lot about her life on Marlboro Street: the name of the synagogue she attended, the name of her grade school, and even her address. But he failed to shake her recollection on any other key point. As a small concession, Amy did testify that when she informed her father and his wife that she distinctly remembered not being in McKeesport the night of the murder, they made no attempt to persuade her to testify otherwise. "The subject was dropped," she said.

The defense might have to withstand a broadside from a confident young woman with a clear memory, but at least Slutzker would not have to face immediate jailing on suspicion of soliciting perjured testimony.

After Amy was excused from the stand, Scarlata argued that he should have an opportunity to have her evaluated psychologically.

"What's a psychological evaluation possibly going to tell the court?" Manning said, as much telling Scarlata what he felt about the request as he was asking a question.

"The motion is denied," he said a moment later. The judge also denied Scarlata's motion to give the prosecution the burden of proving Amy's competency as a witness.

Manning also ruled that he would instruct the jurors to use their judgment in determining how much weight to apply to the suggestion that Slutzker had tried to plant a memory in Amy's mind.

With that, he sent the attorneys back to their tables and summoned the jury. Amy's father and grandfather shot daggers at her as she walked to the front of the room and sat in the witness stand for the second time. Their staring was so intense and unnerving that when Regis Kelly realized what was going on, he positioned himself to block Amy's view of them.

She went on to give testimony that couldn't have been better if it had been scripted, especially considering the eleventh-hour nature of her appearance.

Amy described her memory of December 28, 1975.

Why did she withhold her complete memory from her father? Clark asked.

Because she was afraid of him, Amy said.

Manning interrupted to caution the jury not to assume too much or too little about the meaning of Slutzker's visit with his daughter. Scarlata objected. He said the judge had cast the incident in a light quite different from that intended by the witness.

Manning invited Scarlata to submit proposed language for an additional caution to the jury at the conclusion of the case.

Amy also testified that she remembered John Mudd Jr., playing with him, eating lunch at her house when her mother still lived there. They sat on the tall stools at the Slutzkers' kitchen counter. Debbie Slutzker made sandwiches for them—all of which were details that coincided with Mudd's memories of the Slutzker household.

Scarlata accomplished little in his attempts to shake Amy or undermine her testimony on the crucial details. As before, he forced her to admit she could not remember secondary details, such as the last name of the woman who cared for her the day her father was arrested, how long she stayed with that woman, whether her father got dressed when he got out of bed that night, or what he was wearing when she saw him later. Scarlata's only other apparent success was in getting Amy to testify that she was in her early teens when she had her first baby out of wedlock.

Clark wrapped up the prosecution's case the next day. She put on Mudd's aunt Maureen and uncle Jim, followed by Sandy Catone, who told of Slutzker bragging to her that he'd killed a man. Clark ended with the technical evidence about the path of the bullets and the cause of death of John Mudd Sr.

Scarlata opened the defense with testimony from county police officer Ronald Gratz, the highlight of which was his recollection that James Mudd told him the family "went so far as to have John Mudd Jr. hypnotized."

Scarlata also put on Detective Thomas Glenn, who stood by his written report of the interview with Catone, which diverged somewhat from details of her later statements.

On cross-examination, Clark pointed out that the interviews were brief, that James Mudd was highly emotional during his phone conversation with Gratz, and that Catone was standing beside the car while Glenn and his partner sat inside.

■ ■ ■

Testimony resumed on January 24, the Friday before the Super Bowl, with Dr. Jonathan Himmelhoch testifying for the defense. A University of Pittsburgh Medical School professor, Himmelhoch unabashedly summed up his lengthy credentials with the observation that when a psychiatrist sits on the Board of Medical Examiners, as he did, it means "you're considered the top in your field."

Scarlata used Himmelhoch to try to shoot down the theory that John Mudd experienced a flashback recollection due to posttraumatic stress disorder.

The doctor said the anatomical parts of the human brain—the nerves, fatty matter, and other tissue—required to have full-blown memory don't develop until the person is between seven and ten years old.

"As a result, we now know that the failure to remember things early in life is not just repression, but it's a physical impossibility to remember them. The medial forebrain bundle is the name of the tract that is important in this regard, and it really is not fully developed until twelve, although other tracts are beginning to kick in around eight, nine, or ten," he said.

In addition, Himmelhoch testified, memories that are stored in the brain are not necessarily memories of events that actually happened.

"You can have memories of something that never happened because in order to have memory, all you have to have is something to register. It can be a wish. It can be fantasy. It can be a misinterpretation. Then that gets remembered rather than what actually happened."

Dreams and fantasy can play a big part in childhood memories, because a six-year-old's ability to fantasize is much more developed than his ability to remember. "He is liable to be prey to misinterpretations, mistakes, fantasies, and dreams," he said, and a moment later added suggestion to the list of influences that can prey on the mind of a child. And with that, Himmelhoch arrived at the crux of his testimony.

He said the power of suggestion springs from two sources. One is the repetition of an idea put forth by others. The second is wishful thinking.

These memories can be dredged up when the person experiences extreme emotions "and usually they're wrong. They're called screen memories.

"Let's say a person wants to kill someone and then

suddenly has a memory of a bloody incident that really didn't take place, but it stops his fists or it stops his knife or it stops his gun. That's called a screen memory, and it's one of the blessings that have been placed upon mankind," Himmelhoch said. "But for them, we'd have more bloody streets than we have now."

The University of Pittsburgh psychiatrist studied the records of John's counseling by Catholic Youth Services and he'd read the reports about Mudd's visions on the night of November 23 and the early morning of November 24, 1990, and to the surprise of no one who'd listened to Himmelhoch's explanation of screen memory the doctor testified, "I've never seen a more classic example of a screen memory."

Under questioning by Scarlata, Himmelhoch went on to cut a number of other disctinctions between Mudd's experience and genuine flashback recollection produced by posttraumatic stress syndrome. And as to whether John Mudd Jr. suffered an episode of the syndrome, the doctor concluded, "There is no possibility that he did."

Unfortunately for Slutzker, Himmelhoch at times, especially early in his testimony, used so much jargon, and his attitude seemed so condescending and sanctimonious —in discussing Freud's work on childhood memory, for example, he referred to the renowned psychiatrist as "Sigmund"—that jurors later told Clark they found him overbearing.

In the meantime, Joe Lindsey was wrestling with a memory of his own as he followed the trial through the news. Lindsey was remembering the day in December 1975 when he showed Slutzker how to load the automatic pistol in the basement of the apartment building on Buena Vista Street. The memory affected Lindsey the way a big bucket of greasy buffalo wings with hot sauce and Roquefort dip affects a weak stomach.

Lindsey hadn't talked to Slutzker in all of the intervening years except to bump into him at a flea market in North Park.

The case was building toward a crescendo, and with every step toward a verdict of innocent or guilty, Lindsey was pushed closer to action by the universal human desire to tell what we know, especially if we know that we can change the world, or just one small corner of it.

There was one other powerful force working on Lindsey, his wife. He had told her what he knew, and she wanted him to do the right thing. Some months before the trial began, he almost did. He picked up the phone and called the Allegheny County district attorney's office, but he hung up when someone answered.

But by January 24, time was running out. Clark had entered all of the evidence she had planned on entering, and the defense case reached its climax when Scarlata had Slutzker on the stand.

As that was going on in Judge Manning's courtroom in Pittsburgh, Lindsey was twenty miles north of the city in the rural community of Mars, where he lived. Finally, he had the courage to dial the DA's office. This time he stayed on the line when his call was answered.

Clark was still in the courtroom when Lindsey called. The message he left was an admonition: "Don't let this case go to the jury until I talk to her."

But the newly emboldened informant would have to hold his water because Clark couldn't leave the courtroom for a while, and the question was whether Lindsey's nerve would hold out long enough for Clark to get back to him.

After the prosecutor finished cross-examining Slutzker, the judge dismissed the members of the jury for the weekend with orders to remain silent about the case and to enjoy watching the Super Bowl.

Although the jury was gone, the attorneys had further business with the judge that prevented Clark from talking to Lindsey right away.

That business was to explore the question of whether Manning should grant Scarlata's request and order Arlene Mudd Stewart to testify. The debate was complicated by a state Supreme Court ruling that seemed to require that Manning order her to testify. The judge's staff and Arlene's attorney, Sumner Parker, had only recently discovered the ruling, which was two years old.

"Just when the court thinks you have a pretty good handle on what all the law is in the Commonwealth, the Supreme Court writes a decision that befuddles just about anyone," Manning said.

"I just recently came across it and suspected," Parker was saying when the judge interrupted and finished Parker's thought: ". . . suspected I would discover it sooner or later."

"Well, sooner or later," Parker admitted.

"Hoping I wouldn't, right?"

"Well, Judge, there's nothing wrong in hoping that sleeping dogs don't stay asleep, not to infer that the court is a dog," Parker said.

Manning took no offense, or if he did, he didn't let on.

The 1990 ruling in a case called *Commonwealth v. McGrogan* held that just because others might throw suspicion on a witness like Arlene Stewart, her right not to incriminate herself might not apply if her previous testimony absolved her of any wrongdoing.

Since Arlene had testified at the coroner's inquest in 1976 that she had nothing to do with her husband's murder, her Fifth Amendment right not to incriminate herself didn't necessarily provide her with a means to avoid repeating the testimony.

"That leaves me in the unenviable position of ordering her to testify, I assume, as I read it," Manning told the attorneys.

The Supreme Court ruling had fascinating implications for just about everyone involved.

First of all, Scarlata wanted very much to have Arlene take the stand and once again testify that she had no part in the killing and had no idea who committed the crime. If the jurors believed her, then they'd have great difficulty believing her son's testimony that he remembered seeing her talk to Slutzker immediately after the shooting.

The legal questions also put Arlene in a precarious position. The Supreme Court's ruling noted that to invoke the Fifth Amendment right against self-incrimination, a witness must have a reasonable basis for believing that her testimony will incriminate her. Invoking her right might suggest that Arlene may have told something less than the truth at the coroner's inquest when she claimed total innocence. It suggested that she'd incriminate herself at Slutzker's trial if she told the truth.

"She's between a rock and a hard place," Parker said.

And to an extent, so was Clark. The prosecutor claimed earlier that Arlene had a Fifth Amendment right in this instance. Yet Clark also had publicly identified Arlene as a suspect in the murder. As such, Arlene might give answers to important questions if she could be put on the witness stand.

"Since you chirped earlier and said she had a Fifth Amendment right, it may be your undoing in the end," Manning chided Clark. "The Commonwealth almost shoots itself in the foot here."

■ ■ ■

The judge delayed ruling on whether Arlene would have to testify, and Scarlata went on to score points when Margaret Gillick, Mudd's boyhood psychological counselor, testified that during the period when her counseling sessions with Mudd took place in the boy's home she heard adults talking about the murder. She said she also heard them state their opinion that Slutzker was involved.

Her testimony was intended to reinforce the skepticism that jurors might understandably have about the validity of John Mudd's recollection in light of the boy's vow to take revenge when he became twenty-one.

Scarlata also tried to shake Brendlinger's credibility with testimony that the officer's written report from the night of the murder made no mention of seeing Slutzker with Arlene on the sidewalk.

Then, the defense attorney put Steve on the stand.

In the abstract, Slutzker's testimony would seem like the highlight of the defense case. In reality, though, his words must have seemed to the jurors to be defensive and evasive, and therefore less than wholly believable.

Steve said that Pezzano never showed up for their appointment to pursue the murder plan and after that he dropped the matter entirely.

Slutzker denied in absolute terms any involvement in Mudd's murder.

At 4:30 that afternoon, Clark finally spoke to Lindsey by phone. She brought in her surprise witness when the trial resumed on the Monday, and over the concerns of Scarlata, Manning allowed him to take the stand and recount the gun-loading lesson he gave Slutzker in December 1975.

The attorneys argued some more over Arlene's status.

Parker said he'd let her take the stand if the district attorney's office would grant her immunity from prosecution for anything she might say that incriminated herself.

"We don't wish to immunize Arlene Mudd, Arlene Montgomery, Arlene Stewart because she is still, in our minds, a suspect in this case, and we still may eventually refile the charges against her if we can obtain other evidence," Clark said.

Manning ruled that she should take the stand, but Arlene's testimony was anticlimactic as well.

In the end, the jury did exactly as Manning asked them. They applied their common sense to all they'd heard and determined that neither the extraordinary flashback recollection of John Mudd Jr. nor the startling testimony of Amy Slutzker carried the day. Instead they put great credence in the words of Officer Brendlinger and Cynthia DeMann, the neighbor, both of whom said they saw Slutzker talking to Arlene on the sidewalk minutes after the murder.

The jurors also said they found significance in the absence of Janet and Patrick O'Dea at the trial. They wondered why the two people most able to corroborate Slutzker's alibi were never called to testify.

The jurors simply did not buy Slutzker's claim that as a man who rarely drank alcohol, he just happened to be plastered on the most convenient night.

On January 28, 1992, after nine hours of deliberation over two days, the members of the panel stood at their seats in the jury box and one by one declared that "Yes," they agreed that Steven Slutzker was guilty of murder in the first degree.

Scarlata filed a raft of posttrial motions. Judge Manning politely but firmly shot each one down. In his posttrial opinion, Manning identified one issue where the defense attorney made an oversight that denied him the privilege of raising the issue on appeal. Scarlata was trying to make an issue of the proposed caution that he'd wanted the judge to give to the jurors during the charge. Manning wrote in his opinion that since Scarlata failed to object to the charge at the time the judge delivered it to the jurors, then he couldn't raise it on appeal.

Manning imposed a mandatory sentence of life without parole. Slutzker became a permanent resident of the State Penitentiary at Pittsburgh, a brown stone fortress that stands on the bank of the Ohio River just north of Pittsburgh and is known as "the Wall."

In the halls of the courthouse after the verdict, members of the Mudd family cheered and hugged each other. "Happy days are here again," said Terry Mudd. "We finally got justice after sixteen years," said Maureen Perri.

Joyce Slutzker slipped out of the building unnoticed without commenting on the verdict against her husband.

Slutzker's father, Louis, on the other hand, was eager to talk.

"This court has found my son guilty by a great injustice. God will punish all of them," he said. "The prosecutor had a number of witnesses who perjured themselves, including police.

"I guarantee you that if it takes every last nickel I have, this will be appealed."

Likewise, Norman Slutzker remained convinced of his brother's innocence, and Steve engaged another attorney to pursue possible avenues of appeal.

Amy Slutzker returned to her home near Altoona, where she lives with her four children. She has had little if any contact with her father or his family, believing that the least Steve could have done was contribute to her support while she was growing up without him.

Debbie Slutzker, for whom the entire saga was so painful that she could not bear to talk about it even around Amy, has died of cancer since the trial.

The Pezzanos continue to live in Florida, where Donna says Mike is at peace with himself and the world, despite believing that his life got worse, not better, as a result of his effort to stop a crime and save his friend from committing a ruinous act.

Regis Kelly is one of the few police officers or detectives associated with the Mudd case still on the job as a criminal investigator. He concentrates most of his efforts on ending gang violence, a mission to which he devotes most of his waking thoughts and much of his personal time. Coincidentally, a great deal of the gang activity that draws Kelly's attention takes place in Wilkinsburg.

Kim Clark remains an assistant district attorney for Allegheny County, and Charles Scarlata continues in private practice in Pittsburgh. Since the Mudd case, he has been involved in a number of high-profile cases.

Maureen Perri continues to live in Pittsburgh and to watch after John Jr. as if he were her son.

Arlene was never again charged in connection with the death of John Mudd Sr.

Slutzker stays in touch by mail with Norman and maintains his sense of humor, even joking on occasion about the accident that cost him the tips of two fingers on one hand. It occurred in the prison wood shop, where Steve has a creative outlet in building furniture.

State regulations do not permit him to keep any of the money he could earn by selling the pieces he makes, so his resources are limited in financing further litigation. Knowledgeable observers estimate that Slutzker spent $40,000 on his defense, considering the going rate for an attorney like Scarlata and the caliber of the expert witnesses who testified for the defense.

John Mudd Jr. lives in Lawrenceville. He and Kim married in July 1992. In 1994 they had a strapping, healthy baby boy, whom they named John Lawrence Mudd III. The couple separated later that year. John Jr. is trying to arrange financing for studies that would prepare him to be a medical technician.

John Jr. has custody of the boy, whom he adores, and greatly enjoys being a father despite the extra duty of being a single parent. When his son is five years old, John Jr. will be twenty-eight.